Not your usual founding father.

Not your usual founding father.

Selected Readings from Benjamin Franklin

Edited by Edmund S. Morgan

Yale university press, new haven and london.

Designed by Nancy Ovedovitz and set in Monotype Fournier by Keystone Typesetting, Inc. and printed in the United States of America by R. R. Donnelley & Sons.

Library of Congress Cataloging-in-Publication Data
Franklin, Benjamin, 1706–1790.
Not your usual founding father : selected readings from Benjamin Franklin / edited by Edmund S. Morgan.
p. cm.
Includes index.
ISBN-13: 978-0-300-11394-5 (alk. paper)
ISBN-10: 0-300-11394-3 (alk. paper)
1. Franklin, Benjamin, 1706–1790—Archives. 2. Franklin, Benjamin, 1706–1790—Correspondence. 3. Franklin, Benjamin, 1706–1790—Philosophy. 4. United States—Politics and government—To 1775—Sources. 5. United States—Politics and government—1775–1783—Sources. 6. United States—Politics and government—1783–1789—Sources. 7. United States—Social life and customs—18th century—Sources. 8. Statesmen—United States—Archives. I. Morgan, Edmund Sears. II. Title.
E302.F82 2006
973.3—dc22   2006045706

A catalogue record for this book is available from the British Library.

The paper in this book meets the guidelines for permanence and durability of the Committee on Production Guidelines for Book Longevity of the Council on Library Resources.

10 9 8 7 6 5 4 3 2 1

frontispiece:
Jean-Antoine Houdon, Portrait bust of Benjamin Franklin (detail), 1779

To Nan Elizabeth Norene

Contents.

Preface.

Benjamin Franklin. The name inevitably conveys—it once did to me, anyhow—a benevolent, stuffy old gentleman, complacently mouthing admonitions to diligence and thrift. When you find, instead, a man who challenges your own stuffiness, you wonder where that image came from. I think it may have started with the *Autobiography*, begun as a letter addressed to his pretty stuffy grown son. The *Autobiography* is the man's re-creation of himself, undertaken when he was sixty-five years old, and written with a practiced literary skill in a paternal voice. It is worth study in itself as a work of art and for the unique historical information contained in it, but it can also screen the man himself from us.

The man himself is a puzzle and a prize. He fascinated people at the time and continues to fascinate many of us today. Why? I think because of his combination of common sense and uncommon ideas, of the prosaic and the poetic, plebeian and patrician, expected and unexpected. I shall not attempt to exhibit everything that Franklin did or thought. Instead, I will try first to meet him as an ordinary, gregarious, good-natured human being, welcomed everywhere for a chat, a joke, a drink, a song, an adventure.

The man we will meet is not the precocious youth of the *Autobiography*. We will skip that and cut to the man in his full powers. Apart from a tantalizing glimpse of him as he saw himself at twenty in a unique youthful journal, the earliest single item in this reader is a letter to his parents when he was already thirty-two. The choice is partly a necessity. Franklin's surviving papers will fill forty-seven volumes in the complete edition under way. Only the first two volumes and half of the third were needed for everything he wrote in the first half of his long life (eighty-four years). It was what he did in the second half that mattered, after he had left his business career behind. He was in his forties when he performed the electrical experiments and observations that made him famous throughout the world, in his forties when he dedicated himself to a public career that would last for the rest of his life. He was seventy when he helped write the Declaration of Independence, seventy-six when he signed the peace treaty with England, eighty-one when he helped draft the Constitution of the United States. He was the only founding father to sign all three of these documents. But we should note that none of them was quite what he had wanted it to be.

Indeed he seldom got his way in the public measures he helped to bring about. He was a great proponent of the federal union that now guides us, but not its architect—he would have preferred something a little different. In 1754 he proposed a plan of union for England's North American colonies. It was accepted by a congress of representatives but then rejected by all the colonies. In 1775, at the Continental Congress, he proposed articles of confederation for a continental union. The Congress declined to consider them and later adopted a much weaker set with provisions Franklin had specifically opposed. In 1776, after helping draft the Declaration of Independence, he argued for the United States to defend itself without any foreign assistance. Instead, the Congress sent him to France—to get foreign assistance, which he did very successfully. In 1782, along with John Adams and John Jay, he negotiated the treaty with Great Britain that ended the war, but the treaty contained none of the articles to benefit mankind and his country that he would most have liked to see in it. In 1787 he attended the Constitutional Convention, but the convention rejected the provisions he advocated. In 1776 he had presided at the drafting of the Pennsylvania state constitution, which included unique democratic provisions that he cherished. But as he lay dying in 1790 his fellow Pennsylvanians gave up his constitution for a more conservative one, with provisions to which he had written strenuous objections.

Franklin's willingness to suppress his own wishes in order to carry out what other people wanted tells us something about him, something that will become more comprehensible as we get to know him. This was not your usual founding father, and this reader is not intended to show his achievements as a founder or even as a father. It is directed at the man and what he thought it meant to be a man, a human being: what he made of the natural world he found around him, how he dealt with the joys and sorrows, the puzzles and problems that the company of other human beings brought him, and, more particularly, how he responded to the opportunities and responsibilities that being an American presented to him.

Franklin had a well-honed talent for speaking clearly. Even in writing about complex issues in complex situations, he could cut to the quick and make his point to the most casual reader. So you can read the selections at random if you wish. Each will make sense by itself. But I have arranged them in a sequence, not always chronological, that I believe will exhibit the man as he developed, first as a human being, then as a deservedly renowned scientific thinker, and finally as a visionary striver for a better world. To this end I have divided the selections into four parts. Part I is aimed at getting to know the man as others in his time knew him, to find out what it would have been like to spend time with him and why it would have been such good fun. We want to meet him on equal terms, as he met everyone, before looking at what makes him worth remembering today. Part II is devoted to a characteristic that distinguished him from most of the rest of us then and now: an intellectual curiosity that challenged him to make sense out of things that others took for granted. His ability to ask questions and look for answers made him world famous in his time because of what he found out about electricity. His questions and answers about other things that puzzled him did not have as far-reaching results but show us the man's restless mind, continually challenged by the wonders of everyday life.

The last two parts of the reader may strike some as controversial. They are devoted to what I believe was the driving force in Franklin's public career. Sometime in his forties he decided on a life of public service. At the same time, I believe, he decided that the public he should serve was more than his neighborhood or city or province but something larger: an America that was not yet what we would call a nation but would become one in the not very distant future. In 1751 the idea, or vision as I prefer to say, came to him of America as part of the British Empire but destined to be the foundation and stronghold of a new incarnation of that empire. For the rest of his life, I believe, that vision guided his public career. Part III of the reader is taken up with his campaign to persuade the existing leaders of the empire to recognize Americans for what they were and what they would be.

By 1776 the unwillingness of the British to recognize facts meant that Franklin's efforts would now be directed toward enabling Americans to make the most of their future by themselves. Part IV follows those efforts. Here as elsewhere in the volume, the focus, the principle of selection from his papers, is to show the man, what he wanted rather than what he got, what his America could have been rather than what it became, but also to show his satisfaction with what he and his fellow founders did, however short it fell from what he would have wished.

In selecting the readings and in my introduction to them I have benefited more than I can say from the assistance and collaboration of others. From the beginning Marie Morgan has worked with me, and we have exchanged thoughts so often that the book is as much hers as mine. In choosing the selections I had the advantage of the CD-ROM of the entire body of Franklin's papers, published and unpublished, prepared by the Packard Humanities Institute. The ability to call up any document instantly by author, recipient, date, or subject greatly facilitated making choices. The CD-ROM has now been placed online at franklinpapers.org. The actual text of each document printed here, however, has been taken directly either from one of the thirty-eight volumes of the *Papers* now in print or from the original manuscript or photocopy of those not yet in print. Ellen Cohn, as editor of the definitive *Papers of Benjamin Franklin*, gave her expert advice and supervised the transcriptions from the originals. Lauren Shapiro and Christopher Rogers at Yale University Press made valuable suggestions about format, and Eleanor Goldberg gave valuable assistance in obtaining the illustrations. Susan Laity, in editing the final manuscript as it went to the printer, has given the book a stylistic organization, accessibility, and coherence it could not otherwise have achieved. And Nancy Ovedovitz fitted the book with a typographical design worthy of the man it celebrates.

PART I The man.

I n the *Autobiography* Franklin told his son and the world what he
wanted them to think about him. Some years before he wrote it, he
said in one of the almanacs he published in Philadelphia, "Let all men
know thee, but no man know thee thoroughly." I think he followed that
injunction in the *Autobiography*. In his other writings, he seldom talks about
himself at all, but we can catch him unawares. We can discover him in what
he did talk about, in what he said and how he said it on whatever was
engaging him at the moment—what struck him as good or bad, funny or
foolish, important or silly. In the rest of the reader we will follow him as a
major player in pursuit of what he and his contemporaries considered
important at different times in his life. In this part we try to catch him in the
more mundane, everyday activities, thoughts, and relationships that occupy all of us.

First, a word about what is conspicuously missing here: his role as a
husband and father. One reason for the omission is that his surviving
papers tell us little about the marriage beyond the small details of domestic
life. In 1730 Franklin married Deborah Read, a young Philadelphia widow,
and for the next twenty-seven years they lived together and had few
occasions to exchange letters. From the sparse evidence it appears that they
were happy together. It tells us something about both of them that he had
an illegitimate son, William, born shortly before their marriage—he never

revealed who the mother was—and that Deborah ungrudgingly, though perhaps unhappily, took the boy into the family. Franklin and Deborah had two children of their own, a boy, Francis, and a girl, Sarah (Sally). Franklin seems to have been devoted to all of them. He was deeply grieved when Francis died at the age of four. Thereafter Franklin fastened his affections on William, took him on his mission to London in 1757, and readily forgave him when he had an illegitimate son of his own, William Temple Franklin. Franklin used his influence to get William appointed royal governor of New Jersey in 1762, a position of considerable prestige and power. But he never forgave William for clinging to the office and taking the British side when Americans repudiated royal authority and royal governors in the Revolution. William Temple, the grandson, took the American side and replaced his father as Franklin's favorite.

Franklin has gained a reputation as a womanizer because he had a son out of wedlock, because he had a penchant for ribald humor, and because he carried on extravagant public flirtations with Parisian women of wealth and high birth after Deborah's death. The notion that he had a roving eye is supported by the fact that he was away from home for all but two of her last seventeen years. He was still in England when she died in 1774. But it is well to remember their twenty-seven years together. There is no doubt that Franklin enjoyed the company of women throughout his life, before and after his marriage. But he enjoyed all company, and he made many close friends, both male and female. He was a compulsive joiner of social clubs. He formed a famous men's club of his own, the Junto, in 1727 for weekly talk, song, and drink, as well as serious discussion of moral and political issues with other ambitious young Philadelphians.

That he was ever unfaithful to Deborah or cool or uncaring toward her, even when he was absent for long years, is not borne out by anything he said or wrote, nor did she ever cool toward him. In the flow of letters they exchanged regularly they always addressed each other as "My Dear Child," or "My dear Love," and Deborah occasionally made it "My Dearest Child" or "My Dearest Dear Child." If he suffers from gout, as he often did, she wishes that "I was near aneuf to rube it with a lite hand"—this in 1770, when he had been gone for six years. In the same letter: "When will it be in your power to cume home? How I long to see you but I wold not say one word that wold give you one moments trubel." Franklin never complained of her failure to learn spelling or grammar, never condescended to her. The relationship, whether they were together or apart, was a trusting, affectionate one.

That is about all the letters tell us. They are all much the same. Franklin knew that Deborah was interested in the homely, household, neighborhood things that also interested him. But in the familiar exchanges of news between them we cannot catch the man who charmed and intrigued so many people and can still charm us. I have therefore skipped all the letters to and from Deborah.

It would be hard to measure what his charm had to do with his many achievements. It undoubtedly contributed to his success as a statesman and diplomat. To a sensitive eye it can be detected in virtually everything he wrote, whether in print or in private correspondence. People who write always communicate something of themselves, and Franklin is no exception. What he communicates is often hidden in the message, but it comes out more in some of his writings than in others. I have chosen the selections in Part I for the way they reveal the man, not for the message they happen to contain.

1 The young man and the old man.

We begin with some passages from the journal Franklin kept for a few weeks on a long sea voyage when he was just twenty years old. It is almost the only thing we have, from all his surviving papers, in which he talks to himself about himself. A lot of it, like most of the personal journals of the time, is about wind and weather, and I have included some of those entries just to give a sense of the whole. But other entries include thoughts about a variety of matters that are echoed in his later life. It is a good place to meet an ordinary young man who never lost his ordinary character, even when his exploits raised him to a fame shared by no other American in the intellectual world of his time, and by no other American, Washington excepted, in the political world.

At the time of the journal he has already had a busy, hardworking childhood and adolescence in Boston. Apprenticed to his brother as a printer, he has run away to Philadelphia, worked there for a year, then spent a kind of junior year abroad (actually a year and a half) in London, working as a printer and sowing a few wild oats. Now he is aboard ship, waiting for a favoring wind to carry him back to Philadelphia.

Waiting for the right wind was a common experience for voyagers in the age of sail, especially on vessels that had to clear the English Channel before reaching the open sea. No one wanted to spend needless days aboard a wind-bound ship. So the captain of Franklin's ship inched along the coast, waiting for a fair wind, and allowed his passengers to go ashore at several ports along the way. Thus Franklin's "Albion, farewell!" two days after embarking was a little premature. For the next two weeks he was on and off the ship, visiting towns along the coast, and we get his reactions to them and his account of a small adventure ashore. Then, while he was at sea for sixty-seven days (an unusually long crossing), he recorded his keen observations of what can be seen on an ocean voyage, including the way people cooped up in a ship behave toward one another.

There is nothing quite like the journal in the rest of Franklin's voluminous writings. In the next selection we jump from the energetic young printer confined aboard ship to the man whose mind could not be confined anywhere. The journal contains many hints of the man to come. In his comments on the card sharp's repentance when ostracized, in his search for congenial society among the other passengers, and in his joy at seeing other human faces on the ship that sailed in company with theirs for a time, we get a glimpse of Franklin's need for people, his heartfelt enjoyment of other human beings.

Someone whose company he enjoyed in later life was George Whately, a London merchant who had become a good friend during Franklin's seventeen years in the city. Those years had ended with his departure as the War for American Independence began, with Franklin in a crucial role. But the war is over now, and the two elderly men have resumed their friendship by mail. Franklin, as U.S. minister to France, has sent Whately one of the medallions with which the country honored its supporters abroad. In this long letter to his English friend, ranging over many subjects, we learn something about how, at age seventy-nine, he looks at the world and its ways.

A word about the topics that engaged him. The references to the shocking numbers of abandoned children in both England and France continue an exchange prompted by Whately's appointment as treasurer of London's Foundling Hospital. Franklin was fond of children and ever eager to support efforts for their welfare. The "double spectacles" mentioned are the bifocals that Franklin had just invented—he was always inventing something. The "Cincinnati Institution" is the Society of the Cincinnati, an organization of army officers whose hereditary nature raised his hackles. He gave a more extended criticism of it and of all hereditary honors in a letter to his daughter, included in the last section of this book. "Our Constitution" is the Articles of Confederation, adopted in 1781. Franklin could defend the Articles to Whately for what he thought was good about them. He does not mention the glaring weaknesses that he would be happy to join in correcting two years later at the Constitutional Convention. Read this letter not so much for the details it gives about all these things but for the impression it conveys of the man who wrote it.

Journal of a Voyage, 1726

Friday, July 22, 1726

Yesterday in the afternoon we left London, and came to an anchor off Gravesend about eleven at night. I lay ashore all night, and this morning took a walk up to the Windmill Hill, whence I had an agreeable prospect of the country for above twenty miles round, and two or three reaches of the river with ships and boats sailing both up and down, and Tilbury Fort on the other side, which commands the river and passage to London. This Gravesend is a *cursed biting* place; the chief dependence of the people being the advantage they make of imposing upon strangers. If you buy any thing of them, and give half what they ask, you pay twice as much as the thing is worth. Thank God, we shall leave it to-morrow.

Saturday, July 23

This day we weighed anchor and fell down with the tide, there being little or no wind. In the afternoon we had a fresh gale, that brought us down to Margate, where we shall lie at anchor this night. Most of the passengers are very sick. Saw several Porpoises, &c.

Sunday, July 24

This morning we weighed anchor, and, coming to the Downs, we set our pilot ashore at Deal and passed through. And now whilst I write this, sitting upon the quarter-deck, I have methinks one of the pleasantest scenes in the world before me. 'Tis a fine clear day, and we are going away before the wind with an easy pleasant gale. We have near fifteen sail of ships in sight, and I may say in company. On the left hand appears the coast of France at a distance, and on the right is the town and castle of Dover, with the green hills and chalky cliffs of England, to which we must now bid farewell. Albion, farewell!

Monday, July 25

All the morning calm. Afternoon sprung up a gale at East; blew very hard all night. Saw the Isle of Wight at a distance.

Tuesday, July 26

Contrary winds all day, blowing pretty hard. Saw the Isle of Wight again in the evening.

Wednesday, July 27

This morning the wind blowing very hard at West, we stood in for the land, in order to make some harbour. About noon we took on board a pilot out of a fishing shallop, who brought the ship into Spithead off Portsmouth. The captain, Mr. Denham and myself went on shore, and during the little time we staid I made some observations on the place.

. . . Portsmouth is a place of very little trade in peace time; it depending chiefly on fitting out men of war. Spithead is the place where the fleet commonly anchor, and is a very good riding place. The people of Portsmouth tell strange stories of the severity of one [Sir John] Gibson, who was governor of this place in the Queen's time, to his soldiers, and show you a miserable dungeon by the town gate, which they call *Johnny Gibson's Hole,* where for trifling misdemeanors he used to confine his soldiers till they were almost starved to death. 'Tis a common maxim, that without severe discipline it is impossible to govern the licentious rabble of soldiery. I own indeed that if a commander finds he has not those qualities in him that will make him beloved by his people, he ought by all means to make use of such methods as will make them fear him, since one or the other (or both) is absolutely necessary; but Alexander and Caesar, those renowned generals, received more faithful service, and performed greater actions by means of the love their soldiers bore them, than they could possibly have done, if instead of being beloved and respected they had been hated and feared by those they commanded.

Thursday, July 28

This morning we came on board, having lain on shore all night. We weighed anchor and with a moderate gale stood in for Cowes in the Isle of Wight, and came to an anchor before the town about eleven o'clock. . . .

Friday, July 29

... The island is about sixty miles in circumference, and produces plenty of corn and other provisions, and wool as fine as Cotswold; its militia having the credit of equalling the soldiery, and being the best disciplined in England. [Joseph Dudley, the former royal governor at Massachusetts] was once in King William's time entrusted with the government of this island. At his death it appeared he was a great villain, and a great politician; there was no crime so damnable which he would stick at in the execution of his designs, and yet he had the art of covering all so thick, that with almost all men in general, while he lived, he passed for a saint. What surprised me was, that the silly old fellow, the keeper of the castle, who remembered him governor, should have so true a notion of his character as I perceived he had. In short I believe it is impossible for a man, though he has all the cunning of a devil, to live and die a villain, and yet conceal it so well as to carry the name of an honest fellow to the grave with him, but some one by some accident or other shall discover him. Truth and sincerity have a certain distinguishing native lustre about them which cannot be perfectly counterfeited, they are like fire and flame that cannot be painted.

. . .

Saturday, July 30

This morning about eight o'clock we weighed anchor, and turned to windward till we came to Yarmouth, another little town upon this island, and there cast anchor again, the wind blowing hard and still westerly. Yarmouth is a smaller town than Cowes; yet the buildings being better, it makes a handsomer prospect at a distance, and the streets are clean and neat. There is one monument in the church which the inhabitants are very proud of, and which we went to see. It was erected to the memory of Sir Robert Holmes, who had formerly been governor of the island. It is his statue in armour, somewhat bigger than the life, standing on his tomb with a truncheon in his hand, between the two pillars of porphyry. Indeed all the marble about it is very fine and good; and they say it was designed by the French King for his palace at Versailles, but was cast away upon this island, and by Sir Robert himself in his life-time applied to this use, and that the whole monument was finished long before he died, (though not fixed up in that place); the inscription likewise (which is very much to his honour) being written by himself. One would think either that he had no defect at all, or had a very ill opinion of the world, seeing he was so careful to make sure of a monument to record his good actions and transmit them to posterity.

Having taken a view of the church, town, and fort, (on which there is seven large guns mounted) three of us took a walk up further into the island, and having gone about two miles, we headed a creek that runs up one end of the town, and then went to Freshwater church, about a mile nearer the town, but on the other side of the creek. Having stayed here some time it grew dark, and my companions were desirous to be gone, lest those whom we had left drinking where we dined in the town, should go on board and leave us. We were told that it was our best way to go straight down to the mouth of the creek, and that there was a ferry boy that would carry us over to the town. But when we came to the house the lazy whelp was in bed, and refused to rise and put us over; upon which we went down to the water-side, with a design to take his boat, and go over by ourselves. We found it very difficult to get the boat, it being fastened to a stake and the tide risen near fifty yards beyond it: I stripped all to my shirt to wade up to it; but missing the causeway, which was under water, I got up to my middle in mud. At last I came to the stake; but to my great disappointment found she was locked and chained. I endeavoured to draw the staple with one of the thole-pins, but in vain; I tried to pull up the stake, but to no purpose; so that after an hour's fatigue and trouble in the wet and mud, I was forced to return without the boat. We had no money in our pockets, and therefore began to conclude to pass the night in some hay-stack, though the wind blew very cold and very hard. In the midst of these troubles one of us recollected that he had a horseshoe in his pocket which he found in his walk, and asked me if I could not wrench the staple out with that. I took it, went, tried and succeeded, and brought the boat ashore to them. Now we rejoiced and all got in, and when I had dressed myself we put off. But the worst of all our troubles was to come yet; for, it being high water and the tide over all the banks, though it was moonlight we could not discern the channel of the creek, but rowing heedlessly straight forward, when we were got about half way over, we found ourselves aground on a mud bank, and striving to row her off by putting our oars in the mud, we broke one and there stuck fast, not having four inches water. We were now in the utmost perplexity, not knowing what in the world to do; we could not tell whether the tide was rising or falling; but at length we plainly perceived it was ebb, and we could feel no deeper water within the reach of our oar. It was hard to lie in an open boat all night exposed to the wind and weather; but it was worse to think how foolish we should look in the morning, when the owner of the boat should catch us in that condition, where we must be exposed to the view of all the town. After we had strove and struggled for half an hour and more, we gave all over, and sat down with our hands before us, despairing to get off; for if the tide had left us we had been never the nearer, we must have sat in the boat, as the mud was too deep for us to walk ashore through it, being up to our necks. At last we bethought ourselves of some means of escaping, and two of us stripped and got out, and thereby lightening the boat, we drew her upon our knees near fifty yards into deeper water, and then with much ado, having but one oar, we got safe ashore under the fort; and having dressed ourselves and tied the man's boat, we went with great joy to the Queen's Head, where we left our companions, whom we found waiting for us, though it was very late. Our boat being gone on board, we were obliged to lie ashore all night; and thus ended our walk.

. . .

Friday, August 5

Called up this morning and hurried aboard, the wind being North-West. About noon we weighed and left Cowes a third time, and sailing by Yarmouth we came into the channel through the Needles; which passage is guarded by Hurst Castle, standing on a spit of land which runs out from the main land of England within a mile of the Isle of Wight. Towards night the wind veered to the Westward, which put us under apprehensions of being forced into port again; but presently after it fell a flat calm, and then we had a small breeze that was fair for half an hour, when it was succeeded by a calm again.

Saturday, August 6

This morning we had a fair breeze for some hours, and then a calm that lasted all day. In the afternoon I leaped overboard and swam round the ship to wash myself. Saw several Porpoises this day. About eight o'clock we came to an anchor in forty fathom water against the tide of flood, somewhere below Portland, and weighed again about eleven, having a small breeze.

Sunday, August 7

Gentle breezes all this day. Spoke with a ship, the *Ruby*, bound for London from Nevis, off the Start of Plymouth. This afternoon spoke with Captain Homans in a ship bound for Boston, who came out of the River when we did, and had been beating about in the Channel all the time we lay at Cowes in the Wight.

Monday, August 8

Fine weather, but no wind worth mentioning, all this day; in the afternoon saw the Lizard.

Tuesday, August 9

Took our leave of the land this morning. Calms the fore part of the day. In the afternoon a small gale, fair. Saw a grampus.

. . .

Friday, August 19

This day we have had a pleasant breeze at East. In the morning we spied a sail upon our larboard bow, about two leagues distance. About noon she put out English colours, and we answered with our ensign, and in the afternoon we spoke with her. She was a ship of New York, Walter Kippen Master, bound from Rochelle in France to Boston with salt. Our captain and Mr. D. went on board and stayed till evening, it being fine weather. Yesterday complaints being made that a Mr. G——n one of the passengers had with a fraudulent design marked the cards, a Court of Justice was called immediately, and he was brought to his trial in form. A Dutchman who could speak no English deposed by his interpreter, that when our mess was on shore at Cowes, the prisoner at the bar marked all the court cards on the back with a pen.

I have sometimes observed that we are apt to fancy the person that cannot speak intelligibly to us, proportionably stupid in understanding, and when we speak two or three words of English to a foreigner, it is louder than ordinary, as if we thought him deaf, and that he had lost the use of his ears as well as his tongue. Something like this I imagine might be the case of Mr. G——n; he fancied the Dutchman could not see what he was about because he could not understand English, and therefore boldly did it before his face.

The evidence was plain and positive, the prisoner could not deny the fact, but replied in his defence, that the cards he marked were not those we commonly played with, but an imperfect pack, which he afterwards gave to the cabin-boy. The Attorney-General observed to the court that it was not likely he should take the pains to mark the cards without some ill design, or some further intention than just to give them to the boy when he had done, who understood nothing at all of cards. But another evidence being called, deposed that he saw the prisoner in the main top one day when he thought himself unobserved, marking a pack of cards on the backs, some with the print of a dirty thumb, others with the top of his finger, &c. Now there being but two packs on board, and the prisoner having just confessed the marking of one, the court perceived the case was plain. In fine the jury brought him in guilty, and he was condemned to be carried up to the round top, and made fast there in view of all the ship's company during the space of three hours, that being the place where the act was committed, and to pay a fine of two bottles of brandy. But the prisoner resisting authority, and refusing to submit to punishment, one of the sailors stepped up aloft and let down a rope to us, which we with much struggling made fast about his middle and hoisted him up into the air, sprawling, by main force. We let him hang, cursing and swearing, for near a quarter of an hour; but at length he crying out murder! and looking black in the face, the rope being over-tort [too taut] about his middle, we thought proper to let him down again; and our mess have excommunicated him till he pays his fine, refusing either to play, eat, drink, or converse with him.

. . .

Thursday, August 25

Our excommunicated ship-mate thinking proper to comply with the sentence the court passed upon him, and expressing himself willing to pay the fine, we have this morning received him into unity again. Man is a sociable being, and it is for aught I know one of the worst of punishments to be excluded from society. I have read abundance of fine things on the subject of solitude, and I know 'tis a common boast in the mouths of those that affect to be thought wise, *that they are never less alone than when alone*. I acknowledge solitude an agreeable refreshment to a busy mind; but were these thinking people obliged to be always alone, I am apt to think they would quickly find their very being insupportable to them. I have heard of a gentleman who underwent seven years close confinement, in the Bastile at Paris. He was a man of sense, he was a thinking man; but being deprived of all conversation, to what purpose should he think? for he was denied even the instruments of expressing his thoughts in writing. There is no burden so grievous to man as time that he knows not how to dispose of. He was forced at last to have recourse to this invention: he daily scattered pieces of paper about the floor of his little room, and then employed himself in picking them up and sticking them in rows and figures on the arm of his elbow-chair; and he used to tell his friends, after his release, that he verily believed if he had not taken this method he should have lost his senses. One of the philosophers, I think it was Plato, used to say, that he had rather be the veriest stupid block in nature, than the possessor of all knowledge without some intelligent being to communicate it to.

What I have said may in a measure account for some particulars in my present way of living here on board. Our company is in general very unsuitably mixed, to keep up the pleasure and spirit of conversation: and if there are one or two pair of us that can sometimes entertain one another for half an hour agreeably, yet perhaps we are seldom in the humour for it together. I rise in the morning and read for an hour or two perhaps, and then reading grows tiresome. Want of exercise occasions want of appetite, so that eating and drinking affords but little pleasure. I tire myself with playing at draughts, then I go to cards; nay there is no play so trifling or childish, but we fly to it for entertainment. A contrary wind, I know not how, puts us all out of good humour; we grow sullen, silent and reserved, and fret at each other upon every little occasion. 'Tis a common opinion among the ladies, that if a man is ill-natured he infallibly discovers it when he is in liquor. But I, who have known many instances to the contrary, will teach them a more effectual method to discover the natural temper and disposition of their humble servants. Let the ladies make one long sea voyage with them, and if they have the least spark of ill nature in them and conceal it to the end of the voyage, I will forfeit all my pretensions to their favour. The wind continues fair.

. . .

Wednesday, September 21

This morning our Steward was brought to the geers [jeers: tackle for raising and lowering yards] and whipped, for making an extravagant use of flour in the puddings, and for several other misdemeanors. It has been perfectly calm all this day, and very hot. I was determined to wash myself in the sea to-day, and should have done so had not the appearance of a shark, that mortal enemy to swimmers, deterred me: he seemed to be about five feet long, moves round the ship at some distance in a slow majestic manner, attended by near a dozen of those they call pilot-fish, of different sizes; the largest of them is not so big as a small mackerel, and the smallest not bigger than my little finger. Two of these diminutive pilots keep just before his nose, and he seems to govern himself in his motions by their direction; while the rest surround him on every side indifferently. A shark is never seen without a retinue of these, who are his purveyors, discovering and distinguishing his prey for him; while he in return gratefully protects them from the ravenous hungry dolphin. They are commonly counted a very greedy fish; yet this refuses to meddle with the bait we have thrown out for him. 'Tis likely he has lately made a full meal.

Thursday, September 22

A fresh gale at West all this day. The shark has left us.

Friday, September 23

This morning we spied a sail to windward of us about two leagues. We shewed our jack upon the ensign-staff, and shortened sail for them till about noon, when she came up with us. She was a snow from Dublin, bound to New York, having upwards of fifty servants on board, of both sexes; they all apeared upon deck, and seemed very much pleased at the sight of us. There is really something strangely cheering to the spirits in the meeting of a ship at sea, containing a society of creatures of the same species and in the same circumstances with ourselves, after we had been long separated and excommunicated as it were from the rest of mankind. My heart fluttered in my breast with joy when I saw so many human countenances, and I could scarce refrain from that kind of laughter which proceeds from some degree of inward pleasure. When we have been for a considerable time tossing on the vast waters, far from the sight of any land or ships, or any mortal creature but ourselves (except a few fish and sea birds) the whole world, for aught we know, may be under a second deluge, and we (like Noah and his company in the Ark) the only surviving remnant of the human race. The two Captains have mutually promised to keep each other company; but this I look upon to be only matter of course, for if ships are unequal in their sailing they seldom stay for one another, especially strangers. This afternoon the wind that has been so long contrary to us, came about to the eastward (and looks as if it would hold), to our no small satisfaction. I find our messmates in a better humour, and more pleased with their present condition than they have been since we came out; which I take to proceed from the contemplation of the miserable circumstances of the passengers on board our neighbour, and making the comparison. We reckon ourselves in a kind of paradise, when we consider how they live, confined and stifled up with such a lousy stinking rabble in this sultry latitude.

. . .

Wednesday, September 28

We had very variable winds and weather last night, accompanied with abundance of rain; and now the wind is come about westerly again, but we must bear it with patience. This afternoon we took up several branches of gulf weed (with which the sea is spread all over from the Western Isles to the coast of America); but one of these branches had something peculiar in it. In common with the rest it had a leaf about three quarters of an inch long, indented like a saw, and a small yellow berry filled with nothing but wind; besides which it bore a fruit of the animal kind, very surprising to see. It was a small shell-fish like a heart, the stalk by which it proceeded from the branch being partly of a gristly kind. Upon this one branch of the weed there were near forty of these vegetable animals; the smallest of them near the end contained a substance somewhat like an oyster, but the larger were visibly animated, opening their shells every moment, and thrusting out a set of unformed claws, not unlike those of a crab; but the inner part was still a kind of soft jelly. Observing the weed more narrowly, I spied a very small crab crawling among it, about as big as the head of a ten-penny nail, and of a yellowish colour, like the weed itself. This gave me some reason to think that he was a native of the branch, that he had not long since been in the same condition with the rest of those little embrios that appeared in the shells, this being the method of their generation; and that consequently all the rest of this odd kind of fruit might be crabs in due time. To strengthen my conjecture, I have resolved to keep the weed in salt water, renewing it every day till we come on shore, by this experiment to see whether any more crabs will be produced or not in this manner. I remember that the last calm we had, we took notice of a large crab upon the surface of the sea, swimming from one branch of weed to another, which he seemed to prey upon; and I likewise recollect that at Boston, in New England, I have often seen small crabs with a shell like a snail's upon their backs, crawling about in the salt water; and likewise at Portsmouth in England. It is likely nature has provided this hard shell to secure them till their own proper shell has acquired a sufficient hardness, which once perfected, they quit their old habitation and venture abroad safe in their own strength. The various changes that silk-worms, butterflies, and several other insects go through, make such alterations and metamorphoses not improbable. This day the captain of the snow with one of his passengers came on board us; but the wind beginning to blow, they did not stay dinner, but returned to their own vessel.

Thursday, September 29

Upon shifting the water in which I had put the weed yesterday, I found another crab, much smaller than the former, who seemed to have newly left his habitation. But the weed begins to wither, and the rest of the embrios are dead. This new comer fully convinces me, that at least this sort of crabs are generated in this manner. The snow's Captain dined on board us this day. Little or no wind.

Friday, September 30

. . . I took in some more gulf-weed to-day with the boat-hook, with shells upon it like that before mentioned, and three living perfect crabs, each less than the nail of my little finger. One of them had something particularly observable, to wit, a thin piece of the white shell which I before noticed as their covering while they remained in the condition of embrios, sticking close to his natural shell upon his back. This sufficiently confirms me in my opinion of the manner of their generation. I have put this remarkable crab with a piece of the gulf-weed, shells, &c. into a glass phial filled with salt water, (for want of spirits of wine) in hopes to preserve the curiosity till I come on shore. The wind is South-West.

. . .

Sunday, October 9

We have had the wind fair all the morning: at twelve o'clock we sounded, perceiving the water visibly changed, and struck ground at twenty-five fathoms, to our universal joy. After dinner one of our mess went up aloft to look out, and presently pronounced the long-wished for sound, LAND! LAND! In less than an hour we could descry it from the deck, appearing like tufts of trees. I could not discern it so soon as the rest; my eyes were dimmed with the suffusion of two small drops of joy. By three o'clock we were run in within two leagues of the land, and spied a small sail standing along shore. We would gladly have spoken with her, for our captain was unaquainted with the coast, and knew not what land it was that we saw. We made all the sail we could to speak with her. We made a signal of distress; but all would not do, the ill-natured dog would not come near us. Then we stood off again till morning, not caring to venture too near.

Monday, October 10

This morning we stood in again for land, and we, that had been here before, all agreed that it was Cape Henlopen: about noon we were come very near, and to our great joy saw the pilot-boat come off to us, which was exceeding welcome. He brought on board about a peck of apples with him; they seemed the most delicious I ever tasted in my life: the salt provisions we had been used to, gave them a relish. We had an extraordinary fair wind all the afternoon and ran above an hundred miles up the Delaware before ten at night. The country appears very pleasant to the eye, being covered with woods, except here and there a house and plantation. We cast anchor when the tide turned, about two miles below Newcastle, and there lay till the morning tide.

Tuesday, October 11

This morning we weighed anchor with a gentle breeze, and passed by Newcastle, whence they hailed us and bade us welcome. 'Tis extreme fine weather. The sun enlivens our stiff limbs with his glorious rays of warmth and brightness. The sky looks gay, with here and there a silver cloud. The fresh breezes from the woods refresh us, the immediate prospect of liberty after so long and irksome confinement ravishes us. In short all things conspire to make this the most joyful day I ever knew. As we passed by Chester some of the company went on shore, impatient once more to tread on *terra firma,* and designing for Philadelphia by land. Four of us remained on board, not caring for the fatigue of travel when we knew the voyage had much weakened us. About eight at night, the wind failing us, we cast anchor at Redbank, six miles from Philadelphia, and thought we must be obliged to lie on board that night: but some young Philadelphians happening to be out upon their pleasure in a boat, they came on board, and offered to take us up with them: we accepted of their kind proposal, and about ten o'clock landed at Philadelphia, heartily congratulating each other upon our having happily completed so tedious and dangerous a voyage. Thank God!

To George Whately, 1785

Dear old Friend   Passy, May 23. 1785.

I sent you a few Lines the other Day, with the Medallion, when I should have written more but was prevented by the coming in of a Bavard, who worried me till Evening. I bore with him, and now you are to bear with me: For I shall probably *bavarder* [to babble, prattle, blab] in answering your Letter.

I am not acquainted with the Saying of Alphonsus which you allude to, as a Sanctification of your Rigidity in refusing to allow me the Plea of Old Age as an Excuse for my Want of Exactitude in Correspondence. What was that Saying? You do not it seems, feel any occasion for such an Excuse, tho' you are, as you say, rising 75. But I am rising (perhaps more properly falling) 80. & I leave the Excuse with you till you arrive at that Age; perhaps you may then be more sensible of its Validity, and see fit to use it for your self.

I must agree with you that the Gout is bad, and that the [kidney or bladder] Stone is worse. I am happy in not having them both together: and I join in your Prayer that you may live till you die without either. But I doubt the Author of the Epitaph you send me was a little mistaken, when he speaking of the World, he says that

> he ne'er car'd a pin,
> What they said or may say of the Mortal within,

It is so natural to wish to be well spoken of, whether alive or dead, that I imagine he could not be quite exempt from that Desire, and that at least he wish'd to be thought a Wit, or he would not have given himself the Trouble of writing so good an Epitaph to leave behind him. Was it not as worthy of his Care that the World should say he was an honest and a good Man?—I like better the concluding Sentiment in the old Song call'd the *Old Man's Wish*, wherein after wishing for a warm House in a Country Town, an easy Horse, some good old Authors, ingenious & cheerful Companions, a Pudding on Sundays with stout Ale and a Bottle of Burgundy, &c. &c. in separate Stanzas, each ending with this Burthen

> May I govern my Passions with an absolute Sway,
> Grow wiser and better as my Strength wears away,
> Without Gout, or Stone, by a gentle Decay,

he adds,

> With a Courage undaunted may I face my last day;
> And when I am gone, may the better Sort say,
> In the Morning when sober, in the Evening when mellow,
> He's gone, and has not left behind him his Fellow;
>   For he govern'd his Passions, &c

But what signifys our Wishing. Things happen after all as they will happen. I have sung that *wishing Song* a thousand times when I was young, and now find at Fourscore that the three Contraries have befallen me: being subject to the Gout, and the Stone, and not being yet Master of all my Passions. Like the proud Girl in my Country, who wish'd and resolv'd not to marry a Parson, nor a Presbyterian, nor an Irishman, and at length found herself married to an Irish Presbyterian Parson. You see I have some reason to wish that in a future State I may not only be *as well as I was*, but a little better. And I hope it: For I too, with your Poet, *trust in God*. And when I observe that there is great Frugality as well as Wisdom in his Works, since he has been evidently sparing both of Labour and Materials; for by the various wonderful Inventions of Propagation he has provided for the continual peopling his World with Plants and Animals, without being at the Trouble of repeated new Creations; and by the natural Reduction of compound Substances to their original Elements, capable of being employ'd in new Compositions, he has prevented the Necessity of creating new Matter; for that the Earth, Water, Air & perhaps fire, which, being compounded, from Wood, do when the Wood is dissolved return and again become Air, Earth, Fire and Water: I say that when I see nothing annihilated, and not even a Drop of Water wasted, I cannot suspect the Annihilation of Souls, or believe that he will suffer the daily Waste of Millions of Minds ready made that now exist, and put himself to the continual Trouble of making new ones. Thus finding myself to exist in the World, I believe I shall in some Shape or other always exist: And with all the Inconveniencies human Life is liable to, I shall not object to a new Edition of mine; hoping however that the Errata of the last may be corrected.

I return your Note of Children receiv'd in the Foundling Hospital at Paris from 1741 to 1755 inclusive, and I have added the Years preceding as far back as 1710, together with the general Christnings of the City; and the Years succeeding down to 1770. Those since that Period I have not been able to obtain. I have noted in the Margin the gradual Increase, viz. from every tenth Child so thrown upon the Publick, till it comes to every third. Fifteen Years have pass'd since the last Account, & probably it may now amount to one half. Is it right to encourage this monstrous Deficiency of natural Affection? A Surgeon I met with here, excus'd the Women of Paris, by Saying seriously that they *could not* give Suck, *Car, dit il, ils n'ont point des Tetons.* He assur'd me it was a Fact, and had me look at them, and observe how flat they were on the Breast; they have nothing more there, says he, than I have upon the Back of my Hand. I have since thought that there might be some Truth in his Observation, and that possibly Nature finding they made no use of Bubbies, has left off giving them any. Yet since Rousseau, with admirable Eloquence pleaded for the Rights of Children to their Mother's Milk, the Mode has chang'd a little, and some Ladies of Quality now suckle their Infants and find Milk enough. May the Mode descend to the lower Ranks, till it becomes no longer the Custom to pack their Infants away, as soon as born, to the *Enfans-trouvés* [foundling homes], with the careless Observation that the King is better able to maintain them.

I am credibly inform'd that nine tenths of them die there pretty soon; which is said to be a great Relief to the Institution, whose Funds would not otherwise be sufficient to bring up the Remainder. Except the few Persons of Quality abovementioned, and the Multitude who send to the Hospital, the Practice is to hire Nurses in the Country to carry out the Children and take care of them there. Here is an Office for examining the Health of Nurses and giving them Licences. They come to Town on certain Days of the Week in Companies to receive the Children, and we often meet Trains of them on the Road returning to the neighbouring Villages with each a Child in Arms. But those who are good enough to try this way of raising their Children, are often not able to pay the Expense, so that the Prisons of Paris are crowded with wretched Fathers and Mothers confined [as debtors] *pour mois de Nourice* [during the months of their children being wet-nursed]; tho' it is laudably a favourite Charity to pay for them and set such Prisoners at Liberty. I wish Success to the new Project of assisting the Poor to keep their Children at home, because I think there is no Nurse like a Mother (or not many) and that if Parents did not immediately send their Infants out of their Sight, they would in a few Days begin to love them, and thence be spurr'd to greater Industry for their Maintenance. . . .

The Philadelphia Bank goes on, as I hear, very well. What you call the Cincinnati Institution is no Institution of our Government, but a private Convention among the Officers of our late Army, & so universally dislik'd by the People that it is suppos'd it will be dropt. It was consider'd as an Attempt to establish something like an hereditary Rank or Nobility. I hold with you that it was wrong; may I add that all descending Honours are wrong & absurd; that the Honour of virtuous Actions appertains only to him that performs them, and is in its nature incommunicable. If it were communicable by Descent, it must also be divisible among the Descendants, & the more ancient the Family, the less would be found existing in any one Branch of it; to say nothing of the greater Chance of unlucky Interruptions.

Our Constitution seems not to be well understood with you. If the Congress were a permanent Body, there would be more Reason in being jealous of giving it Powers. But its Members are chosen annually, cannot be chosen more than three Years successively, nor more than three Years in seven, and any of them may be recall'd at any time, when their Constituents shall be dissatisfied with their Conduct. They are of the People & return again to mix with the People, having no more durable Pre-eminence than the different Grains of Sand in an Hourglass. Such an Assembly cannot easily become dangerous to Liberty. They are the Servants of the People, sent together to do the People's Business and promote the public Welfare; their Powers must be sufficient, or their Duties cannot be performed.— They have no profitable Appointments, but a mere Payment of daily Wages, such as are scarcely equivalent to their Expences, so that having no Chance for great Places & enormous Salaries or Pensions as in some Countries, there is no briguing [corrupt electioneering, from *briguer*] or bribing for Elections. I wish old England were as happy in its Government, but I do not see it. Your People however think their Constitution the best in the World, and affect to despise ours.—It is comfortable to have a good Opinion of one's self and of every thing that belongs to us, to think one's own Religion, King and Wife the best of all possible Wives, Kings & Religions. . . .

By Mr Dollond's [John Dolland, a London optician, inventor of the heliometer] Saying that my double Spectacles can only serve particular Eyes, I doubt he has not been rightly inform'd of their Construction. I imagine it will be found pretty generally true, that the same Convexity of Glass through which a Man sees clearest and best at the Distance proper for Reading, is not the best for greater Distances. I therefore had formerly two Pair of Spectacles, which I shifted occasionally, as in travelling I sometimes read and often wanted to regard the Prospects. Finding this Change troublesome and not always sufficiently ready, I had the Glasses cut, and half of each kind associated in the same Circle, thus

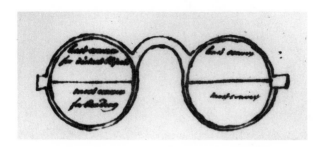

By this means, as I wear my Spectacles constantly, I have only to move my Eyes up or down as I want to see distinctly far or near, the proper Glasses being always ready. This I find more particularly convenient since my being in France, the Glasses that serve me best at Table to see what I eat, not being the best to see the Faces of those on the other Side of the Table who speak to me; and when one's Ears are not well accustomed to the Sounds of a Language, a Sight of the Movements in the Features of him that speaks helps to explain, so that I understand French better by the help of my spectacles.—

. . .

Adieu, my dear Friend, and believe me ever. Yours very affectionately

B. Franklin

2 Friendship and flirtation.

Most of Franklin's correspondence was with other men and had to do with his business interests or his political and intellectual pursuits. There are, unfortunately, few letters as chatty as the one he wrote George Whately, whose conversational style gives a sense of what it would have been like to spend time with Franklin. It also suggests in the first paragraph what he deliberately tried to avoid in himself and in the company he kept. He had a lifelong aversion to babblers, people who talked too much with too little to say, and he always strove to avoid babbling himself. In his early days as a printer in Philadelphia he became famous for his yearly *Poor Richard's Almanack,* with its aphorisms salted through the pages. These are the source of the pithy injunctions to industry, thrift, earnestness, and humility that gave him his reputation as the patron saint of American businessmen and go-getters generally, an ill-deserved image that has stifled understanding of his true qualities. The point here is that one of Poor Richard's most common pieces of advice was, in modern parlance, to just shut up:

Great talkers, little Doers.

Here comes the Orator with his Flood of words, and his Drop of Reason.

None preaches better than the ant, and she says nothing.

Great talkers should be cropt, for they have no need of ears.

Best is the tongue that feels the rein;—
He that talks much, must talk in vain

We from the wordy Torrent fly;
Who listens to the chattering [Mag]Pye?

Here comes Glib-Tongue: who can out-flatter a Dedication, and lie like
an Epitaph.

Franklin published his recipe for comprehensively boring people in his
newspaper, the *Pennsylvania Gazette*.

With women correspondents he was more likely to talk about himself. In
his letters to women we can catch an element of the quality that affected
everyone who enjoyed his company. He treated them all on an equal
footing, men and women, rich and poor, old and young, sophisticated and
ingenuous. They were all human, and they deserved respect for their
humanity, no more and no less than the respect he accorded himself. His
evenhanded posture stands out in letters to women because this was a time
when women were frequently treated as less than equal, and as having
minds ill suited to the contemplation and discussion of anything beyond the
nursery and the garden gate. Franklin himself believed that they should
stay out of politics. There is obviously a play of sexuality—and whatever it
implies—in his relation with younger women. He loved to flirt, and applied
himself to the art with the same energy he brought to other amusements.
But he does not patronize, does not condescend, any more than he did with
Deborah. The lighthearted, jocular tone of these letters conceals a deep
respect for the persons to whom they are addressed. Even flirtation, on
Franklin's terms, is a playful way of saying, "I value you, you are worth the
trouble."

The selections below illuminate Franklin's different relationships with six
women who were important to him over the course of his life: Catharine
Ray Greene, a long-time friend both before and after her marriage; Mary
(Polly) Stevenson Hewson, the daughter of Franklin's landlady in London;
Anna Mordaunt Shipley, the wife of one of Franklin's closest friends in
England; Madame Brillon and Madame Helvétius, rival hostesses in the
elite salons of Paris; and Emma Thompson, a correspondent of Franklin's
old age.

Catharine Ray was one of Franklin's favorites. They met in Boston in
1754, when she was visiting her sister and Franklin was organizing the post

office. Twenty-five years his junior, she was then twenty-three. They were instantly friends and remained so throughout his life. They left Boston together on December 30, 1754, and "Katy" rode with him as far as Westerly, Rhode Island, where they visited her brother-in-law Samuel Ward, the future governor of Rhode Island, and his family. From Westerly, Catharine returned to her home on Block Island, while Franklin made his leisurely way back to Philadelphia. She immediately began their long correspondence by asking him to "love me one thousandth Part so well as I do you," while requesting at the same time his advice about two rival suitors. She accepted neither of them and three years later married William Greene, who became governor of Rhode Island in 1778, during the Revolution. Before her marriage, Franklin's letters were openly flirtatious, like the one below. But we have to remember that expressions of love in the eighteenth century often conveyed affection and esteem more than desire. Nevertheless, his letters after she married stopped being flirtatious and became simply companionable. Franklin and Katy enjoyed a long companionship that included Franklin's wife and daughter.

Franklin's relations with Polly Stevenson were similar to those with Catharine Ray Greene but with an added dimension, and without flirtation. They met in 1757 when Franklin took rooms at the house of her mother on Craven Street in London, his headquarters throughout his many years in London as colonial agent. She was eighteen, thirty-three years his junior, and possessed an inquiring mind that answered to his own. Their earliest letters, written when she was visiting relatives, are mostly on scientific questions. Franklin was already world famous for his work on electricity. He had been elected to the Royal Society, England's most prestigious scientific organization, before he arrived in London. In 1759 the University of St. Andrews in Scotland conferred an honorary doctorate on him. Thereafter he was known everywhere as Doctor Franklin. But he never traded on this fame, with Polly or any other friend. He took her seriously and took her interest in scientific matters seriously. Like his friendship with Katy, their companionship lasted throughout his life. He was present at her marriage to William Hewson, a distinguished physician, in 1770. Hewson died in 1774; and after the Revolutionary War Polly left England for Philadelphia in order to be near Franklin in his old age. The letter to her below has all the newsiness of an exchange between close friends, with no hint to suggest that the author, despite having an audience with the king of France, is in any way older or wiser than the young woman to whom it is sent.

It will scarcely come as a surprise that Franklin got along well with children. The same evenhanded, attentive demeanor that charmed his older friends enabled him to meet with children on their own terms. One of his closest friends in England was Jonathan Shipley, bishop of St. Asaph, who openly espoused the American cause. Shipley had married Anna Mordaunt, niece of the earl of Peterborough. They lived with their son and four daughters at Twyford, their country estate near Southampton, where Franklin spent two weeks in the summer of 1771. (It was in the garden at Twyford that he began composing the *Autobiography*.) When he returned to London, by coach, he took the youngest daughter, Kitty, back with him to her boarding school. On the way, as Kitty and Doctor Franklin selected husbands of appropriate rank and fortune for Kitty's sisters, they explored the realm of fashionable marriages and frank discussion of worldly prospects that would become the preoccupation of Jane Austen. In the selection below Franklin describes their plotting together to Kitty's mother.

As will have become evident, Franklin's devotion to Deborah never prevented him from frankly cherishing the company of women. As minister to France and a widower, he managed quite effortlessly to enchant a large number of the ladies of Paris. When he discovered that they were as fond of raillery as he was, and considerably more practiced at it, he indulged himself without restraint and soon became known as a gallant and a wit. Anne-Louise Boivin d'Hardancourt Brillon de Jouy, known as Madame Brillon, was his near neighbor in Passy, the fashionable suburb of Paris where he lived as minister. He had tea at her house twice a week for four years and carried on an elaborate, somewhat studied dalliance with her in writing, of which the letter below is a sample.

Madame Brillon's principal rival was Anne-Catherine de Ligniville d'Autricourt, otherwise Madame Helvétius, widow of one of France's notable philosophers. At fifty-eight she was only thirteen years Franklin's junior and had been a famous beauty of the previous generation. Madame Helvétius presided over a salon at Auteuil, near Passy, where gallantry and sexual innuendo mixed easily with conversation among France's leading intellectuals and statesmen. Franklin became a regular visitor there, which brought him familiarity with people who mattered to his diplomatic mission. But that was not the only or even the main reason for his frequent appearance at the salons. Madame Helvétius entranced him not only with her fading beauty and her lively conversation but with her "artless simplicity," the casual, confident manners of the born aristocrat heedless of the conventions of bourgeois society. Franklin was always quick to do in Rome as the Romans did, and being shockproof to begin with, he scandalized his colleague in diplomacy, the earnest and upright John Adams. (We will encounter in later pages the difficulties that John Adams brought to their mission.) The consternation of Adams and his wife, Abigail, thoroughpaced Yankees, when presented with the spectacle of "the Doctor" and the plainspeaking female aristocrat gives us an outsider's view of Franklin's relationship with the ladies.

The final letter in this chapter reminds us that Franklin's circle of friends in England extended more widely than we can know. This letter to Emma Thompson, in answer to one of hers, is our only clue to her existence or to that of the friend mentioned. She was apparently visiting France, where Franklin had arrived two months earlier to represent the independent United States. He evidently knew Emma well enough to joke with her about the Revolution and the trip he had made to Quebec the year before in the unsuccessful bid to bring Canada into the union, subjects on which he seldom permitted himself to speak lightly. I include the letter because it gives a picture of Franklin as he saw himself at age seventy-one.

Rules for Making Oneself a Disagreeable Companion, 1750

RULES, by the Observation of which, a Man of Wit and Learning may nevertheless make himself a *disagreeable* Companion.

Your Business is to *shine;* therefore you must by all means prevent the shining of others, for their Brightness may make yours the less distinguish'd. To this End,

1. If possible engross the whole Discourse; and when other Matter fails,

talk much of your-self, your Education, your Knowledge, your Circumstances, your Successes in Business, your Victories in Disputes, your own wise Sayings and Observations on particular occasions, &c. &c. &c.

2. If when you are out of Breath, one of the Company should seize the Opportunity of saying something; watch his Words, and, if possible, find somewhat either in his Sentiment or Expression, immediately to contradict and raise a Dispute upon. Rather than fail, criticise even his Grammar.

3. If another should be saying an indisputably good Thing; either give no Attention to it; or interrupt him; or draw away the Attention of others; or, if you can guess what he would be at, be quick and say it before him; or, if he gets it said, and you perceive the Company pleas'd with it, own it to be a good Thing, and withal remark that it had been said by Bacon, Locke, Bayle, or some other eminent Writer: thus you deprive him of the Reputation he might have gain'd by it, and gain some yourself, as you hereby show your great Reading and Memory.

4. When modest Men have been thus treated by you a few times, they will chuse ever after to be silent in your Company; then you may shine on without Fear of a Rival; rallying them at the same time for their Dullness, which will be to you a new Fund of Wit.

Thus you will be sure to please *yourself*. The polite Man aims at pleasing *others*, but you shall go beyond him even in that. A Man can be present only in one Company, but may at the same time be absent in twenty. He can please only where he is, you wherever you are *not*.

To Catharine Ray, 1755

Philada. Sept. 11. 1755

Begone, Business, for an Hour, at least, and let me chat a little with my Katy.

I have now before me, my dear Girl, three of your Favours, viz. of March the 3d. March the 30th. and May the 1st. The first I receiv'd just before I set out on a long Journey and the others while I was on that Journey, which held me near Six Weeks. Since my Return, I have been in such a perpetual Hurry of publick Affairs of various kinds, as render'd it impracticable for me to keep up my private Correspondencies, even those that afforded me the greatest Pleasure.

You ask in your last, How I do, and what I am doing, and whether every body loves me yet, and why I make 'em do so? In the first place, I am so well Thanks to God, that I do not remember I was ever better. I still relish all the Pleasures of Life that a temperate Man can in reason desire, and thro' Favour I have them all in my Power. This happy Situation shall continue as long as God pleases, who knows what is best for his Creatures, and I hope will enable me to bear with Patience and dutiful Submission any Change he may think fit to make that is less agreable. As to the second Question, I must confess, (but don't you be jealous) that many more People love me now than ever did before: For since I saw you, I have been enabled to do some general Services to the Country, and to the Army, for which both have thank'd and prais'd me; and say they love me; they *say so,* as you us'd to do; and if I were to ask any Favours of them, would, perhaps, as readily refuse me: So that I find little real Advantage in being belov'd, but it pleases my Humour.

Now it is near four Months since I have been favour'd with a single Line from you; but I will not be angry with you, because 'tis my fault. I ran in debt to you three or four Letters, and as I did not pay, you would not trust me any more, and you had some Reason: But believe me, I am honest, and tho' I should never make equal Returns, you shall see I'll keep fair Accounts. Equal Returns I can never make, tho' I should write to you by every Post: For the Pleasure I receive from one of yours, is more than you can have from two of mine. The small News, the domestic Occurrences among our Friends, the natural Pictures you draw of Persons, the sensible Observations and Reflections you make, and the easy chatty Manner in which you express every thing, all contribute to heighten the Pleasure; and the more, as they remind me of those Hours and Miles that we talk'd away so agreably, even in a Winter Journey, a wrong Road, and a soaking Shower.

I long to hear whether you have continu'd ever since in that Monastery; or have broke into the World again, doing pretty Mischief; how the Lady Wards [Samuel Ward's three sisters, Hannah, Margaret, and Elizabeth] do, and how many of them are married, or about it; what is become of Mr. B. and Mr. L. and what the State of your Heart is at this Instant? but that, perhaps I ought not to know; and therefore I will not conjure, as you sometimes say I do. If I could conjure, it should be to know what was that *oddest Question about me that ever was thought of,* which you tell me a Lady had just sent to ask you.

I commend your prudent Resolutions in the Article of granting Favours to Lovers: But if I were courting you, I could not heartily approve such Conduct. I should even be malicious enough to say you were too *knowing,* and tell you the old Story of the Girl and the Miller [this has not been identified].

I enclose you the Songs you write for, and with them your Spanish Letter with a Translation. I honour that honest Spaniard for loving you: It show'd the Goodness of his Taste and Judgment. But you must forget him, and bless some worthy young Englishman.

You have spun a long Thread, 5022 Yards! It will reach almost from Block Island hither. I wish I had hold of one End of it, to pull you to me: But you would break it rather than come. The Cords of Love and Friendship are longer and stronger, and in Times past have drawn me farther; even back from England to Philadelphia. I guess that some of the same kind will one day draw you out of that Island.

I was extreamly pleas'd with the Turff [peat from a Rhode Island bog] you sent me. The Irish People who have seen it, say, 'tis the right Sort; but I cannot learn that we have anything like it here. The Cheeses, particularly one of them, were excellent: All our Friends have tasted it, and all agree that it exceeds any English Cheese they ever tasted. Mrs. Franklin was very proud, that a young Lady should have so much Regard for her old Husband, as to send him such a Present. We talk of you every Time it comes to Table; She is sure you are a sensible Girl, and a notable Housewife; and talks of bequeathing me to you as a Legacy; But I ought to wish you a better, and hope she will live these 100 Years; for we are grown old together, and if she has any faults, I am so us'd to 'em that I don't perceive 'em, as the Song says,

Some Faults we have all, and so may my Joan,
    But then they're exceedingly small;
And now I'm us'd to 'em they're just like my own,
    I scarcely can see 'em at all,
      My dear Friends,
    I scarcely can see them at all.

Indeed I begin to think she has none, as I think of you. And since she is willing I should love you as much as you are willing to be lov'd by me; let us join in wishing the old Lady a long Life and a happy.

With her respectful Compliments to your good Mother and Sisters, present mine, tho' unknown, and believe me to be, Dear Girl, Your affectionate Friend and humble Servant B Franklin

Sally says, Papa, my Love to Miss Katy.

. . .

To Mary Stevenson, 1767

Dear Polly   Paris, Sept. 14. 1767

I am always pleas'd with a Letter from you, and I flatter myself you may be sometimes pleas'd in receiving one from me, tho' it should be of little Importance, such as this, which is to consist of a few occasional Remarks made here and in my Journey hither.

Soon after I left you in that agreable Society at Bromley [the village in which Dr. John Hawkesworth supervised his wife's school for girls; Polly and her friend Dolly Blunt were often guests of the Hawkesworths], I took the Resolution of making a Trip with Sir John Pringle into France. We set out the 28th past. All the way to Dover we were furnished with Post Chaises hung so as to lean forward, the Top coming down over one's Eyes, like a Hood, as if to prevent one's seeing the Country, which being one of my great Pleasures, I was engag'd in perpetual Disputes with the Innkeepers, Hostlers and Postillions about getting the Straps taken up a Hole or two before, and let down as much behind, they insisting that the Chaise leaning forward was an Ease to the Horses, and that the contrary would kill them. I suppose the Chaise leaning forward looks to them like a Willingness to go forward; and that its hanging back shows a Reluctance. They added other Reasons that were no Reasons at all, and made me, as upon a 100 other Occasions, almost wish that Mankind had never been endow'd with a reasoning Faculty, since they know so little how to make use of it, and so often mislead themselves by it; and that they had been furnish'd with a good sensible Instinct instead of it.

At Dover the next Morning we embark'd for Calais with a Number of

Passengers who had never been before at Sea. They would previously make a hearty Breakfast, because if the Wind should fail, we might not get over till Supper-time. Doubtless they thought that when they had paid for their Breakfast they had a Right to it, and that when they had swallowed it they were sure of it. But they had scarce been out half an Hour before the Sea laid Claim to it, and they were oblig'd to deliver it up. So it seems there are Uncertainties even beyond those between the Cup and the Lip. If ever you go to sea, take my Advice, and live sparingly a Day or two before hand. The Sickness, if any, will be the lighter and sooner over. We got to Calais that Evening.

Various Impositions we suffer'd from Boat-men, Porters, &c. on both Sides the Water. I know not which are most rapacious, the English or French; but the latter have, with their Knavery the most Politeness.

The Roads we found equally good with ours in England, in some Places pav'd with smooth Stone like our new Streets for many Miles together, and Rows of Trees on each Side and yet there are no Turnpikes. But then the poor Peasants complain'd to us grievously, that they were oblig'd to work upon the Roads full two Months in the Year without being paid for their Labour; Whether this is Truth, or whether, like Englishmen, they grumble Cause or no Cause, I have not yet been able fully to inform myself.

The Women we saw at Calais, on the Road, at Bouloigne and in the Inns and Villages, were generally of dark Complexions; but arriving at Abbeville we found a sudden Change, a Multitude both of Women and Men in that Place appearing remarkably fair. Whether this is owing to a small Colony of Spinners, Woolcombers and Weavers, &c. brought hither from Holland with the Woollen Manufacture about 60 Years ago; or to their being less expos'd to the Sun than in other Places, their Business keeping them much within Doors, I know not. Perhaps as in some other Cases, different Causes may club in producing the Effect, but the Effect itself is certain. Never was I in a Place of greater Industry, Wheels and Looms going in every House. As soon as we left Abbeville the Swarthiness return'd. I speak generally, for here are some fair Women at Paris, who I think are not whiten'd by Art. As to Rouge, they don't pretend to imitate Nature in laying it on. There is no gradual Diminution of the Colour from the full Bloom in the Middle of the Cheek to the faint Tint near the Sides,

nor does it show itself differently in different Faces. I have not had the
Honour of being at any Lady's Toylette to see how it is laid on, but I fancy I
can tell you how it is or may be done: Cut a Hole of 3 Inches Diameter in a
Piece of Paper, place it on the Side of your Face in such a Manner as that the
Top of the Hole may be just under your Eye; then with a Brush dipt in the
Colour paint Face and Paper together; so when the Paper is taken off there
will remain a round Patch of Red exactly the Form of the Hole. This is the
Mode, from the Actresses on the Stage upwards thro' all Ranks of Ladies to
the Princesses of the Blood, but it stops there, the Queen not using it,
having in the Serenity, Complacence and Benignity that shine so eminently
in or rather through her Countenance, sufficient Beauty, tho' now an old
Woman, to do extremely well without it.

You see I speak of the Queen as if I had seen her, and so I have; for you
must know I have been at Court. We went to Versailles last Sunday, and
had the Honour of being presented to the King [Louis XV], he spoke to
both of us very graciously and chearfully, is a handsome Man, has a very
lively Look, and appears younger than he is. In the Evening we were at the
Grand Couvert, where the Family sup in Publick. The Form of their sitting
at the Table was this:

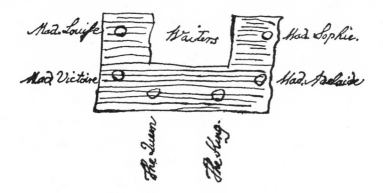

The Table as you see was half a Hollow Square, the Service Gold. When
either made a Sign for Drink, the Word was given by one of the Waiters, *A
boire pour le Roy,* or *A boire pour la Reine* [drink for the king/queen], &c.
then two Persons within the Square approach'd, one with Wine the other
with Water in Caraffes, each drank a little Glass of what they brought, and

then put both the Caraffes with a Glass on a Salver and presented it. Their Distance from each other was such as that other Chairs might have been plac'd between any two of them. An Officer of the Court brought us up thro' the Croud of Spectators, and plac'd Sir John so as to stand between the King and Madame Adelaide, and me between the Queen and Madame Victoire. The King talk'd a good deal to Sir John, asking many Questions about our Royal Family; and did me too the Honour of taking some Notice of me; that's saying enough, for I would not have you think me so much pleas'd with this King and Queen as to have a Whit less Regard than I us'd to have for ours. No Frenchman shall go beyond me in thinking my own King and Queen the very best in the World and the most amiable.

Versailles has had infinite Sums laid out in Building it and Supplying it with Water: Some say the Expence exceeded 80 Millions Sterling. The Range of Building is immense, the Garden Front, most magnificent all of hewn Stone, the Number of Statues, Figures, Urns, &c in Marble and Bronze of exquisite Workmanship is beyond Conception. But the Water-works are out of Repair, and so is great Part of the Front next the Town, looking with its shabby half Brick Walls and broken Windows not much better than the Houses in Durham Yard. There is, in short, both at Versailles and Paris, a prodigious Mixture of Magnificence and Negligence, with every kind of Elegance except that of Cleanliness, and what we call *Tidyness*. Tho' I must do Paris the Justice to say, that in two Points of Cleanliness they exceed us. The Water they drink, tho' from the River, they render as pure as that of the best Spring, by filtring it thro' Cisterns fill'd with Sand; and the Streets by constant Sweeping are fit to walk in tho' there is no pav'd foot Path. Accordingly, many well dress'd People are constantly seen walking in them. The Crouds of Coaches and Chairs for that Reason is not so great; Men as well as Women carry Umbrellas in their Hands, which they extend in case of Rain or two much Sun; and a Man with an Umbrella not taking up more than 3 foot square or 9 square feet of the Street, when if in a Coach he would take up 240 square feet, you can easily conceive that tho' the Streets here are narrower they may be much less encumber'd. They are extreamly well pav'd, and the Stones being generally Cubes, when worn on one Side may be turn'd and become new.

The Civilities we every where receive give us the strongest Impressions of the French Politeness. It seems to be a Point settled here universally that Strangers are to be treated with Respect, and one has just the same Deference shewn one here by being a Stranger as in England by being a Lady. The Custom House Officers at Port St. Denis, as we enter'd Paris, were about to seize 2 Doz. of excellent Bourdeaux Wine given us at Boulogne, and which we brought with us; but as soon as they found we were Strangers, it was immediately remitted on that Account. At the Church of Notre Dame, when we went to see a magnificent Illumination with Figures &c. for the deceas'd Dauphiness, we found an immense Croud who were kept out by Guards; but the Officer being told that we were Strangers from England, he immediately admitted us, accompanied and show'd us every thing. Why don't we practice this Urbanity to Frenchmen? Why should they be allow'd to out-do us in any thing?

Here is an Exhibition of Paintings, &c. like ours in London, to which Multitudes flock daily. I am not Connoisseur enough to judge which has most Merit. Every Night, Sundays not excepted here are Plays or Operas; and tho' the Weather has been hot, and the Houses full, one is not incommoded by the Heat so much as with us in Winter. They must have some Way of changing the Air that we are not acquainted with. I shall enquire into it.

Travelling is one Way of lengthening Life, at least in Appearance. It is but a Fortnight since we left London; but the Variety of Scenes we have gone through makes it seem equal to Six Months living in one Place. Perhaps I have suffered a greater Change too in my own Person then I could have done in Six Years at home. I had not been here Six Days before my Taylor and Peruquier [wigmaker] had transform'd me into a Frenchman. Only think what a Figure I make in a little Bag Wig and naked Ears! They told me I was become 20 Years younger, and look'd very galante; so being in Paris where the Mode is to be sacredly follow'd, I was once very near making Love to my Friend's Wife.

This Letter shall cost you a Shilling [in the eighteenth century it was the recipient of a letter who paid the postage], and you may think it cheap when you consider that it has cost me at least 50 Guineas to get into the Situation that enables me to write it. Besides, I might, if I had staid at home, have won perhaps two shillings of you at Cribbidge. By the Way, now I mention Cards, let me tell you that Quadrille is quite out of Fashion here, and English Whisk all the Mode, at Paris and the Court.

And pray look upon it as no small Matter, that surrounded as I am by the Glories of this World and Amusements of all Sorts, I remember you and Dolly and all the dear good Folks at Bromley. 'Tis true I can't help it, but must and ever shall remember you all with Pleasure. Need I add that I am particularly, my dear good Friend Yours most affectionately   B Franklin

To Anna Mordaunt Shipley, *1771*

Dear Madam,   London, Aug. 13, 1771

This is just to let you know that we arriv'd safe and well in Marlborough Street about Six, where I deliver'd up my Charge.

The above seems too short for a Letter; so I will lengthen it by a little Account of our Journey. The first Stage we were rather pensive. I tried several Topics of Conversation, but none of them would hold. But after Breakfast, we began to recover Spirits, and had a good deal of Chat. Will you hear some of it? We talk'd of her Brother, and she wish'd he was married. And don't you wish your Sisters married too? Yes. All but Emily; I would not have her married. Why? Because I can't spare her, I can't part with her. The rest may marry as soon as they please, so they do but get good Husbands. We then took upon us to consider for 'em what sort of Husbands would be fittest for every one of them. We began with Georgiana. She thought a Country Gentleman, that lov'd Travelling and would take her with him, that lov'd Books and would hear her read to him; I added, that had a good Estate and was a Member of Parliament and lov'd to see an Experiment now and then. This she agreed to; so we set him down for Georgiana, and went on to Betsy. Betsy, says I, seems of a sweet mild Temper, and if we should give her a Country Squire, and he should happen to be of a rough, passionate Turn, and be angry now and then, it might break her Heart. O, none of 'em must be so; for then they would not be good Husbands. To make sure of this Point, however, for Betsey, shall we give her a Bishop? O no, that won't do. They all declare against the Church, and against the Army; not one of them will marry either a Clergyman or an Officer; that they are resolv'd upon. What can be their reason for that? Why you know, that when a Clergyman or an Officer dies, the Income goes with 'em; and then what is there to maintain the Family? there's the Point. Then suppose we give her a good honest, sensible City Merchant, who will love her dearly and is very rich? I don't know but that may do. We proceeded to Emily, her dear Emily, I was afraid we should hardly find any thing good enough for Emily; but at last, after first settling that, if she did marry, Kitty was to live a good deal with her; we agreed that as Emily was very handsome we might expect an Earl for her: So having fix'd her, as I thought, a Countess, we went on to Anna-Maria. She, says Kitty, should have a rich Man that has a large Family and a great many things to take care of; for she is very good at managing, helps my Mama very much, can look over bills, and order all sorts of Family Business. Very well; and as there is a Grace and Dignity in her Manner that would become the Station, what do you think of giving her a Duke? O no! I'll have the Duke for Emily. You may give the Earl to Anna-Maria if you please: But Emily shall have the Duke. I contested this Matter some time; but at length was forc'd to give up the point, leave Emily in Possession of the Duke, and content myself with the Earl for Anna Maria. And now what shall we do for Kitty? We have forgot her, all this Time. Well, and what will you do for her? I suppose that tho' the rest have resolv'd against the Army, she may not yet have made so rash a Resolution. Yes, but she has: Unless, now, an old one, an old General that has done fighting, and is rich, such a one as General Rufane; I like him a good deal; You must know I like an old Man, indeed I do: And some how or other all the old Men take to me, all that come to our House like me better than my other Sisters: I go to 'em and ask 'em how they do, and they like it mightily; and the Maids take notice of it, and say when they see an old Man come, there's a Friend of yours, Miss Kitty. But then as you like an old General, hadn't you better take him while he's a young Officer, and let him grow old upon your Hands, because then, you'll like him better and better every Year as he grows older and older. No, that won't do. He must be an old Man of 70 or 80, and take me when I am about 30: And then you know I may be a rich young Widow. We din'd at Staines, she was Mrs. Shipley, cut up the Chicken pretty handily (with a little Direction) and help'd me in a very womanly Manner. Now, says she, when I commended her, my Father never likes to see me or Georgiana carve, because we do it, he says, so badly: But how should we learn if we never try? We drank good Papa and Mama's Health, and the Health's of the Dutchess, the Countess, the Merchant's Lady, the Country Gentlewoman, and our Welsh Brother. This brought their Affairs again under Consideration. I doubt, says she, we have not done right for Betsey. I don't think a Merchant will do for her. She is much inclin'd to be a fine Gentlewoman; and is indeed already more of the fine Gentlewoman, I think, than any of my other Sisters; and therefore she shall be a Vice Countess.

Thus we chatted on, and she was very entertaining quite to Town.

I have now made my Letter as much too long as it was at first too short. The Bishop would think it too trifling, therefore don't show it him. I am afraid too that you will think it so, and have a good mind not to send it. Only it tells you Kitty is well at School, and for that I let it go. My Love to the whole amiable Family, best Respects to the Bishop, and 1000 Thanks for all your Kindnesses, and for the happy Days I enjoy'd at Twyford. With the greatest Esteem and Respect, I am, Madam, Your most obedient humble Servant   B Franklin

To Madame Brillon, 1778

Passy, March 10, 1778

I am charm'd with the Goodness of my Spiritual Guide, and resign myself implicitly to her Conduct, as she promises to lead me to Heaven in a Road so delicious, when I could be content to travel thither even in the roughest of all the Ways with the Pleasure of her Company.

How kindly partial to her Penitent, in finding him, on examining his Conscience, guilty of only one capital Sin, and to call that by the gentle Name of a *Foible!*

I lay fast hold of your Promise to absolve me of all Sins past, present, and *future*, on the easy and pleasing Condition of loving God, America, and my Guide above all things. I am in Raptures when I think of being absolv'd of the FUTURE.

People commonly speak of *Ten* Commandments. I have been taught that there are *twelve*. The *first* was, *Increase and multiply* and replenish the Earth. The *twelfth* is, A new Commandment I give unto you, *that ye love one another.* It seems to me that they are a little misplac'd, and that the last should have been the first. However, I never made any Difficulty about that, but was always willing to obey them both whenever I had an Opportunity. Pray tell me, my dear Casuist, whether my keeping religiously these two Commandments, tho' not in the Decalogue, may not be accepted in Compensation for my breaking so often one of the Ten, I mean that which forbids Coveting my Neighbour's Wife, and which *I confess* I break constantly, God forgive me, as often as I see or think of my lovely Confessor: And I am afraid I should never be able to repent of the Sin, even if I had the full Possession of her.

And now I am consulting you upon a Case of Conscience, I will mention the Opinion of a certain Father of the Church, which I find myself willing to adopt, tho' I am not sure it is orthodox. It is this, That the most effectual Way to get rid of a certain Temptation, is, as often as it returns, to comply with and Satisfy it. Pray instruct me how far, I may venture to practice upon this Principle?

But why should I be so scrupulous, when you have promised to absolve me of the *future!* Adieu, my charming Conductress, and believe me ever, with the sincerest Esteem and Affection, Your most obedient humble Servant.

Abigail Adams on Madame Helvétius, 1784

She entered the Room with a careless jaunty air. Upon seeing Ladies who were strangers to her, she bawled out ah Mon dieu! where is Frankling, why did you not tell me there were Ladies here? You must suppose her speaking all this in French. How said she I look? takeing hold of a dressing chimise made of tiffanny which She had on over a blew Lutestring, and which looked as much upon the decay as her Beauty, for she was once a handsome woman. Her Hair was fangled, over it she had a small straw hat with a dirty half gauze hankerchief round it, and a bit of dirtyer gauze than ever my maids wore was sewed on behind. She had a black gauze Skarf thrown over her shoulders. She ran out of the room. When she returned, the Dr. [Franklin] entered at one door she at the other, upon which she ran forward to him, caught him by the hand, helas Frankling, then gave him a

Louis-Michel Vanloo, *Madame Helvétius*, date unknown

double kiss one upon each cheek and an other upon his forehead. When we went into the room to dine she was placed between the Dr. and Mr. Adams. She carried on the chief of the conversation at dinner, frequently locking her hand into the Drs. and sometimes spreading her Arms upon the Backs of both the Gentlemans Chairs, then throwing her Arm carelessly upon the Drs. Neck.

I should have been greatly astonished at this conduct, if the good Doctor had not told me that in this Lady I should see a genuine French Woman, wholy free from affectation or stifness of behaviour and one of the best women in the world. For this I must take the Drs. word, but I should have set her down for a very bad one altho Sixty years of age and a widow. I own I was highly disgusted and never wish for an acquaintance with any Ladies of this cast. After dinner she threw herself upon a settee where she shew more than her feet. She had a little Lap Dog who was next to the Dr. her favorite. This She kisst and when he wet the floor she wiped it up with her chimise. This is one of the Drs. most intimate Friends, with whom he dines once every week and She with him. She is rich and is my near Neighbour, but I have not yet visited her.

To Emma Thompson, *1777*

Paris, Feb. 8, 1777

You are too early, Hussy, (as well as too saucy) in calling me Rebel; you should wait for the event, which will determine whether it is a Rebellion or only a Revolution. Here the Ladies are more civil; they call us *les Insurgens*, a Character that usually pleases them: And methinks you, with all other Women who smart or have smarted under the Tyranny of a bad Husband, ought to be fix'd in *Revolution* Principles, and act accordingly.

In my way to Canada last Spring, I saw dear Mrs. Barrow at New York. Mr. Barrow had been from her two or three Months, to keep Gov. Tryon and other Tories Company, on board the Asia one of the King's Ships which lay in the Harbour; and in all that time, naughty Man, had not ventur'd once on shore to see her. Our Troops were then pouring into the Town, and she was packing up to leave it; fearing as she had a large House they would incommode her by quartering Officers in it. As she appear'd in great Perplexity, scarce knowing where to go I persuaded her to stay, and I went to the General Officers then commanding there, and recommended her to their Protection, which they promis'd, and perform'd. On my Return from Canada, (where I was a Piece of a Governor, and I think a very good one, for a Fortnight; and might have been so till this time if your wicked Army, Enemies to all good Government, had not come and driven me out) I found her still in quiet Possession of her House. I enquired how our People had behav'd to her; she spoke in high Terms of the respectful Attention they had paid her, and the Quiet and Security they had procur'd her. I said I was glad of it; and that if they had us'd her ill, I would have turn'd Tory. *Then*, says she, (with that pleasing Gaiety so natural to her) *I wish they had.* For you must know she is a Toryess as well as you and can as flippantly call Rebel. . . . I know you wish you could see me, but as you can't, I will describe my self to you. Figure me in your mind as jolly as formerly, and as strong and hearty, only a few Years older, very plainly dress'd, wearing my thin grey strait Hair, that peeps out under my only Coiffure, a fine Fur Cap, which comes down my Forehead almost to my Spectacles. Think how this must appear among the Powder'd Heads of Paris. I wish every Gentleman and Lady in France would only be so obliging as to follow my Fashion, comb their own Heads as I do mine, dismiss their Friseurs, and pay me half the Money they paid to them. You see the Gentry might well afford this; and I could then inlist those Friseurs, who are at least 100,000; and with the Money I would maintain them, make a Visit with them to England, and dress the Heads of your Ministers and Privy Counsellors, which I conceive to be at present *un peu dérangées,* Adieu, Mad-cap, and believe me ever Your affectionate Friend and humble Servant   BF

PS. Don't be proud of this long Letter. A fit of the Gout which has confin'd me 5 Days, and made me refuse to see any Company, has given me a little time to trifle. Otherwise it would have been very short. Visitors and Business would have interrupted. And perhaps, with Mrs. Barrow, *you wish they had.*

3 The uses of laughter.

Flirtation, like flattery, is a mode of exaggeration. In Franklin exaggeration spoke to a special talent of his for imaginative and humorous inflation resulting in deflation. It comes out so often in his writing that we have to count it as part of his character or personality, something that he used to make people smile, to laugh away disagreements, and to make light of the pretensions of human beings, himself included. We have seen it in his "Rules for Making Oneself a Disagreeable Companion." He could employ humor, as we shall see, for more serious purposes, but he could also use it just for fun, as in "The Speech of Miss Polly Baker," one of the hoaxes for which he became famous, a deadpan account of an event that did not actually happen. When it appeared anonymously as a news item in a London paper, people accepted it as factual, and it was widely reprinted. Franklin did not reveal his authorship until thirty years later, when a friend in France regaled him with the story as a piece of American history. Although Franklin wrote it for fun, to make people laugh at their own assumptions about themselves and their society, he would doubtless have been pleased if he could have believed that Polly Baker's speech had helped to laugh out of existence the laws of which she complained.

When Franklin became a spokesman for America in the contest with Great Britain, laughter was his first weapon of choice. If he could laugh the British out of their flagrant misconceptions of America, there need be no contest. In 1765 the British were beginning to worry about their colonies becoming competitors instead of customers in the manufacture of woolens. Franklin and others had already written straightforward essays to discount the danger of such competition, citing the high cost of colonial labor and the small supply of raw wool. The selection I call "Leaping Whales," a letter to the *Public Advertiser*, turned the soberly factual approach on its head in a mode of humorous exaggeration that was to become an American specialty: the tall tale.

Franklin wrote many more newspaper pieces in the attempt to laugh the British out of the colonial policies that alienated Americans. And although he gave up the attempt in disgust after 1775, he never stopped sending up human pretensions. He liked to take common assumptions (that he himself may have shared) and hold them up to the unforgiving light of common sense. In an essay he wrote during his mission to France, and printed himself on a press he acquired there, he let American Indians represent the voice of common sense and candor in their interchanges with his white countrymen.

There is more than meets the eye in this placement of simplicity against civilized pretensions. In France, Franklin encountered among the literati two opposing views of America and its original inhabitants. On the one hand, disciples of Jean-Jacques Rousseau saw the Indian as a Noble Savage, endowed with the grave courtesy and guileless but penetrating sagacity that Franklin celebrates here. On the other hand, disciples of the comte de Buffon, the famous naturalist, held to a theory that residence on the American continent had resulted in a diminished stature and vigor in animals and much reduced physical and mental strength in its human inhabitants, including, by implication, Europeans who settled there. Despite its demonstrable absurdity, belief in inexorable American dwindling and debilitation was widely held. Franklin once amused a dinner party of mixed Europeans and Americans by asking the company to rise. As it happened, the Americans were taller than any of the French. But Buffon's "scientific" dogma was still going strong when Jefferson replaced Franklin as minister. Jefferson's riposte was to have the carcass of a moose shipped to France to show the size of American deer.

Franklin may have intended his "Remarks" for distribution among the habitués of Madame Helvétius's salon. It can be read as supporting evidence for Rousseau, as a good-natured refutation of Buffon, or as a mild mockery of the pretensions of civilized society, whether European or

American. The characterization of Indians as masters of oratory may be a sly reference to the contemporary fame accorded oratory in British and American legislative assemblies. We have already noticed Franklin's personal preference for brevity and pungency of speech.

The Speech of Miss Polly Baker, 1747

The SPEECH of Miss POLLY BAKER, before a Court of Judicature, at Connecticut near Boston in New-England; where she was prosecuted the Fifth Time, for having a Bastard Child: Which influenced the Court to dispense with her Punishment, and induced one of her Judges to marry her the next Day.

MAY it please the Honourable Bench to indulge me in a few Words: I am a poor unhappy Woman, who have no Money to fee Lawyers to plead for me, being hard put to it to get a tolerable Living. I shall not trouble your Honours with long Speeches; for I have not the Presumption to expect, that you may, by any Means, be prevailed on to deviate in your Sentence from the Law, in my Favour. All I humbly hope is, That your Honours would charitably move the Governor's Goodness on my Behalf, that my Fine may be remitted. This is the Fifth Time, Gentlemen, that I have been dragg'd before your Court on the same Account; twice I have paid heavy Fines, and twice have been brought to Publick Punishment, for want of Money to pay those Fines. This may have been agreeable to the Laws, and I don't dispute it; but since Laws are sometimes unreasonable in themselves, and therefore repealed, and others bear too hard on the Subject in particular Circumstances; and therefore there is left a Power somewhat to dispense with the Execution of them; I take the Liberty to say, That I think this Law, by which I am punished, is both unreasonable in itself, and particularly severe with regard to me, who have always lived an inoffensive Life in the Neighbourhood where I was born, and defy my Enemies (if I have any) to say I ever wrong'd Man, Woman, or Child. Abstracted from the Law, I cannot conceive (may it please your Honours) what the Nature of my Offence is. I have brought Five fine Children into the World, at the Risque of my Life; I have maintain'd them well by my own Industry, without burthening the Township, and would have done it better, if it had not been for the heavy

Charges and Fines I have paid. Can it be a Crime (in the Nature of Things I mean) to add to the Number of the King's Subjects, in a new Country that really wants People? I own it, I should think it a Praise-worthy, rather than a punishable Action. I have debauched no other Woman's Husband, nor enticed any Youth; these Things I never was charg'd with, nor has any one the least Cause of Complaint against me, unless, perhaps, the Minister, or Justice, because I have had Children without being married, by which they have missed a Wedding Fee. But, can ever this be a Fault of mine? I appeal to your Honours. You are pleased to allow I don't want Sense; but I must be stupified to the last Degree, not to prefer the Honourable State of Wedlock, to the Condition I have lived in. I always was, and still am willing to enter into it; and doubt not my behaving well in it, having all the Industry, Frugality, Fertility, and Skill in Oeconomy, appertaining to a good Wife's Character. I defy any Person to say, I ever refused an Offer of that Sort: On the contrary, I readily consented to the only Proposal of Marriage that ever was made me, which was when I was a Virgin; but too easily confiding in the Person's Sincerity that made it, I unhappily lost my own Honour, by trusting to his; for he got me with Child, and then forsook me: That very Person you all know; he is now become a Magistrate of this Country; and I had Hopes he would have appeared this Day on the Bench, and have endeavoured to moderate the Court in my Favour; then I should have scorn'd to have mention'd it; but I must now complain of it, as unjust and unequal, That my Betrayer and Undoer, the first Cause of all my Faults and Miscarriages (if they must be deemed such) should be advanc'd to Honour and Power in the Government, that punishes my Misfortunes with Stripes [lashes] and Infamy. I should be told, 'tis like, That were there no Act of Assembly in the Case, the Precepts of Religion are violated by my Transgresions. If mine, then, is a religious Offence, leave it to religious Punishments. You have already excluded me from the Comforts of your Church-Communion. Is not that sufficient? You believe I have offended Heaven, and must suffer eternal Fire: Will not that be sufficient? What Need is there, then, of your additional Fines and Whipping? I own, I do not think as you do; for, if I thought what you call a Sin, was really such, I could not presumptuously commit it. But, how can it be believed, that Heaven is angry at my having Children, when to the little done by me towards it, God has been pleased to add his Divine Skill and admirable Workmanship in the Formation of their Bodies, and crown'd it, by furnishing them with rational and immortal Souls. Forgive me, Gentlemen, if I talk a little extravagantly on these Matters; I am no Divine [minister], but if you, Gentlemen, must be making Laws, do not turn natural and useful Actions into Crimes, by your Prohibitions. But take into your wise Consideration, the great and growing Number of Batchelors in the Country, many of whom from the mean Fear of the Expences of a Family, have never sincerely and honourably courted a Woman in their Lives; and by their Manner of Living, leave unproduced (which is little better than Murder) Hundreds of their Posterity to the Thousandth Generation. Is not this a greater Offence against the Publick Good, than mine? Compel them, then, by Law, either to Marriage, or to pay double the Fine of Fornication every Year. What must poor young Women do, whom Custom have forbid to solicit the Men, and who cannot force themselves upon Husbands, when the Laws take no Care to provide them any; and yet severely punish them if they do their Duty without them; the Duty of the first and great Command of Nature, and of Nature's God, *Encrease and Multiply.* A Duty, from the steady Performance of which, nothing has been able to deter me; but for its Sake, I have hazarded the Loss of the Publick Esteem, and have frequently endured Publick Disgrace and Punishment; and therefore ought, in my humble Opinion, instead of a Whipping, to have a Statue erected to my Memory.

Leaping Whales, 1765

Sir,

In your Paper of Wednesday last, an ingenious Correspondent that calls himself the SPECTATOR, and dates from Pimlico, under the Guise of Good-Will to the News-Writer, whom he allows to be "an useful Body of Men in this great City," has, in my Opinion artfully attempted to turn them and their Works into Ridicule; wherein, if he could succeed, great Injury might be done to the Public, as well as to those good People.

Supposing, Sir, that the *We hears* they give us of this and t'other intended Voyage, or Tour of this and t'other great Personage, were mere Inventions, yet they at least afford us an innocent Amusement while we read, and useful Matter of Conversation when we are disposed to converse. Englishmen, Sir, are too apt to be silent when they have nothing to say; too apt to be sullen when they are silent, and when they are sullen to h[an]g themselves. But by these *We hears* we are supplied with abundant Fund of Discourse: We discuss the Motives to such Voyages, the Probability of their being undertaken and the Practicability of their Execution. Here we can display our Judgment in Politics, our Knowledge of the Interests of Princes, and our Skill in Geography; and (if we have it) shew our Dexterity more-over in Argumentation. In the mean time, the tedious Hour is killed; we go home pleased with the Applauses we have received from others, or at least with those we secretly give to ourselves; we sleep soundly, and live on, to the Comfort of our Families.

But, Sir, I beg leave to say, that all the Articles of News, that seem improbable, are not mere Inventions. Some of them, I can assure you on the Faith of a Traveller, are serious Truths. And here, quitting Mr. Spectator of Pimlico, give me Leave to instance the various numberless Accounts the News-Writers have given us (with so much honest Zeal for the Welfare of Poor Old England!) of the establishing Manufactures in the Colonies to the Prejudice of those of this Kingdom. It is objected by superficial Readers, who yet pretend to some Knowledge of those Countries, that such Estab-lishments are not only improbable but impossible; for that their Sheep have but little Wool, not in the whole sufficient for a Pair of Stockings a Year to each Inhabitant; and that, from the universal Dearness of Labour among them, the working of Iron and other Materials, except in some few coarse Instances, is impracticable to any Advantage. Dear Sir, do not let us suffer ourselves to be amused with such groundless Objections. The very Tails of the American Sheep are so laden with Wool, that each has a Car or Waggon on four little Wheels to support and keep it from trailing on the Ground. Would they caulk their Ships? would they fill their Beds? would they even litter their Horses with Wool, if it was not both plenty and cheap? And what signifies Dearness of Labour, where an English Shilling passes for Five-and-twenty? Their engaging three hundred Silk Throwsters [who twist silk into thread] here in one Week for New York was treated as a Fable, because, forsooth, they have "no Silk there to throw." Those who made this Objection perhaps did not know, that at the same Time the

Agents from the King of Spain were at Quebec contracting for 1000 Pieces of Cannon to be made there for the Fortifications of Mexico, with 25,000 Axes for their Industrious Logwood-Cutters; and at New-York engaging an annual Supply of warm Floor-Carpets for their West-India Houses; other Agents from the Emperor of China were at Boston in New-England treating about an Exchange of Raw-Silk for Wool, to be carried on in Chinese Jonks through the Straits of Magellan. And yet all this is as certainly true as the Account, said to be from Quebec, in the Papers of last Week, that the Inhabitants of Canada are making Preparations for a Cod and Whale Fishery this Summer in the Upper Lakes. Ignorant People may object that the Upper Lakes are fresh, and that Cod and Whale are Salt-water Fish: But let them know, Sir, that Cod, like other Fish, when attacked by their Enemies, fly into any Water where they think they can be safest; that Whales, when they have a Mind to eat Cod, pursue them wherever they fly; and that the grand Leap of the Whale in that Chace up the Fall of Niagara is esteemed by all who have seen it, as one of the finest Spectacles in Nature! Really, Sir, the World is grown too incredulous: Pendulum-like, it is ever swinging from one Extream to another. Formerly every Thing printed was believed, because it was in Print: Now Things seem to be disbelieved for just the very same Reason. Wise Men wonder at the present Growth of Infidelity! They should have consider'd, when they taught People to doubt the Authority of News-papers, and the Truth of Predictions in Almanacs, that the next Step might be a Disbelief in the well-vouch'd Accounts of Ghosts and Witches, and Doubts even of the Truth of the A[thanasia]n Creed.

Thus much I thought it necessary to say in favour of an honest Set of Writers, whose comfortable Living depends on collecting and supplying the Printers with News, at the small Price of Six-pence an Article; and who always show their Regard to Truth, by contradicting such as are wrong in a subsequent Article—for another Six-pence, to the great Satisfaction and Improvement of us Coffee-house Students in History and Politics, and the infinite Advantage of all future Livies, Rapins, Robertsons, Humes, Smollets, and Macaulays, who may be sincerely inclin'd to furnish the World with that *rara Avis*, a true History. I am, sir, Your humble Servant

A Traveller

Remarks Concerning the Savages of North-America, ca. 1783

SAVAGES we call them, because their manners differ from ours, which we think the Perfection of Civility; they think the same of theirs.

Perhaps if we could examine the manners of different Nations with Impartiality, we should find no People so rude as to be without any Rules of Politeness; nor any so polite as not to have some remains of Rudeness.

The Indian Men, when young, are Hunters and Warriors; when old, Counsellors; for all their Government is by the Counsel or Advice of the Sages; there is no Force, there are no Prisons, no Officers to compel Obedience, or inflict Punishment. Hence they generally study Oratory; the best Speaker having the most Influence. The Indian Women till the Ground, dress the Food, nurse and bring up the Children, and preserve and hand down to Posterity the Memory of Public Transactions. These Employments of Men and Women are accounted natural and honorable. Having few Artificial Wants, they have abundance of Leisure for Improvement by Conversation. Our laborious manner of Life compared with theirs, they esteem slavish and base; and the Learning on which we value ourselves; they regard as frivolous and useless. An Instance of this occurred at the Treaty of Lancaster in Pennsylvania, Anno 1744, between the government of Virginia & the Six Nations. After the principal Business was settled, the Commissioners from Virginia acquainted the Indians by a Speech, that there was at Williamsburg a College with a Fund for Educating Indian Youth, and that if the Chiefs of the Six-Nations would send down half a dozen of their Sons to that College, the Government would take Care that they should be well provided for, and instructed in all the Learning of the white People. It is one of the Indian Rules of Politeness not to answer a public Proposition the same day that it is made; they think it would be treating it as a light Matter; and that they show it Respect by taking time to consider it, as of a matter important. They therefore deferred their Answer till the day following; when their Speaker began by expressing their deep Sense of the Kindness of the Virginia Government, in making them that Offer; for we know, says he, that you highly esteem the kind of Learning taught in those Colleges, and that the Maintenance of our Young Men while with you, would be very expensive to you. We are convinced therefore that you mean to do us good by your Proposal, and we thank you heartily. But you who are wise must know, that different Nations have different Conceptions of things; and you will therefore not take it amiss, if our Ideas of this Kind of Education happen not to be the same with yours. We have had some Experience of it: Several of our Young People were formerly brought up at the Colleges of the Northern Provinces; they were instructed in all your Sciences; but when they came back to us, they were bad Runners, ignorant of every means of living in the Woods, unable to bear either Cold or Hunger, knew neither how to build a Cabin, take a Deer, or kill an Enemy, spoke our Language imperfectly; were therefore neither fit for Hunters, Warriors, or Counsellors; they were totally good for nothing. We are however not the less obliged by your kind Offer, tho' we decline accepting it; and to show our grateful Sense of it, if the Gentlemen of Virginia will send us a dozen of their Sons, we will take great Care of their Education, instruct them in all we know, and make *Men* of them.

Having frequent Occasions to hold public Councils, they have acquired great Order and Decency in conducting them. The old Men sit in the foremost Ranks, the Warriors in the next, and the Women and Children in the hindmost. The Business of the Women is to take exact notice of what passes, imprint it in their Memories, for they have no Writing, and communicate it to their Children. They are the Records of the Council, and they preserve Tradition of the Stipulations in Treaties a hundred Years back, which when we compare with our Writings we always find exact. He that would speak, rises. The rest observe a profound Silence. When he has finished and sits down, they leave him five or six Minutes to recollect, that if he has omitted any thing he intended to say, or has any thing to add, he may rise again and deliver it. To interrupt another, even in common Conversation, is reckoned highly indecent. How different this is from the Conduct of a polite British House of Commons, where scarce a Day passes without some Confusion that makes the Speaker hoarse in calling *to order;* and how different from the mode of Conversation in many polite Companies of Europe, where if you do not deliver your Sentence with great Rapidity, you are cut off in the middle of it by the impatient Loquacity of those you converse with, & never suffer'd to finish it.

The Politeness of these Savages in Conversation is indeed carried to excess, since it does not permit them to contradict, or deny the Truth of what is asserted in their Presence. By this means they indeed avoid Disputes, but then it becomes difficult to know their Minds, or what Impression you make upon them. The Missionaries who have attempted to convert them to Christianity, all complain of this as one of the great Difficulties of their Mission. The Indians hear with Patience the Truths of the Gospel explained to them, and give their usual Tokens of Assent and Approbation: you would think they were convinced. No such Matter. It is mere Civility.

A Suedish Minister having assembled the Chiefs of the Sasquehanah Indians, made a Sermon to them, acquainting them with the principal historical Facts on which our Religion is founded, such as the Fall of our first Parents by Eating an Apple, the Coming of Christ to repair the Mischief, his Miracles and Suffering, &c. When he had finished, an Indian Orator stood up to thank him. What you have told us, says he, is all very good. It is indeed bad to eat Apples. It is better to make them all into Cyder. We are much obliged by your Kindness in coming so far to tell us those things which you have heard from your Mothers. In Return I will tell you some of those we have heard from ours.

In the Beginning our Fathers had only the Flesh of Animals to subsist on, and if their Hunting was unsuccessful, they were starving. Two of our young Hunters having killed a Deer, made a Fire in the Woods to broil some Parts of it. When they were about to satisfy their Hunger, they beheld a beautiful young Woman descend from the Clouds, and seat herself on that Hill which you see yonder among the blue Mountains. They said to each other, it is a Spirit that perhaps has smelt our broiling Venison, & wishes to eat of it: let us offer some to her. They presented her with the Tongue: She was pleased with the Taste of it, & said, your Kindness shall be rewarded. Come to this Place after thirteen Moons, and you shall find something that will be of great Benefit in nourishing you and your Children to the latest Generations. They did so, and to their Surprise found Plants they had never seen before, but which from that ancient time have been constantly cultivated among us to our great Advantage. Where her right Hand had touch'd the Ground, they found Maize; where her left Hand had touch'd it, they found Kidney-beans; and where her Backside had sat on it, they found Tobacco. The good Missionary, disgusted with this idle

Tale, said, what I delivered to you were sacred Truths; but what you tell me is mere Fable, Fiction & Falsehood. The Indian offended, reply'd, my Brother, it seems your Friends have not done you Justice in your Education; they have not well instructed you in the Rules of common Civility. You saw that we who understand and practise those Rules, believed all your Stories; why do you refuse to believe ours?

When any of them come into our Towns, our People are apt to croud round them, gaze upon them, and incommode them where they desire to be private; this they esteem great Rudeness, and the Effect of want of Instruction in the Rules of Civility and good Manners. We have, say they, as much Curiosity as you, and when you come into our Towns we wish for Opportunities of looking at you; but for this purpose we hide ourselves behind Bushes where you are to pass, and never intrude ourselves into your Company.

Their Manner of entring one anothers Villages has likewise its Rules. It is reckon'd uncivil in travelling Strangers to enter a Village abruptly, without giving Notice of their Approach. Therefore as soon as they arrive within hearing, they stop and hollow [shout "hello"], remaining there till invited to enter. Two old Men usually come out to them, and lead them in. There is in every Village a vacant Dwelling, called the Strangers House. Here they are placed, while the old Men go round from Hut to Hut acquainting the inhabitants that Strangers are arrived, who are probably hungry and weary; and every one sends them what he can spare of Victuals and Skins to repose on. When the Strangers are refresh'd, Pipes & Tobacco are brought; and then, but not before, Conversation begins, with Enquiries who they are, whither bound, what News, &c. and it usually ends with Offers of Service, if the Strangers have Occasion of Guides or any Necessaries for continuing their Journey; and nothing is exacted for the Entertainment.

The same Hospitality, esteemed among them as a principal Virtue, is practised by private Persons; of which *Conrad Weiser,* our Interpreter, gave me the following Instance. He had been naturaliz'd among the Six-Nations, and spoke well the Mohock Language. In going thro' the Indian Country, to carry a Message from our Governor to the Council at *Onondaga,* he called at the Habitation of *Canassetego,* an old Acquaintance, who embraced him, spread Furs for him to sit on, placed before him some boiled

Beans and Venison, and mixed some Rum and Water for his Drink. When he was well refresh'd, and had lit his Pipe, Canassetego began to converse with him, ask'd how he had fared the many Years since they had seen each other, whence he then came, what occasioned the Journey, &c. &c. Conrad answered all his Questions; and when the Discourse began to flag, the Indian, to continue it, said, Conrad, you have liv'd long among the white People, and know something of their Customs; I have been sometimes at Albany, and have observed that once in seven Days, they shut up their Shops and assemble all in the great House; tell me, what is it for? what do they do there? They meet there, says Conrad, to hear & learn *good things*. I do not doubt, says the Indian, that they tell you so; they have told me the same; but I doubt the Truth of what they say, & I will tell you my Reasons. I went lately to Albany to sell my Skins, & buy Blankets, Knives, Powder, Rum, &c. You know I used generally to deal with Hans Hanson; but I was a little inclined this time to try some other Merchants. However I called first upon Hans, and ask'd him what he would give for Beaver; He said he could not give more than four Shillings a Pound; but, says he, I cannot talk on Business now; this is the Day when we meet together to learn *good things*, and I am going to the Meeting. So I thought to myself since I cannot do any Business to day, I may as well go to the Meeting too; and I went with him. There stood up a Man in black, and began to talk to the People very angrily. I did not understand what he said; but perceiving that he looked much at me, & at Hanson, I imagined he was angry at seeing me there; so I went out, sat down near the House, struck Fire & lit my Pipe; waiting till the Meeting should break up. I thought too, that the Man had mentioned something of Beaver, and I suspected it might be the Subject of their Meeting. So when they came out I accosted my Merchant; well Hans, says I, I hope you have agreed to give more than four Shillings a Pound. No, says he, I cannot give so much. I cannot give more than three Shillings and six Pence. I then spoke to several other Dealers, but they all sung the same Song, three & six Pence, three & six Pence. This made it clear to me that my Suspicion was right; and that whatever they pretended of Meeting to learn *good things*, the real Purpose was to consult, how to cheat Indians in the Price of Beaver. Consider but a little, Conrad, and you must be of my Opinion. If they met so often to learn *good things*, they would certainly have learnt some before this time. But they are still ignorant. You know our Practice. If a white Man in travelling thro' our Country, enters one of our Cabins, we all treat him as I treat you; we dry him if he is wet, we warm him if he is cold, and give him Meat & Drink that he may allay his Thirst and Hunger, & we spread soft Furs for him to rest & sleep on: We demand nothing in return.* But if I go into a white Man's House at Albany, and ask for Victuals & Drink, they say, where is your Money? and if I have none, they say, get out, you Indian Dog. You see they have not yet learnt those little *good things,* that we need no Meetings to be instructed in, because our Mothers taught them to us when we were Children. And therefore it is impossible their Meetings should be as they say for any such purpose, or have any such Effect; they are only to contrive *the Cheating of Indians in the Price of Beaver.*

It is remarkable that in all Ages and Countries, Hospitality has been allowed as the Virtue of those, whom the civiliz'd were pleased to call Barbarians; the Greeks celebrated the Scythians for it. The Saracens possess'd it eminently; and it is to this day the reigning Virtue of the wild Arabs. St. Paul too, in the Relation of his Voyage & Shipwreck, on the Island of Melita, says, The Barbarous People shew'd us no little Kindness; for they kindled a Fire, and received us every one, because of the present Rain & because of the Cold.

4 Religion.

We have been approaching our subject somewhat obliquely, letting the reader infer the man from what he said and how he said it to other people (in letters and in print), and in what he said to himself in the journal of his transatlantic crossing. We have been trying to take him unawares, to catch him in unguarded moments, as well as in his attempts to make people laugh with him at human follies. Before turning to the extraordinary things he did as a scientist and statesman, we should let him speak directly to a profound question he had to ask himself. Franklin had been brought up in a devout Congregational family in Boston, where he had been taught the prevailing religious doctrine that doing good was mere self-indulgence, leading to perdition unless it was performed in response to a declared faith in Christ. And that faith could be had only after a hard-won, soul-searching recognition of utter personal worthlessness, including the worthlessness of any previous good deeds. Franklin discarded that belief when still in his teens and never returned to it. After briefly indulging in what amounted to atheism, he decided that doing good was itself the essence of true religion and was all that God demanded of man, without any requirement of searching and battling for some elusive faith.

Franklin's way of doing good was something that developed quietly over the years and eventuated in a dedication to the future of the American continent and its people that we will follow in the rest of this volume. As a young adult in Philadelphia he briefly attended the Presbyterian church when a new young minister's sermons seemed to express his own beliefs about doing good. But the new minister was quickly dismissed, and after a futile attempt to defend him, Franklin gave up on churches. In 1731 he joined the Freemasons and became a leading figure in the organization and in its benevolent enterprises at home and abroad. He never again attended church.

Franklin was no atheist. Atheism was not a belief system that appealed to him, either intellectually or ethically. As we have seen in his letter to George Whately, he believed in the immortality of souls as part of God's plan for the universe. He was on cordial terms with many orthodox ministers, including George Whitefield, the great British evangelist, without accepting any of their beliefs. Although he tells us in the *Autobiography* that he devised private services expressing his devotion to an omnipotent God, there is no evidence in the rest of his writings and papers that he ever performed them. His religious devotion lay in doing good, as he saw it, to others. He put in the mouth of Poor Richard his impatience with churches and their theology, which elevated thinking right above doing right:

> Sin is not hurtful because it is forbidden but it is forbidden because it's hurtful.

> Nor is Duty beneficial because it is commanded, but it is commanded, because it's beneficial.

> Many a long dispute among Divines may be thus abridged, It is so: It is not so.

> Many have quarrel'd about Religion, that never practis'd it.

> Serving God is Doing Good to Man, But Praying is thought an easier Service,
> And therefore more generally chosen.

Franklin knew that his contempt for the doctrines taught him in childhood was distressing to his parents. In the letter printed below he apologized to them. He explained himself in more detail in a letter to Joseph Huey, who is otherwise unknown. (Since the eighteenth century this has been one of his most frequently reprinted letters.) And he later wrote more boldly to his sister Jane.

To Josiah and Abiah Franklin, 1738

Honour'd Father and Mother   April 13, 1738

I have your Favour of the 21st of March in which you both seem concern'd lest I have imbib'd some erroneous Opinions. Doubtless I have my Share, and when the natural Weakness and Imperfection of Human Understanding is considered, with the unavoidable Influences of Education, Custom, Books and Company, upon our Ways of thinking, I imagine a Man must have a good deal of Vanity who believes, and a good deal of Boldness who affirms, that all the Doctrines he holds, are true; and all he rejects, are false. And perhaps the same may be justly said of every Sect, Church and Society of men when they assume to themselves that Infallibility which they deny to the Popes and Councils. I think Opinions should be judg'd of by their Influences and Effects; and if a Man holds none that tend to make him less Virtuous or more vicious, it may be concluded he holds none that are dangerous; which I hope is the Case with me. I am sorry you should have any Uneasiness on my Account, and if it were a thing possible for one to alter his Opinions in order to please others, I know none whom I ought more willingly to oblige in that respect than your selves: But since it is no more in a Man's Power *to think* than *to look* like another, methinks all that should be expected from me is to keep my Mind open to Conviction, to hear patiently and examine attentively whatever is offered me for that end; and if after all I continue in the same Errors, I believe your usual Charity will induce you rather to pity and excuse than blame me. In the mean time your Care and Concern for me is what I am very thankful for.

As to the Freemasons, unless she will believe me when I assure her that they are in general a very harmless sort of People; and have no principles or Practices that are inconsistent with Religion or good Manners, I know no Way of giving my Mother a better Opinion of them than she seems to have at present, (since it is not allow'd that Women should be admitted into that secret Society). She has, I must confess, on that Account, some reason to be displeas'd with it; but for any thing else, I must entreat her to suspend her Judgment till she is better inform'd, and in the mean time exercise her Charity.

My Mother grieves that one of her Sons is an Arian, another an Arminian. [Franklin was actually both.] What an Arminian or an Arian is, I cannot say that I very well know; the Truth is, I make such Distinctions very litle my Study; I think vital Religion has always suffer'd, when Orthodoxy is more regarded than Virtue. And the Scripture assures me, that at the last Day, we shall not be examin'd what we *thought*, but what we *did;* and our Recommendation will not be that we said *Lord, Lord,* but that we did GOOD to our Fellow Creatures. See Matth. 26 [should be 25: the parable of the wise and foolish virgins].

We have had great Rains here lately, which with the Thawing of Snow in the Mountains back of our Country has made vast Floods in our Rivers, and by carrying away Bridges, Boats, &c. made travelling almost impracticable for a Week past, so that our Post has entirely mist making one Trip. . . .

. . . I am Your dutiful Son   B F

To Joseph Huey, 1753

Sir,   Philada. June 6, 1753

I received your kind Letter of the 2d Inst. and am glad to hear that you increase in Strength; I hope you will continue mending till you recover your former Health and Firmness. Let me know whether you still use the cold Bath, and what Effect it has.

As to the Kindness you mention, I wish it could have been of more Service to you. But if it had, the only Thanks I should desire is, that you would always be equally ready to serve any other person that may need your Assistance, and so let good Offices go round, for Mankind are all of a Family.

For my own Part, when I am employed in serving others, I do not look upon my self as conferring Favours, but as paying Debts. In my Travels and since my Settlement I have received much Kindness from Men, to whom I shall never have any Opportunity of making the least direct Return. And numberless Mercies from God, who is infinitely above being benefited by our Services. These Kindnesses from Men I can therefore only return on their Fellow-Men; and I can only show my Gratitude for those Mercies from God, by a Readiness to help his other Children and my

Brethren. For I do not think that Thanks, and Compliments, tho' repeated Weekly, can discharge our real Obligations to each other, and much less those to our Creator.

You will see in this my Notion of Good Works, that I am far from expecting (as you suppose) that I shall merit Heaven by them. By Heaven we understand, a State of Happiness, infinite in Degree, and eternal in Duration: I can do nothing to deserve such Reward: He that for giving a Draught of Water to a thirsty Person should expect to be paid with a good Plantation, would be modest in his Demands, compar'd with those who think they deserve Heaven for the little Good they do on Earth. Even the mix'd imperfect Pleasures we enjoy in this World are rather from God's Goodness than our Merit; how much more such Happiness of Heaven. For my own part, I have not the Vanity to think I deserve it, the Folly to expect it, nor the Ambition to desire it; but content myself in submitting to the Will and Disposal of that God who made me, who has hitherto preserv'd and bless'd me, and in whose fatherly Goodness I may well confide, that he will never make me miserable, and that even the Afflictions I may at any time suffer shall tend to my Benefit.

The Faith you mention has doubtless its use in the World; I do not desire to see it diminished, nor would I endeavour to lessen it in any Man. But I wish it were more productive of Good Works than I have generally seen it: I mean real good Works, Works of Kindness, Charity, Mercy, and Publick Spirit; not Holiday-keeping, Sermon-Reading or Hearing, performing Church Ceremonies, or making long Prayers, fill'd with Flatteries and Compliments, despis'd even by wise Men, and much less capable of pleasing the Deity. The Worship of God is a Duty, the hearing and reading of Sermons may be useful; but if Men rest in Hearing and Praying, as too many do, it is as if a Tree should value itself on being water'd and putting forth Leaves, tho' it never produc'd any Fruit.

Your great Master tho't much less of these outward Appearances and Professions than many of his modern Disciples. He prefer'd the Doers of the Word to the meer Hearers; the Son that seemingly refus'd to obey his Father and yet perform'd his Commands, to him that profess'd his Readiness but neglected the Works; the heretical but charitable Samaritan, to the uncharitable tho' orthodox Priest and sanctified Levite: and those who gave

Food to the hungry, Drink to the Thirsty, Raiment to the Naked, Entertainment to the Stranger, and Relief to the Sick, &c. tho' they never heard of his Name, he declares shall in the last Day be accepted, when those who cry Lord, Lord; who value themselves on their Faith tho' great enough to perform Miracles but have neglected good Works shall be rejected. He profess'd that he came not to call the Righteous but Sinners to Repentance; which imply'd his modest Opinion that there were some in his Time so good that they need not hear even him for Improvement; but now a days we have scarce a little Parson, that does not think it the Duty of every Man within his Reach to sit under his petty Ministrations, and that whoever omits them offends God. I wish to such more Humility, and to you Health and Happiness, being Your Friend and Servant   B Franklin

To Jane Mecom, 1758

Dear Sister   London Sept 16 1758

  . . .

We have been together over a great part of England this Summer; and among other places visited the Town our Father was born in and found some Relations in that part of the Country Still living. Our Cousin Jane Franklin, daughter of our Unkle John, died but about a Year ago. We saw her Husband Robert Page, who gave us some old Letters to his Wife from unkle Benjamin. In one of them, dated Boston July 4. 1723 he writes "Your Unkle Josiah has a Daughter Jane about 12 years Old, a good humour'd Child." So Jenny keep up your Character, and don't be angry when you have no Letters.

In a little Book he sent her, call'd *None but Christ*, he wrote an Acrostick on her Name, which for Namesakes' Sake, as well as the good Advice it contains, I transcribe and send you

  Illuminated from on High,
  And shining brightly in your Sphere
  Nere faint, but keep a steady Eye
  Expecting endless Pleasures there
  Flee Vice, as you'd a Serpent flee,
  Raise Faith and Hope three Stories higher
  And let Christ's endless Love to thee

> N-ere cease to make thy Love Aspire.
> Kindness of Heart by Words express
> Let your Obedience be sincere,
> In Prayer and Praise your God Address
> Nere cease 'till he can cease to hear.

After professing truly that I have a great Esteem and Veneration for the pious Author, permit me a little to play the Commentator and Critic on these Lines. The Meaning of *Three Stories* higher seems somewhat obscure, you are to understand, then, that *Faith*, *Hope* and *Charity* have been called the three Steps of Jacob's Ladder, reaching from Earth to Heaven. Our Author calls them *Stories,* likening Religion to a Building, and those the three Stories of the Christian Edifice; Thus Improvement in Religion, is called *Building Up,* and *Edification. Faith* is then the Ground-floor, *Hope* is up one Pair of Stairs. My dearly beloved Jenny, don't delight so much to dwell in these lower Rooms, but get as fast as you can into the Garret; for in truth the best Room in the House is *Charity.* For my part, I wish the House was turn'd upside down; 'tis so difficult (when one is fat) to get up Stairs; and not only so, but I imagine *Hope* and *Faith* may be more firmly built on *Charity,* than *Charity* upon *Faith* and *Hope.* However that be, I think it a better reading to say

> Raise Faith and Hope *one Story* higher

correct it boldly and I'll support the Alteration. For when you are up two Stories already, if you raise your Building three Stories higher, you will make five in all, which is two more than there should be, you expose your upper Rooms more to the Winds and Storms, and besides I am afraid the Foundation will hardly bear them, unless indeed you build with such light Stuff as Straw and Stubble, and that you know won't stand Fire.

Again where the Author Says

> Kindness of Heart by Words express,

Stricke out *Words* and put in *Deeds.* The world is too full of Compliments already; they are the rank Growth of every Soil, and Choak the good Plants of Benevolence and Benificence, Nor do I pretend to be the first in this comparison of Words and Actions to Plants; you may remember an

Ancient Poet whose Words we have all Studied and Copy'd at School, said long ago,

> A Man of Words and not of Deeds,
> Is like a Garden full of Weeds.

'Tis pity that *Good Works* among some sorts of People are so little Valued, and *Good Words* admired in their Stead; I mean seemingly *pious Discourses* instead of *Humane Benevolent Actions.* These they almost put out of countenance, by calling Morality *rotten Morality*, Righteousness, *ragged Righteousness* and even *filthy Rags;* and when you mention *Virtue*, they pucker up their Noses as if they smelt a Stink; at the same time that they eagerly snuff up an empty canting Harangue, as if it was a Posie of the Choicest Flowers. So they have inverted the good old Verse, and say now

> A Man of Deeds and not of Words
> Is like a Garden full of——

I have forgot the Rhime, but remember 'tis something the very Reverse of a Perfume. So much by Way of Commentary.

. . . My Love to Brother and all your Children, concludes at this time from Dear Jenny your affectionate Brother   B Franklin

PART II

Nature observed.

Curiosity has always been the engine of scientific discovery, as of all intellectual progress. When Franklin was born, in 1706, the world as we know it had scarcely begun to reveal its secrets to curious eyes. It had been established that the world was a globe and that it revolved, like other planets, around the sun. The great Isaac Newton had formulated the laws of motion that governed its movements. But people still commonly thought in terms of the four elements, earth, air, fire, and water, that the ancients had identified as what the world was made of. It was assumed that God had created not only the world but everything in it at a single stroke. Since he would not have made any mistakes, creating something that was not in his plan for eternity, it followed, as Franklin observed more than once, that "no species or Genus of Plants was ever lost, or ever will be while the World continues." It would be another century before Charles Darwin suggested a different origin and duration of species.

But Franklin recognized how little was actually known about the world and was continually thrilled by new discoveries, his own and other men's, that revealed facts and forces, hitherto unknown or unnoticed. He once lamented that he had been born too soon to "have the Happiness of knowing what will be known 100 years hence" or even better 1,000 years: "We may perhaps learn to deprive large Masses of their Gravity and give them absolute Levity, for the sake of easy Transport. Agriculture may diminish its Labour and double its Produce. All diseases may by sure means be prevented or cured, not excepting even that of Old Age, and our Lives lengthened at pleasure even beyond the antediluvian Standard."

So much has been discovered since Franklin's time that it is difficult to look at the world and its wonders through his eyes. Human ingenuity has devised instruments to probe farther into space and deeper into matter than he or anyone else could have imagined. But it is still the mark of genius to ask questions that reveal new truths behind everyday things and events that people take for granted. The world that excited Franklin's curiosity is the same world that meets our own senses. It has the same oceans and mountains, the same clouds and winds. It is warmed by the same sun, lighted at night by the same moon and stars. For his electrical experiments he had to use special equipment, much as scientists today need laboratories and special instruments, to look beyond what the eye can see. But most of Franklin's discoveries were the result of looking at what anyone could see and asking why. In Part II we will watch him doing just that: asking himself about a variety of everyday phenomena and then asking the questions about electric sparks that made him famous in his own time.

I have grouped the selections, written over the course of his life, under different headings: "Sickness and Health," "Wind, Weather, and Air," "Ships and the Sea," "Electric Fire," and "Geology and Cosmology." When something piqued Franklin's curiosity, he was likely to keep wondering about it and to make notes on it whenever it popped into his head. So the selections come from widely different times, in no logical or chronological sequence. Many of Franklin's observations, and the conclusions he drew from them, will appear to the modern reader as elementary, but he was among the first to give them systematic attention as subjects worthy of study. Other of his inquiries may seem outlandish or as leading to dead ends. But our purpose is simply to follow an extraordinary mind, to see

Franklin thinking, meeting the challenges that his curiosity continuously presented to him, trying to make sense out of the way things behaved, poking and prodding them, and trying to make use of what he found out. He always hoped and expected that knowledge would be useful, as it proved to be in the invention of lightning rods and dampers for chimneys. But it was the quest that excited him and made him who he was.

5 Sickness and health.

We begin with some of Franklin's experiences with his own body, a strong, athletic one in his youth, an overweight one by middle age, and troubled with psoriasis, gout, and painful, crippling kidney or bladder stones in old age. He never conquered these afflictions, but in an age that had not yet discovered the germ theory of disease, his experience of the common cold led him to discard the folk wisdom about it that still prevails. At the same time he discarded his contemporaries' strange aversion to fresh air. In 1773 he was considering writing a pamphlet on the causes of the common cold and made extensive notes for it. He never wrote the pamphlet but expressed his opinions on "vain Terrors" in letters to friends. The first selection is from one such letter, to Thomas Percival, a Manchester physician, on the benefits of moist fresh air. The next, on fresh air in general, is taken from a parenthetical passage in a long letter to his friend Jan Ingenhousz, physician to the emperor of Austria, on the subject of smoky chimneys that he wrote at sea on his last voyage home. I have also included an extract from John Adams's autobiography describing the occasion in September 1776 when Adams and Franklin were part of a delegation sent by the Continental Congress to meet with Lord Howe, commander of the British naval forces. Howe had hoped for some kind of voluntary submission from the Americans and did not get it; but en route to the meeting Franklin and Adams shared a bed in a tavern and bickered amiably about whether to open the window. (We will find them quarreling not so amiably a couple of years later.)

It seemed appropriate to include in this section Franklin's observations on two public health issues, lead poisoning and Mesmerism. Lead poisoning was a phenomenon he had first observed in the toxic effects of rum distilled in vessels made of lead. It is a good example of the way Franklin not only noticed things but took pains to notice them. The final selection is on a health fad that possessed Europeans in the 1780s, Mesmerism. Like many a later fashionable quack, Franz Anton Mesmer claimed the power to cure any number of diseases through a force he called animal magnetism. Mesmer's popularity in France and the testimony of many well-placed dupes (including the marquis de Lafayette) led Louis XVI to appoint a commission to investigate his claims. He named Franklin to the commission, along with the great chemist Lavoisier. The commission pronounced Mesmerism to be a total fraud. "Comus," mentioned along with Mesmer in Franklin's letter, was the name assumed by another charlatan, who claimed to cure epilepsy by electric shocks. Franklin declined to argue the case beyond the royal commission's report, but he had stated his own views earlier in this letter, which may be read as a caution against the many medical fads and frauds, then and since, that have won popular acclaim.

On the Benefits of Moist Fresh Air, 1773

The Gentry of England are remarkably afraid of Moisture, and of Air. But Seamen who live in perpetually moist Air, are always Healthy if they have good Provisions. The Inhabitants of Bermuda, St. Helena, and other Islands far from Continents, surrounded with Rocks against which the Waves continually dashing fill the Air with Spray and Vapour, and where no wind can arrive that does not pass over much Sea, and of course bring much Moisture, these People are remarkably healthy. And I have long thought that mere moist Air has no ill Effect on the Constitution; Tho' Air impregnated with Vapours from putrid Marshes is found pernicious, not from the Moisture but the Putridity. It seems strange that a Man whose Body is compos'd in great Part of moist Fluids, whose Blood and Juices are so watery, who can swallow Quantities of Water and Small Beer daily without Inconvenience, should fancy that a little more or less Moisture in the Air should be of such Importance. But we abound in Absurdity and Inconsistency. Thus, tho' it is generally agreed that *taking the Air* is a good

Thing, yet what Caution against Air, what stopping of Crevices, what wrapping-up in warm Clothes, what Shutting of Doors and Windows! even in the midst of Summer! Many London Families go out once a Day to take the Air; three or four Persons in a Coach, one perhaps Sick; these go three or four Miles or as many Turns in Hide [Hyde] Park, with the Glasses both up close, all breathing over and over again the same Air they brought out of Town with them in the Coach with the least change possible, and render'd worse and worse every moment. And this they call taking the Air. From many Years Observations on my self and others, I am persuaded we are on a wrong Scent in supposing Moist, or cold Air, the Causes of that Disorder we call a Cold. Some unknown Quality in the Air may perhaps sometimes produce Colds, as in the *Influenza:* but generally I apprehend they are the Effects of too full Living in proportion to our Exercise.

On Fresh Air, 1785

Some are as much afraid of fresh Air as Persons in the Hydrophobia are of fresh Water. I myself had formerly this Prejudice, this *Aerophobia*, as I now account it, and dreading the suppos'd dangerous Effects of cool Air, I consider'd it as an Enemy, & clos'd with extreme Care every Crevice in the Rooms I inhabited. Experience has convinced me of my Error. I now look upon fresh Air as a Friend. I even sleep with an open Window. I am persuaded that no common Air from without, is so unwholesom as the Air within a close Room, that has been often breath'd and not changed. Moist Air, too, which formerly I thought pernicious, gives me now no Apprehensions: For considering that no Dampness of Air apply'd to the Outside of my Skin, can be equal to what is apply'd to and touches it within, my whole Body being full of Moisture; and finding that I can lie two hours in a Bath twice a Week, cover'd with Water, which certainly is much damper than any Air can be, and this for Years together, without catching Cold, or being in any other manner disorder'd by it, I no longer dread mere Moisture, either in Air or Sheets or Shirts: And I find it of Importance to the Happiness of Life, the being freed from vain Terrors, especially of Objects, that we are every day exposed inevitably to meet with. You Physicians have of late happily discover'd, after a contrary Opinion had prevail'd some Ages, that fresh and cool Air does good to Persons in the Small Pox and other Fevers. It is to be hop'd that in another Century or two we may all find out, that it is not bad even for People in Health. And as to moist Air, here I am at this present Writing in a Ship with above 40 Persons, who have had no other but moist Air to breathe for 6 Weeks past, every thing we touch is damp, and nothing dries; yet we are all as healthy as we should be on the Mountains of Switzerland, whose Inhabitants are not more so than those of Bermuda or St. Helena, Islands on whose Rocks the Waves are dash'd into Millions of Particles, which fill the Air with Damp, but produce no Diseases, the Moisture being pure, unmix'd with the poisonous Vapours arising from putrid Marshes, and stagnant Pools, in which many Insects die & corrupt the Water. These Places only, in my Opinion, (which however I submit to yours) afford unwholsome Air; and that it is not the mere Water contain'd in damp Air, but the volatile Particles of corrupted animal Matter mix'd with that Water, which renders such Air pernicious to those who breathe it. And I imagine it a Cause of the same kind that renders the Air in close Rooms, where the perspirable Matter is breath'd over and over again by a number of assembled People, so hurtful to Health. After being in such a Situation, many find themselves affected by that *Febricula,* which the English alone call *a Cold,* and perhaps from the Name imagine that they caught the Malady by *going out* of the Room when it was in fact by being in it.

The Open Window: From the Autobiography of John Adams, 1776

The Taverns were so full We could with difficulty obtain Entertainment. At Brunswick, but one bed could be procured for Dr. Franklin and me, in a Chamber little larger than the bed, without a Chimney and with only one small Window. The Window was open, and I, who was an invalid and afraid of the Air in the night (*blowing upon me*), shut it close. Oh! says Franklin dont shut the Window. We shall be suffocated. I answered I was afraid of the Evening Air. Dr. Franklin replied, the Air within this Chamber will soon be, and indeed is now worse than that without Doors: come! open the Window and come to bed, and I will convince you: I believe you are not acquainted with my Theory of Colds. Opening the Window and leaping into Bed, I said I had read his Letters to Dr. Cooper in which he had advanced, that Nobody ever got cold by going into a cold Church, or any other cold Air: but the Theory was so little consistent with my experience, that I thought it a Paradox: However I had so much curiosity to hear his reasons, that I would run the risque of a cold. The Doctor then began an harrangue, upon Air and cold and Respiration and Perspiration, with which I was so much amused that I soon fell asleep, and left him and his Philosophy together: but I believe they were equally sound and insensible, within a few minutes after me, for the last Words I heard were pronounced as if he was more than half asleep. . . . [ellipsis Adams's] I remember little of the Lecture, except, that the human Body, by Respiration and Perspiration, destroys a gallon of Air in a minute: that two such Persons, as were now in that Chamber, would consume all the Air in it, in an hour or two: that by breathing over again the matter thrown off, by the Lungs and the Skin, We should imbibe the real Cause of Colds, not from abroad but from within. I am not inclined to introduce here a dissertation on this Subject. There is much Truth I believe, in some things he advanced: but they warrant not the assertion that a Cold is never taken from cold air. I have often conversed with him since on the same subject: and I believe with him that Colds are often taken in foul Air, in close Rooms: but they are often taken from cold Air, abroad too. I have often asked him, whether a Person heated with Exercise, going suddenly into cold Air or standing still in a current of it, might not have his Pores suddenly contracted, his Perspiration stopped, and that matter thrown into the Circulations or cast upon the Lungs which he acknowledged was the Cause of Colds. To this he never could give me a satisfactory Answer. And I have heard that in the Opinion of his own able Physician Dr. Jones he fell a Sacrifice at last, not to the Stone but to his own Theory; having caught the violent Cold, which finally choaked him, by sitting for some hours at a Window, with the cool Air blowing upon him.

To Benjamin Vaughan, 1786

Dear Friend,   Philada. July 31, 1786
    I recollect that when I had the great Pleasure of seeing you at South-ampton, now a 12 month since, we had some Conversation on the bad Effects of Lead taken inwardly; and that at your Request I promis'd to send

you in writing a particular Account of several Facts I then mention'd to you, of which you thought some good Use might be made. I now sit down to fulfill that Promise.

The first Thing I remember of this kind, was a general Discourse in Boston when I was a Boy, of a Complaint from North Carolina against New England Rum, that it poison'd their People, giving them the Dry-Belly ach, with a Loss of the Use of their Limbs. The Distilleries being examin'd on the Occasion, it was found that several of them used leaden Still-heads and Worms [coils], and the Physicians were of Opinion that the Mischief was occasioned by that Use of Lead. The Legislature of the Massachusetts thereupon pass'd an Act prohibiting under severe Penalties the Use of such Still-Heads & Worms thereafter. Inclos'd I send you a Copy of the Act, taken from my printed Law book.

In 1724, being in London, I went to work in the Printing-House of Mr Palmer, Bartholomew Close, as a Compositor. I there found a Practice I had never seen before, of drying a Case of Types, (which are wet in Distribution) by placing it sloping before the Fire. I found this had the additional Advantage, when the Types were not only dry'd but heated, of being comfortable to the Hands working over them in cold weather. I therefore sometimes heated my Case when the Types did not want drying. But an old Workman observing it, advis'd me not to do so, telling me I might lose the Use of my Hands by it, as two of our Companions had nearly done, one of whom that us'd to earn his Guinea a Week could not then make more than ten Shillings and the other, who had the Dangles, but Seven & sixpence. This, with a kind of obscure Pain that I had sometimes felt as it were in the Bones of my Hand when working over the Types made very hot, induc'd me to omit the Practice. But talking afterwards with Mr James, a Letterfounder in the same Close, and asking him if his People, who work'd over the little Furnaces of melted Metal, were not subject to that Disorder; he made light of any Danger from the Effluvia, but ascrib'd it to Particles of the Metal swallow'd with their Food by slovenly Workmen, who went to their Meals after handling the Metal, without well-washing their Fingers, so that some of the metalline Particles were taken off by their Bread and eaten with it. This appear'd to have some Reason in it. But the Pain I had experienc'd made me still afraid of those Effluvia.

Being in Derbishire at some of the Furnaces for Smelting of Lead Ore, I was told that the Smoke of those Furnaces was pernicious to the neighbouring Grass and other Vegetables. But I do not recollect to have heard any thing of the Effect of such Vegetables eaten by Animals. It may be well to make the Enquiry.

In America I have often observ'd that on the Roofs of our shingled Houses where Moss is apt to grow in northern Exposures, if there be any thing on the Roof painted with white Lead, such as Balusters, or Frames of dormant Windows, &c. there is constantly a Streak on the Shingles from such Paint down to the Eaves, on which no Moss will grow, but the Wood remains constantly clean & free from it.—We seldom drink Rain Water that falls on our Houses; and if we did, perhaps the small Quantity of Lead descending from such Paint, might not be sufficient to produce any sensible ill Effect on our Bodies. But I have been told of a Case in Europe, I forget the Place, where a whole Family was afflicted with what we call the Dry-Belly ach, or *Colica Pictorum*, by drinking Rain Water. It was at a Country Seat, which being situated too high to have the Advantage of a Well, was supply'd with Water from a Tank which receiv'd the Water from the leaded Roofs. This had been drank several Years without Mischief; but some young Trees planted near the House, growing up above the Roof, and shedding their Leaves upon it, it was suppos'd that an Acid in those Leaves had corroded the Lead they cover'd, and furnish'd the Water of that Year with its baneful Particles &c Qualities.

When I was in Paris with Sir John Pringle in 1767, he visited *La Charité*, a Hospital particularly famous for the Cure of that Malady, and brought from thence a Pamphlet, containing a List of the Names of Persons, specifying their Professions or Trades, who had been cured there. I had the Curiosity to examine that List, and found that all the Patients were of Trades that some way or other use or work in Lead; such as Plumbers, Glasiers, Painters, &c. excepting only two kinds, Stonecutters and Soldiers. These I could not reconcile to my Notion that Lead was the Cause of that Disorder. But on my mentioning this Difficulty to a Physician of that Hospital, he inform'd me that the Stone cutters are continually using melted Lead to fix the ends of Iron Balustrades in Stone; and that the Soldiers had been employ'd by Painters as Labourers in Grinding of Colours.

This, my dear Friend, is all I can at present recollect on the Subject. You will see by it, that the Opinion of this mischievous Effect from Lead, is at least above Sixty Years old; and you will observe with Concern how long a useful Truth may be known, and exist, before it is generally receiv'd and practis'd on. I am, ever, Yours most affectionately   B Franklin

Mesmerism, 1784

You [a M. La Sablière de la Condamine] desire my Sentiments concerning the Cures perform'd by Comus, & Mesmer. I think that in general, Maladies caus'd by Obstructions may be treated by Electricity with Advantage. As to the Animal Magnetism, so much talk'd of, I am totally unacquainted with it, and must doubt its Existence till I can see or feel some Effect of it. None of the Cures said to be perform'd by it, have fallen under my Observation, and there being so many Disorders which cure themselves, and such a Disposition in Mankind to deceive themselves and one another on these Occasions; and this living long having given me frequent Opportunities of seeing certain Remedies cry'd up as curing every thing, and yet soon after totally laid aside as useless, I cannot but fear that the Expectations of great Advantage from this new Method of treating Diseases, will prove a Delusion. That Delusion may how ever in some cases be of use while it lasts. There are in every great rich City, a Number of Persons who are never in health, because they are fond of Medicines and always taking them, whereby, they derange the natural Functions, and hurt their Constitutions. If these people can be persuaded to forbear their Drugs in Expectation of being cured by only the Physician's Finger or an Iron Rod pointing at them, they may possibly find good Effects tho' they mistake the Cause.

6 Wind, weather, and air.

Everybody talks about the weather, but nobody does anything about it. And nobody can, but Franklin did what he could to make sense of it. The letter to his friend Jared Eliot, a learned Connecticut farmer who shared his curiosity about the world, is my favorite example of the way Franklin discovered things that people had had before their eyes for centuries without asking questions about them. Northeast storms were a familiar thing to Americans living near the Atlantic coast, but Franklin was probably the first to determine that, contrary to commonsense assumptions, they did not originate in the northeast. The letter to Peter Collinson, the London physician with whom Franklin frequently corresponded on scientific subjects, gives his only direct experience of a whirlwind, a subject about which he had already written extensive conjectures and hypotheses based on other people's observations. He always valued observation, experience, and experiment above the speculations prompted by them and made a point of never trying to defend his own arguments when others challenged them. It does not follow that he was averse to speculation and theory. The point of observing something was to make accurate notations and then make sense of them, but it was important to distinguish theory from fact.

As important as making sense of an observation was making use of it. The letter to Edward Nairne, begun in 1780, mislaid, and completed in 1783, is another example of the way Franklin's ever-active curiosity extracted new ideas from a common experience—wood expanding across the grain in times of high humidity (such as doors sticking in wet summer weather)—and then finding a way to make the idea yield something useful. The letter to Nairne is also a good example of the lucidity with which he described his ideas. (Compare this with the incomprehensible instructions that accompany those devices that arrive at your door labeled "Some assembly required.") Nairne was an instrument maker and a fellow member of England's Royal Society. There is no evidence that he ever made a hygrometer according to the design Franklin suggested.

In addition to observing and speculating about the movements of the atmosphere, Franklin became an expert on the movement of air indoors. Heating a house was always a big problem for people in the eighteenth century. It was done entirely by open fireplaces and stoves, fireplaces being the most common among the colonists. Heating an ordinary New England house took up to 25 cords of wood. Most of the heat went up the chimney, and sometimes the smoke did not. The fire required plenty of air to burn properly, and much of that went up the chimney too.

Franklin began thinking about air and observing its behavior inside houses in the 1740s. He used what he found out to invent a new combined stove and fireplace that consumed less air and less wood while still giving people the cheery view of the flames that they found so enjoyable. The Franklin stove, made by craftsmen following his published instructions, became very popular. When the governor of Pennsylvania offered him a patent on the stove, Franklin declined on the ground that "as we enjoy great Advantage from the Inventions of others, we should be glad of an Opportunity to serve others by any Invention of ours, and this we should do freely and generously."

When Franklin went to England, where people burned coal more than they did wood, he invented a device for increasing the efficiency of existing fireplaces. It was what we now call a damper, which apparently had not been in use before. In a letter to his Boston friend James Bowdoin, who shared his interest in scientific experiments, he described the damper he had designed for his lodgings in London, explained how it worked, and then went on to suggest a way of using chimneys for ventilation and cooling in summer. He had already made a number of experiments to test the cooling effects of evaporation and here put them to use.

Franklin's curiosity about air and its properties received a new stimulus late in life. While concluding his mission to France in 1783, after the peace with England was signed, he witnessed the first balloon ascensions by Joseph and Jacques Montgolfier. He found them exciting. When someone in the crowd of spectators at one of the ascensions asked scoffingly what good a hot-air balloon could be, Franklin answered, "What good is a newborn baby?" He kept his old friend Sir Joseph Banks, president of the Royal Society, informed about the succession of trials with ever larger balloons floating ever longer distances in the air currents. As he says in the letter below, he looked for the newborn baby to "pave the Way to some Discoveries in Natural Philosophy of which at present we have no Conception."

To Jared Eliot, 1750

Dear Sir   Philada. Feb. 13, 1750

You desire to know my Thoughts about the N. E. Storms beginning to Leeward. Some years since [on Oct. 21, 1743] there was an Eclipse of the Moon at 9 in the Evening, which I intended to observe, but before 8 a Storm blew up at N. E. and continued violent all Night and all next Day, the Sky thick clouded, dark and rainy, so that neither Moon nor Stars could be seen. The Storm did a great deal of Damage all along the Coast, for we had Accounts of it in the News Papers from Boston, Newport, New York, Maryland and Virginia. But what surpriz'd me, was to find in the Boston Newspapers an Account of an Observation of that Eclipse made there: For I thought, as the Storm came from the N. E. it must have begun sooner at Boston than with us, and consequently have prevented such Observation. I wrote to my Brother about it, and he inform'd me, that the Eclipse was over there, an hour before the Storm began. Since which I have made Enquiries from time to time of Travellers, and of my Correspondents N Eastward and S. Westward, and observ'd the Accounts in the Newspapers from N England, N York, Maryland, Virginia and South Carolina, and I find it to be a constant Fact, that N East Storms begin to Leeward; and are often more violent there than farther to Windward. Thus the last October Storm, which with you was on the 8th. began on the 7th in Virginia and N Carolina, and was most violent there. As to the Reason of this, I can only give you my Conjectures. Suppose a great Tract of Country, Land and Sea, to wit Florida and the Bay of Mexico, to have clear Weather for several Days, and to be heated by the Sun and its Air thereby exceedingly rarified; Suppose the Country North Eastward, as Pensilvania, New England, Nova Scotia, Newfoundland, &c. to be at the same time cover'd with Clouds, and its Air chill'd and condens'd. The rarified Air being lighter must rise, and the Dense Air next to it will press into its Place; that will be follow'd by the next denser Air, that by the next, and so on. Thus when I have a Fire in my Chimney, there is a Current of Air constantly flowing from the Door to the Chimney: but the beginning of the Motion was at the Chimney, where the Air being rarified by the Fire, rising, its Place was supply'd by the cooler Air that was next to it, and the Place of that by the next, and so on to the Door. So the Water in a long Sluice or Mill Race, being stop'd by a Gate, is at Rest like the Air in a Calm; but as soon as you open the Gate at one End to let it out, the Water next the Gate begins first to move, that which is next to it follows; and so tho' the Water proceeds forward to the Gate, the Motion which began there runs backwards, if one may so speak, to the upper End of the Race, where the Water is last in Motion. We have on this Continent a long Ridge of Mountains running from N East to S. West; and the Coast runs the same Course. These may, perhaps, contribute towards the Direction of the winds or at least influence them in some Degree. If these Conjectures do not satisfy you, I wish to have yours on the Subject.

. . . I am, Sir, Your obliged humble Servant   B Franklin

To Peter Collinson, 1755

Dear Sir,   Philadelphia, Aug. 25, 1755.

As you have my former papers on Whirlwinds, &c. [sent in June] I now send you an account of one which I had lately an opportunity of seeing and examining myself.

Being in Maryland, riding with Col. Tasker, and some other gentlemen to his country-seat, where I and my son were entertained by that amiable and worthy man, with great hospitality and kindness, we saw in the vale below us, a small whirlwind beginning in the road, and shewing itself by the dust it raised and contained. It appeared in the form of a sugar-loaf, spinning on its point, moving up the hill towards us, and enlarging as it came forward. When it passed by us, its smaller part near the ground, appeared not bigger than a common barrel, but widening upwards, it seemed, at 40 or 50 feet high, to be 20 or 30 feet in diameter. The rest of the company stood looking after it, but my curiosity being stronger, I followed it, riding close by its side, and observed its licking up, in its progress, all the dust that was under its smaller part. As it is a common opinion that a shot, fired through a waterspout, will break it, I tried to break this little whirlwind, by striking my whip frequently through it, but without any effect. Soon after, it quitted the road and took into the woods, growing every moment larger and stronger, raising, instead of dust, the old dry leaves with which the ground was thick covered, and making a great noise with them and the branches of the trees, bending some tall trees round in a circle swiftly and very surprizingly, though the progressive motion of the whirl was not so swift but that a man on foot might have kept pace with it, but the circular motion was amazingly rapid. By the leaves it was now filled with, I could plainly perceive that the current of air they were driven by, moved upwards in a spiral line; and when I saw the trunks and bodies of large trees invelop'd in the passing whirl, which continued intire after it had left them, I no longer wondered that my whip had no effect on it in its smaller state. I accompanied it about three quarters of a mile, till some limbs of dead trees, broken off by the whirl, flying about, and falling near me, made me more apprehensive of danger; and then I stopped, looking at the top of it as it went on, which was visible, by means of the leaves contained in it, for a very great height above the trees. Many of the leaves, as they got loose from the upper and widest part, were scattered in the wind; but so great was their height in the air, that they appeared no bigger than flies. My son, who was, by this time, come up with me, followed the whirlwind till it left the woods, and crossed an old tobacco-field, where, finding neither dust nor leaves to take up, it gradually became invisible below as it went away over that field. The course of the general wind then blowing was along with us as we travelled, and the progressive motion of the whirlwind was in a direction nearly opposite, though it did not keep a strait line, nor was its progressive motion uniform, it making little sallies on either hand as it went, proceeding sometimes faster, and sometimes slower, and seeming sometimes for a few seconds almost stationary, then starting forwards pretty fast again. When we rejoined the company, they were admiring the vast height of the leaves, now brought by the common wind, over our heads. These leaves accompanied us as we travelled, some falling now and then round about us, and some not reaching the ground till we had gone near three miles from the place where we first saw the whirlwind begin. Upon my asking Col. Tasker if such whirlwinds were common in Maryland, he answered pleasantly, *No, not at all common; but we got this on purpose to treat Mr. Franklin.* And a very high treat it was, to Dear Sir, Your affectionate friend, and humble servant   B. F.

To Edward Nairne, 1780–83

Sir,   Passy, near Paris Nov. 13. 1780.[–October 18, 1783]

The Qualities hitherto sought in a Hygrometer, or Instrument to discover the Degrees of Moisture & Dryness in the Air, seem to have been, an Aptitude to receive Humidity readily from a moist Air, and to part with it as readily to a dry Air. Different Substances have been found to possess more or less of this Quality; but when we shall have found the Substance that has it in the greatest Perfection, there will still remain some Uncertainty in the Conclusions to be drawn from the Degree shown by the Instrument, arising from the actual state of the Instrument itself as to Heat & Cold. Thus if two Bottles or vessels of Glass or Metal being filled, the one with cold & the other with hot-Water, are brought into a Room; the Moisture of the Air in the Room will attach itself in Quantities to the Surface of the cold Vessel, while if you actually wet the surface of the hot Vessel, the Moisture will immediately quit it, and be absorbed by the same Air. And thus in a sudden Change of the Air from cold to warm, the Instrument remaining longer Cold may condense & absorb more Moisture, and mark the Air as having become more humid than it is in Reality; and the contrary in a Change from warm to cold.

But if such a suddenly changing Instrument could be freed from these Imperfections, yet when the Design is to discover the different Degrees of Humidity in the Air of different Countries; I apprehend the quick Sensibility of the Instrument to be rather a Disadvantage; since to draw the desired Conclusions from it, a constant & frequent Observation Day &

Night in each Country will be necessary for a Year or Years, and the mean of each different Set of Observations is to be found & determined. After all which some Uncertainty will remain respecting the different Degrees of Exactitude with which different Persons may have made and taken Notes of their Observations.

For these Reasons I apprehend that a Substance which tho' capable of being distended by Moisture & contracted by Dryness, is so slow in receiving and parting with its Humidity that the frequent Changes in the Atmosphere have not time to affect it sensibly, and which therefore should gradually take nearly the Medium of all those Changes & preserve it constantly, would be the most proper Substance of which to make Such an Hygrometer.

Such an Instrument, you my dear Sir, tho' without intending it, have made for me; and I without desiring or expecting it have received from you. It is therefore with Propriety that I address to you the following Account of it, and the more as you have both a Head to contrive and a hand to execute the Means of perfecting it. And I do this with greater Pleasure as it affords me the Opportunity of renewing that antient Correspondence & Acquaintance with you, which to me was always so pleasing & so instructive.

You may possibly remember that in or about the Year 1758, you made for me a Set of artificial Magnets, Six in Number, each 5½ Inches Long, ½ an Inch broad, & ⅙ of an Inch thick. These with two Pieces of Soft Iron which together equalled one of the Magnets were inclos'd in a little Box of Mahogony Wood, the Grain of which ran with, & not across, the Length of the Box; and the Box was clos'd by a Little Shutter of the same Wood, the Grain of which ran across the Box; and the Ends of this shutting Piece were bevel'd so as to fit & slide in a kind of Dovetail Groove when the Box was to be shut or open'd.

I had been of Opinion that good Mahogony Wood was not affected by Moisture so as to change its Dimensions, & that it was always to be found as the Tools of the Workman left it. Indeed the Difference at different Times in the same Country is so small as to be scarcely in a common Way observable. Hence the Box which was made so as to allow sufficient Room for the Magnets to Slide out and in freely, and when in, afforded them so much Play that by shaking the Box one could make them strike the opposite

Sides alternately, continued in the same State all the Time I remain'd in England, which was four Years, without any apparent Alteration. I left England in August 1762 and arriv'd at Philadelphia in October the same Year. In a few Weeks after my Arrival, being desirous of showing your Magnets to a Philosophical Friend, I found them so tight in the Box, that it was with Difficulty I got them out; and constantly during the two Years I remain'd there, Viz till November 1764, this Difficulty of getting them out and in continued. The little Shutter too, as Wood does not shrink length-ways of the Grain, was found too long to enter in Grooves, & not being us'd was mislaid and Lost, and I afterwards had another made that fitted.

In December 1764 I returned to England and after some time I observed that my Box was become full big enough for my Magnets, and too wide for my new Shutter; which was so much too Short for its Grooves, that it was apt to fall out; and to make it keep in, I lengthen'd it by adding to each End a little Coat of Sealing Wax.

I continued in England more than 10 Years, and During all that time after the first Change, I perceived no Alteration. The Magnets had the same Freedom in their Box, and the little Shutter continued with the added Sealing Wax to fit its Grooves, till some Weeks after my second Return to America.

As I could not imagine any other Cause for this Change of Dimensions in the Box, when in the different Countries, I concluded first generally that the Air of England was moister than that of America. And this I supposed an Effect of its being an Island, where every Wind that blew must neces-sarily pass over some Sea before it arrived, and of Course lick up some Vapour. I afterwards indeed doubted whether I had not been too general in my Conclusion; and whether it might not be just only so far as related to the City of London, where I resided; because there are many Causes of Moisture in the City Air, which do not exist to the same Degree in the Country; such as the Brewers' & Dyers' boiling Cauldrons, and the great Number of Pots and Teakettles continually on the Fire, sending forth abundance of Vapour; and also the Number of Animals who by their Breath constantly increase it, to which may be added that even the vast Quantity of Sea Coals burnt there, in kindling discharge a great deal of Moisture.

When I was in England the last time, you also made for me a little

Achromatic Pocket Telescope. The Body was Brass, and it had a round Case (I think of thin Wood) covered with Shagrin [shagreen: a kind of leather]. All the while I remained in England, tho' possibly there might be some small Changes in the Dimensions of this Case, I neither perceived nor suspected any. There was always comfortable Room for the Telescope to slip in and out. But soon after I arrived in America, which was in May 1775, the Case became too small for the Instrument, it was with much Difficulty & various Contrivances that I got it out, and I could never after get it in again; during my Stay there, which was 18 Months. I brought it with me to Europe, but left the Case as useless, imagining that I should find the continental Air of France as dry as that of Pensilvania where my Magnet Box had also returned a second time to its Narrowness, & pinched the Pieces as heretofore, obliging me, too, to scrape the Sealing Wax off the Ends of the Shutter.

I had not been long in France, before I was surprized to find, that my Box was become as large as it had always been in England, the Magnets enter'd and came out with the same Freedom, and when in, I could rattle them against its Sides; this has continued to be the Case without sensible Variation. My Habitation is out of Paris, distant almost a league, so that the moist Air of the City cannot be supposed to have much Effect upon the Box: & I am on a high dry Hill in a free Air, as likely to be dry as any Air in France. Whence it seems probable, that the Air of England in general may, as well as that of London, be moister than the Air of America, since that of France is so, and in a Part so distant from the Sea.

. . .

Now what I would beg leave to recommend to you, is, that you would recollect if you can, the Species of Mahogony of which you made my Box, for you know there is a good deal of Difference in Woods that go under that Name, or if that cannot be, that you would take a Number of Pieces of the closest and finest grain'd Mahogony that you can meet with, plane them to the thinness of about a Line, and the Width of about two Inches across the Grain; and fix each of the Pieces in some Instrument that you can contrive, which will permit them to contract & dilate, and will show in sensible Degrees, by a moveable Hand upon a marked Scale, the otherwise less sensible Quantities of such Contraction and Dilatation. If these Instruments are all kept in the same Place while making, and are graduated together while subject to the same Degrees of Moisture or Dryness, I apprehend you will have so many comparable Hygrometors which being sent into different Countries, and continued there for some time will find and show there the Mean of the different Dryness & Moisture of the Air of those Countries; and that with much less Trouble than by any other Hygrometer hitherto in use. With great Esteem I am, dear Sir, Your most obedient & most humble Servant   B Franklin

To James Bowdoin, 1758

Dear Sir,   London, Dec. 2, 1758.

I have executed here an easy simple contrivance, that I have long since had in speculation, for keeping rooms warmer in cold weather than they generally are, and with less fire. It is this. The opening of the chimney is contracted, by brick-work faced with marble slabs, to about two feet between the jambs, and the breast [the wall between the chimney flue and the room above the fireplace opening] brought down to within about three feet of the hearth. An iron frame is placed just under the breast, and extending quite to the back of the chimney, so that a plate of the same metal may slide horizontally backwards and forwards in the grooves on each side of the frame. This plate is just so large as to fill the whole space, and shut the chimney entirely when thrust quite in, which is convenient when there is no fire; drawing it out, so as to leave a space between its farther edge and the back, of about two inches; this space is sufficient for the smoke to pass; and so large a part of the funnel being stopt by the rest of the plate, the passage of warm air out of the room, up the chimney, is obstructed and retarded, and by that means much cold air is prevented from coming in through crevices, to supply its place. This effect is made manifest three ways. First, when the fire burns briskly in cold weather, the howling or whistling noise made by the wind, as it enters the room through the crevices, when the chimney is open as usual, ceases as soon as the plate is slid in to its proper distance. Secondly, opening the door of the room about half an inch, and holding your hand against the opening, near the top of the door, you feel the cold air coming in against your hand, but weakly, if the plate be in. Let another person suddenly draw it out, so as to let the air of the room go up the chimney, with its usual freedom where chimneys are open, and you immediately feel the cold air rushing in strongly. Thirdly, if something be set against the door, just sufficient, when the plate is in, to keep the door nearly shut, by resisting the pressure of the air that would force it open: Then, when the plate is drawn out, the door will be forced open by the increased pressure of the outward cold air endeavouring to get in to supply the place of the warm air, that now passes out of the room to go up the chimney. In our common open chimneys, half the fuel is wasted, and its effect lost, the air it has warmed being immediately drawn off. Several of my acquaintances having seen the simple machine in my room, have imitated it at their own houses, and it seems likely to become pretty common. I describe it thus particularly to you, because I think it would be useful in Boston, where firing is often dear.

Mentioning chimneys puts me in mind of a property I formerly had occasion to observe in them, which I have not found taken notice of by others; it is, that in the summer time, when no fire is made in the chimneys, there is, nevertheless, a regular draft of air through them; continually passing upwards from about five or six o'clock in the afternoon, till eight or nine o'clock the next morning, when the current begins to slacken and hesitate a little, for about half an hour, and then sets as strongly down again, which it continues to do till towards five in the afternoon, then slackens and hesitates as before, going sometimes a little up, then a little down, till in about half an hour it gets into a steady upward current for the night, which continues till eight or nine the next day; the hours varying a little as the days lengthen and shorten, and sometimes varying from sudden changes in the weather; as if, after being long warm, it should begin to grow cool about noon, while the air was coming down the chimney, the current will then change earlier than the usual hour, &c.

This property in chimneys I imagine we might turn to some account, and render improper, for the future, the old saying, *as useless as a chimney in summer*. If the opening of the chimney, from the breast down to the hearth, be closed by a slight moveable frame, or two in the manner of doors, covered with canvas, that will let the air through, but keep out the flies; and another little frame set within upon the hearth, with hooks on which to hang joints of meat, fowls, &c. wrapt well in wet linen cloths, three or four fold, I am confident that if the linen is kept wet, by sprinkling it once a day, the meat would be so cooled by the evaporation, carried on continually by means of the passing air, that it would keep a week or more in the hottest weather. Butter and milk might likewise be kept cool, in vessels or bottles covered with wet cloths. A shallow tray, or keeler, should be under the frame to receive any water that might drip from the wetted cloths. I think, too, that this property of chimneys might, by means of smoak-jack vanes [a machine for turning a roasting-spit using the power generated by the ascending current of heated air in the flue], be applied to some mechanical purposes, where a small but pretty constant power only is wanted.

If you would have my opinion of the cause of this changing current of air in chimneys, it is, in short, as follows. In summer time there is generally a great difference in the warmth of the air at mid-day and midnight, and, of course, a difference of specific gravity in the air, as the more it is warmed the more it is rarefied. The funnel of a chimney being for the most part surrounded by the house, is protected, in a great measure, from the direct action of the sun's rays, and also from the coldness of the night air. It thence preserves a middle temperature between the heat of the day, and the coldness of the night. This middle temperature it communicates to the air contained in it. If the state of the outward air be cooler than that in the funnel of the chimney, it will, by being heavier, force it to rise, and go out at the top. What supplies its place from below, being warmed, in its turn, by the warmer funnel, is likewise forced up by the colder and weightier air below, and so the current is continued till the next day, when the sun gradually changes the state of the outward air, makes it first as warm as the funnel of the chimney can make it, (when the current begins to hesitate) and afterwards warmer. Then the funnel being cooler than the air that comes into it, cools that air, makes it heavier than the outward air; of course it descends; and what succeeds it from above, being cool'd in its turn, the descending current continues till towards evening, when it again hesitates and changes its course, from the change of warmth in the outward air, and the nearly remaining same middle temperature in the funnel.

Upon this principle, if a houe were built behind Beacon-hill, an adit [tunnel] carried from one of the doors into the hill horizontally, till it met with a perpendicular shaft sunk from its top, it seems probable to me, that those who lived in the house, would constantly, in the heat even of the calmest day, have as much cool air passing through the house, as they should chuse; and the same, though reversed in its current, during the stillest night.

I think, too, this property might be made of use to miners; as where several shafts or pits are sunk perpendicularly into the earth, communicating at bottom by horizontal passages, which is a common case, if a chimney of thirty or forty feet high were built over one of the shafts, or so near the shaft, that the chimney might communicate with the top of the shaft, all air being excluded but what should pass up or down by the shaft, a constant change of air would, by this means, be produced in the passages below, tending to secure the workmen from those damps which so frequently incommode them. For the fresh air would be almost always going down the open shaft, to go up the chimney, or down the chimney to go up the shaft. Let me add one observation more, which is, That if that part of the funnel of a chimney, which appears above the roof of a house, be pretty long, and have three of its sides exposed to the heat of the sun successively, *viz.* when he is in the east, in the south, and in the west; while the north side is sheltered by the building from the cool northerly winds. Such a chimney will often be so heated by the sun, as to continue the draft strongly upwards, through the whole twenty-four hours, and often for many days together. If the outside of such a chimney be painted black, the effect will be still greater, and the current stronger. I am, dear Sir, yours, &c.   B.F.

To Sir Joseph Banks, *1783*

Sir,   Passy, August 30, 1783

On Wednesday the 27th. Instant, the new aerostatic Experiment, invented by Messrs. Mongolfier of Annonay, was repeated by Mr. Charles, Professor of experimental Philosophy at Paris.

A hollow Globe 12 feet Diameter was formed of what is called in

Ascension of Montgolfier balloon, September 19, 1783

England Oiled Silk, here *Taffetas gommé*, the Silk being impregnated with a Solution of Gum elastic in Lintseed Oil, as is said. The Parts were sewed together while wet with the Gum, and some of it was afterwards passed over the Seams, to render it as tight as possible.

It was afterwards filled with the inflammable Air that is produced by pouring Oil of Vitriol upon Filings of Iron, when it was found to have a tendency upwards so strong as to be capable of lifting a Weight of 39 Pounds, exclusive of its own Weight which was 25 lb, and the Weight of the Air contain'd.

It was brought early in the Morning to the *Champ de Mars,* a Field in which [military] Reviews are sometimes made, lying between the Military School and the River. There it was held down by a Cord till 5 in the afternoon, when it was to be let loose. Care was taken before the Hour to replace what Portion had been lost, of the inflammable Air, or of its Force, by injecting more.

It is supposed that not less than 50,000 People were assembled to see the Experiment. The Champ de Mars being surrounded by Multitudes, and vast Numbers on the opposite Side of the River.

At 5 a Clock Notice was given to the Spectators by the Firing of two Cannon, that the Cord was about to be cut. And presently the Globe was seen to rise, and that as fast as a Body of 12 feet Diameter with a force only of 39 Pounds, could be suppos'd to move the resisting Air out of its Way. There was some Wind, but not very strong. A little Rain had wet it, so that it shone, and made an agreable Appearance. It diminish'd in Apparent Magnitude as it rose, till it enter'd the Clouds when it seem'd to me scarce bigger than an Orange, and soon after became invisible, the Clouds concealing it.

The Multitude separated, all well satisfied and delighted with the Success of the Experiment, and amusing one another with discourses of the various Uses it may possibly be apply'd to, among which many were very extravagant. But possibly it may pave the Way to some Discoveries in Natural Philosophy of which at present we have no Conception.

A Note secur'd from the Weather had been affix'd to the Globe, signifying the Time & Place of its Departure, and praying those who might happen to find it, to send an Account of its State to certain Persons at Paris. No News was heard of it till the next Day, when Information was receiv'd, that it fell a little after 6 aClock at Gonesse, a Place about 4 Leagues Distance, and that it was rent open, and some say had Ice in it. It is suppos'd to have burst by the Elasticity of the contain'd Air when no longer compress'd by so heavy an Atmosphere.

One of 38 feet Diameter is preparing by Mr. Mongolfier himself, at the

Expence of the Academy [Académie royale des sciences], which is to go up in a few Days. I am told it is constructed of Linen & Paper, and is to be filled with a different Air, not yet made Public, but cheaper than that produc'd by the Oil of Vitriol, of which 200 Paris Pints were consum'd in filling the other.

It is said that for some Days after its being filled, the Ball was found to lose an eighth Part of its Force of Levity in 24 Hours; Whether this was from Imperfection in the Tightness of the Ball, or a Change in the Nature of the Air, Experiments may easily discover.

I thought it my Duty, Sir, to send an early Account of this extraordinary Fact, to the [Royal] Society which does me the honour to reckon me among its Members; and I will endeavour to make it more perfect, as I receive farther Information.

With great Respect, I am, Sir, Your most obedient and most humble Servant

B Franklin

P.S. . . . I just now learn, that some observers say, the Ball was 150 seconds in rising, from the Cutting of the Cord till hid in the Clouds; that its height was then about 500 Toises [fathoms], but, being moved out of the Perpendicular by the Wind, it had made a Slant so as to form a Triangle, whose Base on the Earth was about 200 Toises. It is said the Country People who saw it fall were frightned, conceiv'd from its bounding a little, when it touch'd the Ground, that there was some living Animal in it, and attack'd it with Stones and Knives, so that it was much mangled; but it is now brought to Town and will be repaired.

The great one of M. Mongolfier, is to go up, as is said, from Versailles, in about 8 or 10 Days; It is not a Globe but of a different Form, more convenient for penetrating the Air. It contains 50,000 cubic Feet, and is supposed to have a Force of Levity equal to 1500 pounds weight. A Philosopher here, M. Pilatre du Rozier, has seriously apply'd to the Academy for leave to go up with it, in order to make some Experiments. He was complimented on his Zeal and Courage for the Promotion of Science, but advis'd to wait till the Management of those Balls was made by Experience more certain & safe. They say the filling of it in M. Mongolfier's Way will not Cost more than half a Crown [one-eighth of an English pound]. One is talk'd of to be 110 feet Diameter. Several Gentlemen have ordered small ones to be made for their Amusement. One has ordered four of 15 feet Diameter each; I know not with what Purpose; But such is the present Enthusiasm for promoting and improving this Discovery, that probably we shall soon make considerable Progress in the art of constructing and using the Machines.

Among the Pleasanteries Conversation produces on this Subject, Some suppose Flying to be now invented, and that since Men may be supported in the Air, nothing is wanted but some light handy Instruments to give and direct Motion. Some think Progressive Motion on the Earth may be Advanc'd by it, and that a Running Footman or a Horse slung and suspended under such a Globe so as to have no more of Weight pressing the Earth with their Feet, than Perhaps 8 or 10 Pounds, might with a fair Wind run in a straight Line across Countries as fast as that Wind, and over Hedges, Ditches & even Waters. It has been even fancied that in time People will keep such Globes anchored in the Air, to which by Pullies they may draw up Game to be preserved in the Cool, & Water to be frozen when Ice is wanted. And that to get Money, it will be contrived to give People an extensive View of the Country, by running them up in an Elbow Chair a Mile high for a Guinea &c. &c.

B F

A Pamphlet is printing, in which we are to have a full & perfect Acct of the Experiments hitherto made, &c. I will send it to you. M. Mongolfier's Air to fill the Globe has hitherto been kept secret; some suppose it to be only common Air heated by passing thro' the Flame of burning Straw, and thereby extreamly rarefied. If so, its Levity will soon be diminish'd, by Condensation, when it comes into the cooler Region above.

7 Ships and the sea.

During his lifetime Franklin made eight transatlantic voyages. On the last one, returning from France to Philadelphia in 1785, he evidently spent much of his time writing at a desk in his cabin. In Paris he had begun a letter to a friend, Julien-David LeRoy, about possible improvements in the rigging of ships, a subject that the two had discussed. At sea Franklin continued the letter until it turned into a lengthy discursive treatise on everything that had occurred to him over the years about ships and the sea. Sailors, he knew, "have a little repugnance to the advice of landmen, whom they esteem ignorant and incapable of giving any worth notice," but, he reminded them, "Most of their instruments were the invention of landmen. At least the first vessel ever made to go on the water was certainly such." On December 3, 1785, having arrived in Philadelphia, he read this paper to a meeting of the American Philosophical Society, the organization that had grown from his initiative forty-three years earlier. The term *philosophical,* as used in Franklin's time, had less to do with metaphysics or formal logic than with what we would now label science and technology. Moreover, the full name of Franklin's brainchild was the American Philosophical Society Held at Philadelphia for Promoting Useful Knowledge. The society published his paper in its *Transactions* under the title "Maritime Observations." I have selected two passages that show what useful knowledge a landsman could teach seamen and shipbuilders and one passage that tells landsmen how to cope with ocean voyages.

The first selection is about ways of propelling ships. At the time human and animal muscle were the only alternatives to wind, and wind power was notoriously changeable or apt to die away altogether, as Franklin's journal of his first London-to-Philadelphia crossing shows. Here he suggests several new methods of applying muscle: circular paddle wheels, propellers in either air or water, or jet propulsion by pumped air or water. It occurred to him that a fire engine might be used for the jet. He presumably means the two-man pump developed in England that generated a powerful stream for fighting fires, but *fire-engine* was later applied to steam engines, and Franklin was already familiar with the steam engine that Matthew Boulton and James Watt had developed in Birmingham in the 1760s.

When Franklin arrived in Philadelphia in 1785, James Rumsey and John Fitch were already experimenting with steam engines to move boats on the Delaware River. Fitch heard of Franklin's "Maritime Observations," and Franklin arranged for him to copy out useful passages. By 1787 Fitch had a steamship working on the river with paddle wheels that would drive it upstream against a headwind. Franklin mistakenly doubted its practicality, probably for the reasons he gives here against paddle wheels. In 1788 he helped organize a company in support of Rumsey's proposal for a steamship that would use jet propulsion. Rumsey's design never took off, while Fitch's did, though Robert Fulton, rather than Fitch, was the gainer by it.

Franklin's suggestion of a propeller may conceivably have contributed to John Stevenson's trial of a craft with twin screws in 1804. The possible, if tenuous, connection lies in the fact that Stevenson was elected to membership in the American Philosophical Society at a meeting in 1789 when Franklin was probably present.

The piece I have titled "The Gulf Stream" records Franklin's most notable contribution to navigation, mapping the Gulf Stream, which he had accomplished earlier with help from American sea captains and continued to refine as more data became available to him. This is his first systematic presentation of the information he had previously collated and formed into charts that were engraved and given to mariners. In the present selection he writes up the results of additional work carried out by his greatnephew Jonathan Williams, Jr., who accompanied him home. Differences in water temperature were the signature of the Gulf Stream's presence. The chart shown here, engraved to accompany the "Maritime Observations" in the Philosophical Society's *Transactions,* does not reflect Williams's measurements, as it was not intended for navigation but simply to demonstrate the location of the Gulf Stream to the world at large.

The third selection is practical advice to those contemplating an ocean voyage. The paragraph on the character of the ship's captain may or may not have been prompted by Franklin's impression of Thomas Truxtun, the commander of the London packet on which Franklin was a passenger. Truxtun had a career in the U.S. Navy ahead of him as captain of the frigate *Constellation*, which took part in the quasi-war with France. In the passage on conditions in steerage Frankin shows something of his customary humanity. And in the closing he dwells on some of the larger goals that had eluded him in the peace negotiations, related in Part IV.

On the Motion of Vessels, 1784–85

It is remarkable that the People we consider as Savages, have improv'd the Art of Sailing & Rowing Boats in several Points beyond what we can pretend to. We have no Sailing Boats equal to the flying Proas of the S. Seas; no rowing or Paddling Boat equal to that of the Greenlanders for Swiftness and Safety. The Birch Canoes of the North American Indians have also some advantageous Properties. They are so light that two Men may carry one of them over Land which is capable of carrying a dozen upon the Water; and in heeling they are not so subject to take in Water as our Boats, the Sides of which are lowest in the Middle where it is most likely to enter, they being highest in that Part, in this form

The Chinese are an enlightned People, the most antiently civiliz'd of any existing, and their Arts are antient; a Presumption in their favour: their Method of Rowing their Boats differs from ours, the Oars being work'd either two a-stern as we skull, or on the Sides with the same kind of Motion, being hung parallel to the Keel on a Rail and always acting in the Water, not perpendicular to the Side as ours are, nor lifted out at every Stroke, which is a loss of Time, & the Boat in the Interval loses Motion. They see our Manner, & we theirs, but neither are disposed to learn of or copy the other.

To the several Means of moving Boats mention'd above, may be added, the singular One lately exhibited at Javelle on the Seine below Paris, where a clumsy Boat was mov'd across that River in three Minutes, by Rowing not in the Water but in the Air, that is, by whirling round a Set of Windmill Vanes fix'd to a horizontal Axis parallel to the Keel, and plac'd at the Head of the Boat. The Axis was bent into an Elbow at the End, by the Help of which it was turn'd by One Man at a time. I saw the Operation at a Distance. The four Vanes appear'd to be about 5 feet long, & perhaps 2½ wide. The Weather was calm. The Labour appear'd to be great for one man, as the two several times reliev'd each other: But the Action upon the Air by the oblique Surfaces of the Vanes must have been considerable, as the Motion of the Boat appear'd tolerably quick going & returning, and she return'd to the same Place from whence she first set out, notwithstanding the Current. This Machine is since apply'd to the Moving of Air Balloons: An Instrument similar may be contriv'd to move a Boat by turning under Water.

Several mechanical Projectors have at different times proposed to give Motion to Boats and even to Ships by means of circular Rowing, or Paddles plac'd on the Circumference of Wheels to be turn'd constantly on each side of the Vessel: but this Method tho' frequently tried has never been found so effectual as to encourage a continuance of the Practice. I do not know that the Reason has hitherto been given. Perhaps it may be this, that great part of the Force

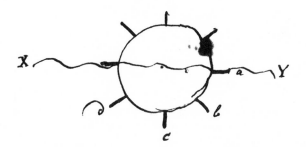

employ'd contributes little to the Motion. For instance, of the 4 Paddles a, b, c, d, all under Water, and turning to move a Boat from X to Y, c has the most Power, b nearly tho' not quite as much; their motion being nearly horizontal, but the Force employ'd in moving a, is consum'd in pressing almost downright upon the Water till it comes to the Place of b; and the Force employ'd in moving d is consum'd in lifting the Water till d arrives at the Surface: by which means much of the Labour is lost. It is true that by placing the Wheels higher out of the Water, this waste Labour will be diminished in a Calm, but where a Sea runs, the Wheels must unavoidably be often dipt deep in the Waves, and the Turning of them thereby render'd very laborious to little purpose.

Among the various means of giving Motion to a Boat that of M. Bernoulli appears one of the most singular, which was to have fix'd in the Boat a Tube in the Form of an L, the upright Part to have a Funnel-kind of Opening at Top, convenient for filling the Tube with Water; which descending and passing thro' the lower horizontal Part, and issuing in the Middle of the Stern, but under the Surface of the River, should push the Boat forward. There is no doubt that the Force of the descending Water would have a considerable Effect, greater in proportion to the Height from which it descended; but then it is to be considered, that every Bucket-full pump'd or dipp'd up into the Boat from its Side or thro' its Bottom must have its *Vis inertiæ* overcome so as to receive the Motion of the Boat before it can come to give Motion by its Descent; and that will be a Deduction from the moving Power. To remedy this, I would propose the Addition of another such L Pipe, and that they should stand Back to Back in the Boat thus

the forward one being work'd as a Pump, and sucking in the Water at the Head of the Boat should draw it forward while push'd in the same Direction by the Force at the Stern. And after all it should be calculated whether the Labour of Pumping would be less than that of Rowing. A Fire-Engine might possibly in some Cases be apply'd in this Operation with Advantage.

Perhaps this Labour of raising Water might be spar'd, and the whole Force of a Man apply'd to the Moving of a Boat, by the Use of Air instead of Water. Suppose the Boat constructed in this Form

A Tube round or square of 2 feet Diameter, in which a Piston may move up and down. The Piston to have Valves in it opening inwards to admit Air when the Piston rises, and shutting when it is forc'd down by means of the Lever B, turning on the Center C.—The Tube to have a Valve D, to open when the Piston is forc'd down, and let the Air pass out at E, which striking forcibly against the Water abaft, must push the Boat forward. If there is added an Air Vessel F, properly valved and placed the Force would continue to act while a fresh Stroke is taken with the Lever. The Boatman might stand with his Back to the Stern, and putting his Hands behind him, work the Motion by taking hold of the Cross Bar at B. while another should steer, or if he had two such Pumps one on each side the Stern, with a Lever for each Hand, he might steer himself by working occasionally more or harder with either hand, as Watermen now do with a Pair of Sculls.—There is no Position in which the Body of a Man can exert more Strength than in pulling right upwards.

To obtain more Swiftness, Greasing the Bottom of a Vessel is sometimes used, and with good Effect. I do not know that any Writer has hitherto attempted to explain this. At first Sight one would imagine, that tho' the Friction of a hard Body sliding on another hard Body, and the Resistance occasion'd by that Friction, might be diminish'd by putting Grease between them, yet that a Body sliding on a Fluid, such as Water, should have no need of, nor receive any Advantage from such Greasing. But the Fact is not disputed. And the Reason perhaps may be this. The Particles of Water have a mutual Attraction called the Attraction of Adhesion. Water also adheres to Wood, and to many other Substances; but not to Grease. On the contrary they have a mutual Repulsion, so that it is a question whether when Oil is pour'd on Water, they ever actually touch each other: for a Drop of Oil upon Water, instead of sticking to the Spot where it falls, as it would if it fell on a Looking Glass, spreads instantly to an immense Distance in a Film extreamly thin, which it could not easily do if it touch'd & rubb'd or adher'd even in a small Degree to the Surface of the Water. Now the Adhesive Force of Water to itself, and to other Substances, may be estimated from the Weight of it necessary to separate a Drop, which adheres, while growing, till it has Weight enough to force the Separation, and break the Drop off. Let us suppose the Drop to be the Size of a Pea, then there will be as many of these Adhesions as there are Drops of that Size touching the Bottom of a Vessel, and these must be broken by the moving Power, every Step of her Motion that amounts to a Drop's Breadth: And there being no such Adhesions to break between the Water and a greas'd Bottom, may occasion the Difference.

The Gulf Stream, 1784–85

Vessels are sometimes retarded, and sometimes forwarded in their Voyages, by Currents at Sea, which are often not perceived. About the Year 1769 or 70, there was an Application made by the Board of Customs at Boston to the Lords of the Treasury in London, complaining that the Packets between Falmouth & New-York were generally a Fortnight longer in their Passages than Merchant Ships from London to Rhodeisland, and proposing that for the future they should be ordered to Rhodeisland instead of N. York. Being then concern'd in the Management of the American Post Office, I happened to be consulted on the Occasion, and it appearing strange to me that there should be such a Difference between two Places scarce a Days Run asunder, especially when the Merchant Ships are generally deeper laden, and more weakly mann'd than the Packets, & had from London the whole length of the River and Channel to run before they left the Land of England, while the Packets had only to go from Falmouth. I could not but think the Fact misunderstood or misrepresented.—There

happened to be then in London, a Nantucket Sea Captain of my Acquaintance, to whom I communicated the Affair. He told me he believ'd the Fact
might be true; but the Difference was owing to this, that the Rhodeisland
Captains were acquainted with the Gulph Stream, which those of the
English Packets were not. We are well acquainted with that Stream, says
he, because in our Pursuit of Whales, which keep near the Sides of it but are
not to be met with in it, we run down along the Sides, and frequently cross
it to change our Side: and in crossing it have sometimes met and spoke with
those Packets, who were in the middle of it, and stemming it. We have
inform'd them, that they were stemming a Current that was against them to
the Value of three Miles an Hour; and advis'd them to cross it & get out of
it; but they were too wise to be counsell'd by simple American Fishermen.
When the Winds are but slight, he added, they are carried back by the
Current more than they are forwarded by the Wind: and if the Wind be
good, the Subtraction from their Course of 70 Miles a day is of some
Importance. — I then observ'd that it was a Pity no Notice was taken of this
Current upon the Charts, and requested him to mark it out for me, which
he readily comply'd with, adding Directions for avoiding it in sailing from
Europe to North America. I procur'd it to be engrav'd by Order from the
General Post Office on the Old Chart of the Atlantic at Mount and Page's,
Tower Hill; and Copies were sent down to Falmouth for the Captains of the
Pacquets, who slighted it however; but it is since printed in France of which
Edition I hereto annex a Copy.

This Stream is probably generated by the great Accumulation of Water
on the Eastern Coast of America between the Tropics by the Trade Winds
which constantly blow there. It is known that a large Piece of Water 10
miles broad and generally only three feet deep, has by a strong Wind had
its Waters driven to one Side and sustained so as to become Six feet deep,
while the Windward Side was laid dry. This may give some Idea of the
Quantity heap'd up on the American Coast, and the reason of its running
down in a strong Current thro' the Islands into the Bay of Mexico, and from
thence issuing thro' the Gulph of Florida and proceeding along the Coast
to the Banks of Newfoundland, where it turns off towards and runs down
through the Western Islands. Having since cross'd this Stream several
Times in passing between America & Europe, I have been attentive to

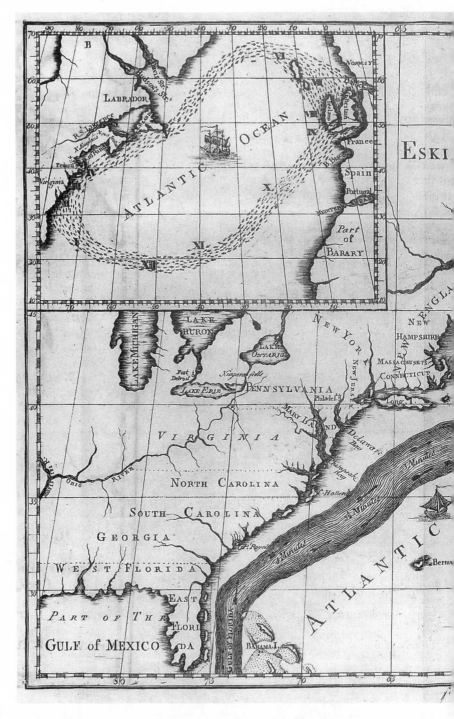

James Poupard after George-Louis Le Rouge, *A Chart of the Gulf Stream*, 1786

Plate 5.

Hudson Straits

's or LABRADOR

Bell Isle

GULF
of
St. LAURENCE

NEW
FOUNDLAND

E.St. JOHN

C. Breton

Gt BANK
Sable I. of Newfoundland.

George's Bank

3¼ Minutes   2 Minutes

COTIA

EAN

A
CHART
of The
GULF STREAM

James Poupard. Sculp.

sundry Circumstances relating to it, by which to know when one is in it; and besides the Gulph Weed with which it is interspers'd, I find that it is always warmer than the Sea on each side of it, & that it does not sparkle in the Night: I annex hereto the Observations made with the Thermometer in two Voyages, and possibly may add a third. It will appear from them, that the Thermometer may be an useful Instrument to a Navigator, since Currents coming from the Northward into Southern Seas, will probably be found colder than the Water of those Seas, as the Currents from Southern Seas into Northern are found warmer. And it is not to be wonder'd that so vast a Body of deep warm Water several Leagues wide coming from between the Tropics and issuing out of the Gulph into the Northern Seas should retain its Warmth longer than the 20 or 30 Days requir'd to its passing the Banks of Newfoundland: The Quantity is too great, and it is too deep to be suddenly cool'd by passing under a cooler Air. The Air immediately over it, however, may receive so much Warmth from it as to be rarified & rise, being render'd lighter than the Air on each Side the Stream; Hence those Airs must flow in to supply the Place of the rising warm Air, and meeting with each other, form those Tornado's and Watersprouts frequently met with & seen near & over the Stream. And as the Vapour from a Cup of Tea in a warm Room, and the Breath of an Animal in the same Room, are hardly visible, but become sensible immediately when out in the cold Air, so the Vapour from the Gulph Stream in the warm Latitudes is scarcely visible, but when it comes into the cool Air from Newfoundland, it is condensed into the Fogs for which those Parts are so remarkable. —

The Power of Wind to raise Water above its common Level in the Sea, is known to us in America, by the High Tides occasion'd in all our Sea Ports, when a Strong North Easter blows against the Gulph Stream.

The Conclusion from these Remarks is, that a Vessel from Europe to North America may shorten her Passage by avoiding to stem the Stream, in which the Thermometer will be very useful. And a Vessel from America to Europe, may do the same by the same Means of keeping in it. It may have often happen'd accidentally, that Voyages have been shortened by these Circumstances. It is well to have the Command of them.

Advice for Travelers, 1784–85

When you intend a long Voyage, you may do well to keep your Intention as much as possible a Secret, or at least the Time of your Departure; otherwise you will be continually interrupted in your Preparations by the Visits of Friends and Acquaintance, who will not only rob you of the Time you want, but put Things out of your mind, so that when you come to Sea, you have the Mortification to recollect Points of Business that ought to have been done, Accounts you had intended to settle, and Conveniences you had propos'd to bring with you, &c. &c. all which have been omitted thro' the Effect of these officious Friendly Visits. Would it not be well if this Custom could be changed; if the Voyager after having without Interruption made all his Preparations should use some of the time he has left, in going himself to take leave of his Friends at their own Houses, and let them come to congratulate him on his happy Return.

It is not always in your Power to make a Choice in your Captain, tho' much of your Comfort in the Passage may depend on his Personal Character as you must for so long a time be confin'd to his Company, and under his Direction. If he be a sensible, sociable, good-natur'd, obliging Man, you will be so much the happier. Such there are. But if he happens to be otherwise, and is only skilful, careful, watchful & active in the Conduct of his Ship, excuse the rest, for these are the Essentials.

Whatever Right you may have by Agreement, in the Mass of Stores laid in by him for the Passengers, it is good to have some particular Things in your own Possession, so as to be always at your own Command.

1 Good Water, that of the Ship being often bad. You can be sure of having it good, only by Bottling it from a clear Spring or Well & in clean Bottles.

2 Good Tea.

3 Coffee ground.

4 Chocolate.

5 Wine of the sort you particularly like, & Cyder.

6 Raisins.

7 Almonds.

  8 Sugar.

  9 Capillaire [infusion of maidenhair fern, used to treat coughs].

10 Lemons.

11 Jamaica Spirits.

12 Eggs greas'd.

13 Diet Bread.

14 Portable Soup.

15 Rusk.

As to Fowls, it is not worth while to have any call'd yours, unless you could have the Feeding and Managing of them according to your own Judgment under your own Eye. As they are generally treated at present in Ships, they are for the most part, sick and their flesh as tough & hard as Whitleather. All Seamen have an Opinion broach'd I suppos'd at first prudently for saving of Water when short, that Fowls do not know when they have drank enough, and will kill themselves if you give them too much, so they are serv'd with a little only once in two Days. This is pour'd into Troughs that lie sloping, and therefore immediately runs down to the lower end. There the Fowls ride upon one another's Backs to get at it, and some are not happy enough to reach and once dip their Bills in it. Thus tantaliz'd, and tormented with Thirst, they cannot digest their dry Food, they fret, pine, sicken & die. Some are found dead, & thrown overboard every Morning, and those kill'd for the Table are not eatable. Their Troughs should be in little Divisions like Cups to hold the Water separately. But this is never done. The Sheep & Hogs are therefore your best Dependance for fresh Meat at Sea, the Mutton being generally tolerable, & the Pork excellent. —

It is possible your Captain may have provided so well in the general Stores, as to render some of the Particulars above recommended of little or no Use to you. But there are frequently in the Ship poorer Passengers, who are taken at a lower Price, lodge in the Steerage, and have no Claim to any of the Cabbin Provisions, or to any but those kinds that are allow'd the Sailors. These People are sometimes dejected, sometimes sick, there may be Women & Children among them. In a Situation where there is no going to Market to purchase such Necessaries, a few of these your Superfluities distributed occasionally may be of great Service, restore Health, save Life, make the miserable happy, and thereby afford you infinite Pleasure.

The worst thing in ordinary Merchant Ships is the Cookery. They have no profess'd Cook, and the worst hand as a Seaman is appointed to that Office, in which he is not only very ignorant but very dirty. — The Sailors have therefore a Saying, that *God sends Meat and the Devil Cooks.* Passengers more piously dispos'd, and willing to believe Heaven orders all things for the best, may suppose that knowing the Sea Air & constant Exercise by Motion of the Vessel would give us extraordinary Appetites, bad Cooks were kindly sent to prevent our Eating too much; or, that foreseeing we should have bad Cooks, good Appetites were furnish'd to prevent our starving. — If you cannot trust to these Circumstances, a Spirit Lamp, with a Blaze-Pan, may enable you to cook some little Things for yourself; such as a Hash, a Soup, &c. And it might be well also to have among your Stores some potted Meats, which if well put up will keep long good. — A small Tin Oven to place with the open Side before the Fire, may be another good Utensil, in which your own Servant may roast for you a Bit of Pork or Mutton. You will sometimes be induc'd to eat of the Ship's Salt Beef, as it is often good. You will find Cyder the best Quencher of that Thirst which Salt Meat or Fish occasions. — The Ship Biscuit is too hard for some Sets of Teeth. It may be softned by Toasting. But Rusk is better; for being made of good fermented Bread, slic'd & bak'd a second time, the pieces imbibe the Water easily, soften immediately, digest more kindly and are therefore more wholesome than the unferment'd Biscuit. — By the Way, Rusk is the true original Biscuit, so prepar'd to keep for Sea, Biscuit in French signifying twice bak'd. If your dry Peas boil hard, a two Pound Iron Shot put with them into the Pot, will by the Motion of the Ship grind them as fine as Mustard.

The Accidents I have seen at Sea with large Dishes of Soup upon a Table, from the Motion of the Ship, have made me wish that our Potters or Pewterers would make Soup Dishes in Divisions, like a Set of small Bowls united together, each containing about sufficient for one Person, in some such Form as this,

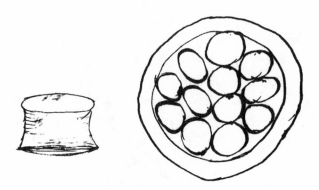

for then when the Ship should make a sudden Heel, the Soup would not in a Body flow over one Side & fall into People's Laps & scald them, as is sometimes the Case, but would be retain'd in the separate Divisions, as in this Figure.

After these Trifles, permit the Addition of a few general Reflections. Navigation when employ'd in supplying necessary Provisions to a Country in Want, and thereby preventing Famines, which were more frequent & destructive before the Invention of that Art, is undoubtedly a Blessing to Mankind. When employ'd merely in transporting Superfluities, it is a question whether the Advantage of the Employment it affords is equal to the Mischief of hazarding so many Lives on the Ocean. But when employ'd in pillaging Merchants and transporting Slaves, it is clearly the means of augmenting the mass of human Misery. It is amazing to think of the Ships & Lives risqu'd in fetching Tea from China, Coffee from Arabia, Sugar & Tobacco from America; all which our Ancestors did well without. Sugar employs near 1000 Ships, Tobacco almost as many. For the Utility of Tobacco there is little to be said; and for that of Sugar, how much more commendable would it be if we could give up the few minutes Gratification afforded once or twice a day by the Taste of Sugar in our Tea, rather than encourage the Cruelties exercis'd in producing it. An eminent French Moralist says, that when he considers the Wars we excite in Africa to obtain Slaves, the Numbers necessarily slain in those Wars, the many Prisoners who perish at Sea by Sickness, bad Provisions, foul Air, &c &c in the Transportation, and how many afterwards die from the Hardships of Slavery, he cannot look on a Piece of Sugar without conceiving it stain'd with Spots of Human Blood! Had he added the Consideration of the Wars we make to take & retake the Sugar Islands from one another, & the Fleets & Armies that perish in those Expeditions, he might have seen his Sugar not merely spotted, but thoroughly dyed Scarlet in grain. It is these Wars that make the maritime Powers of Europe, the Inhabitants of London & Paris, pay dearer for Sugar than those of Vienna a 1000 miles from the Sea; because their Sugar costs not only the Price they pay for it by the Pound, but all they pay in Taxes to maintain the Fleets & Armies that fight for it.

8 Electric fire.

Franklin became famous in his own time for his experiments in electricity, a subject that had excited the curiosity of many learned Europeans in the early eighteenth century. The only form of electricity then recognized was static electricity, the kind that produces a spark when a person shuffles across a rug on a winter's day and touches somebody else. Experimenters had already found a way of generating this kind of electricity by rubbing a glass tube or bottle with a dry cloth; and a Dutch scientist had invented a way of storing the charge in a foil-lined bottle, the so-called Leyden jar. In 1745 Franklin's London correspondent Peter Collinson sent the apparatus and an account of European experiments to the Library Company, which Franklin had founded in 1731. Franklin was fascinated by it, and for the next several years he immersed himself in experiments to find out what the "electrical fluid" was and how it behaved. He described these experiments in a succession of letters to Collinson that were then gathered in a book, *Experiments and Observations on Electricity*, which was printed in London in 1751 and reprinted with many additions and revisions from 1753 to 1774.

Franklin never gave an account of his famous experiment with the kite, and it has been the subject of much controversy. What is certain is that he wished to test whether lightning was a form of electricity, as many had conjectured. In November 1749 he made a note of the similarities between the two, reprinted below. In the first edition of *Experiments and Observations* he suggested a way to test this supposed identity, which follows the note in this reader. In May 1752 French scientists, following his suggestion, made the test. Before hearing of it, Franklin (according to his friend Joseph Priestley) made the kite experiment in June. However the experiment was performed, or by whom, it made Franklin famous. He had already surmised that lightning strikes, whether electric or not, could be prevented from hitting buildings by lightning rods. In the 1753 *Poor Richard's Almanack* he included instructions for the making and use of lightning rods, expanded in a paper written in 1767 and published in the 1769 edition of *Experiments and Observations.*

As always Franklin's great aim in conducting experiments of any kind was to make himself and his discoveries useful to his fellow human beings, particularly in the everyday realm. In describing to Collinson his earliest electrical experiments, many of which may have seemed calculated more for theatrical display than for scientific investigation, he regretted that "We have hitherto been able to discover Nothing in this Way of Use to Mankind." He was highly gratified that the lightning rod proved so useful. Franklin's experiments demonstrated properties of electricity that had no immediate use or application in his time, but they advanced the understanding of a force that would transform the world. A sample of some of his observations, including those with and about lightning, suffices to show how his mind worked. We end this chapter with one of his last reports to Collinson.

Note on the Similarities Between Electricity and Lightning, 1749

Nov. 7, 1749. Electrical fluid agrees with lightning in these particulars: 1. Giving light. 2. Colour of the light. 3. Crooked direction. 4. Swift motion. 5. Being conducted by metals. 6. Crack or noise in exploding. 7. Subsisting in water or ice. 8. Rending bodies it passes through. 9. Destroying animals. 10. Melting metals. 11. Firing inflammable substances. 12. Sulphureous smell. The electric fluid is attracted by points. We do not know whether this property is in lightning. But since they agree in all the particulars wherein we can already compare them, is it not probable they agree likewise in this? Let the experiment be made.

Experiment to Determine Whether the Clouds That Contain Lightning Are Electrified, 1750

On the Top of some high Tower or Steeple, place a Kind of Sentry Box big enough to contain a Man and an electrical Stand. From the Middle of the Stand let an Iron Rod rise, and pass bending out of the Door, and then upright 20 or 30 feet, pointed very sharp at the End. If the Electrical Stand be kept clean and dry, a Man standing on it when such Clouds are passing low, might be electrified, and afford Sparks, the Rod drawing Fire to him from the Cloud. If any Danger to the Man should be apprehended (tho' I think there would be none) let him stand on the Floor of his Box, and now and then bring near to the Rod, the Loop of a Wire, that has one End

fastened to the Leads; he holding it by a Wax-Handle. So the Sparks, if the Rod is electrified, will Strike from the Rod to the Wire and not affect him.

Before I leave this Subject of Lightning, I may mention some other Similarities between the Effects of that and those of Electricity. Lightning has often been known to strike People blind. A Pigeon that we struck dead to Appearance by the Electrical Shock, recovering Life, droopt about the Yard several Days, ate Nothing, tho' Crums were thrown to it, but declined and dyed. We did not then think of it's being deprived of Sight; but afterwards a Pullet [hen] struck dead in like Manner, being recover'd by repeated blowing into it's Lungs, when set down on the Floor, ran head-long against the Wall, and on Examination appear'd perfectly blind. Hence we concluded, that the Pigeon had been absolutely blinded by the Shock. The biggest Animal we have yet killed, or try'd to kill with the Electrical Stroke was a well grown Pullet.

Joseph Priestley's Account of Franklin's Kite Experiment, 1752

To demonstrate, in the completest manner possible, the sameness of the electric fluid with the matter of lightning, Dr. Franklin, astonishing as it must have appeared, contrived actually to bring lightning from the heavens, by means of an electrical kite, which he raised when a storm of thunder was perceived to be coming on. This kite had a pointed wire fixed upon it, by which it drew the lightning from the clouds. This lightning descended by the hempen string, and was received by a key tied to the extremity of it; that part of the string which was held in the hand being of silk, that the electric virtue might stop when it came to the key. He found that the string would conduct electricity even when nearly dry, but that when it was wet, it would conduct it quite freely; so that it would stream out plentifully from the key, at the approach of a person's finger.

At this key he charged phials, and from electric fire thus obtained, he kindled spirits, and performed all other electrical experiments which are usually exhibited by an excited globe or tube.

As every circumstance relating to so capital a discovery as this (the greatest, perhaps, that has been made in the whole compass of philosophy, since the time of Sir Isaac Newton) cannot but give pleasure to all my readers, I shall endeavour to gratify them with the communication of a few particulars which I have from the best authority.

The Doctor, after having published his method of verifying his hypothesis concerning the sameness of electricity with the matter of lightning, was waiting for the erection of a spire in Philadelphia to carry his views into execution; not imagining that a pointed rod, of a moderate height, could answer the purpose; when it occurred to him, that, by means of a common kite, he could have a readier and better access to the regions of thunder than by any spire whatever. Preparing, therefore, a large silk handkerchief, and two cross sticks, of a proper length, on which to extend it; he took the opportunity of the first approaching thunder storm to take a walk into a field, in which there was a shed convenient for his purpose. But dreading the ridicule which too commonly attends unsuccessful attempts in science, he communicated his intended experiment to no body but his son, who assisted him in raising the kite.

The kite being raised, a considerable time elapsed before there was any appearance of its being electrified. One very promising cloud had passed over it without any effect; when, at length, just as he was beginning to despair of his contrivance, he observed some loose threads of the hempen string to stand erect, and to avoid one another, just as if they had been suspended on a common conductor. Struck with this promising appearance, he immediately presented his knucle to the key, and (let the reader judge of the exquisite pleasure he must have felt at that moment) the discovery was complete. He perceived a very evident electric spark. Others succeeded, even before the string was wet, so as to put the matter past all dispute, and when the rain had wet the string, he collected electric fire very copiously. This happened in June 1752, a month after the electricians in France had verified the same theory, but before he heard of any thing they had done.

How to Secure Houses, &c. from Lightning, 1753

It has pleased God in his Goodness to Mankind, at length to discover to them the Means of securing their Habitations and other Buildings from Mischief by Thunder and Lightning. The Method is this: Provide a small

Iron Rod (it may be made of the Rod-iron used by the Nailers) but of such a Length, that one End being three or four Feet in the moist Ground, the other may be six or eight Feet above the highest Part of the Building. To the upper End of the Rod fasten about a Foot of Brass Wire, the Size of a common Knitting-needle, sharpened to a fine Point; the Rod may be secured to the House by a few small Staples. If the House or Barn be long, there may be a Rod and Point at each End, and a middling Wire along the Ridge from one to the other. A House thus furnished will not be damaged by Lightning, it being attracted by the Points, and passing thro the Metal into the Ground without hurting any Thing. Vessels also, having a sharp pointed Rod fix'd on the Top of their Mass, with a Wire from the Foot of the Rod reaching down, round one of the Shrouds, to the Water, will not be hurt by Lightning.

Of Lightning, and the Method (Now Used in America) of Securing Buildings and Persons from Its Mischievous Effects, 1767

Experiments made in electricity first gave philosophers a suspicion that the matter of lightning was the same with the electric matter. Experiments afterwards made on lightning obtained from the clouds by pointed rods, received into bottles, and subjected to every trial, have since proved this suspicion to be perfectly well founded; and that whatever properties we find in electricity, are also the properties of lightning.

This matter of lightning, or of electricity, is an extream subtile fluid, penetrating other bodies, and subsisting in them, equally diffused.

When by any operation of art or nature, there happens to be a greater proportion of this fluid in one body than in another, the body which has most, will communicate to that which has least, till the proportion becomes equal; provided the distance between them be not too great; or, if it is too great, till there be proper conductors to convey it from one to the other.

If the communication be through the air without any conductor, a bright light is seen between the bodies, and a sound is heard. In our small experiments we call this light and sound the electric spark and snap; but in the great operations of nature, the light is what we call *lightning*, and the sound (produced at the same time, tho' generally arriving later at our ears than the light does to our eyes) is, with its echoes, called *thunder.*

If the communication of this fluid is by a conductor, it may be without either light or sound, the subtle fluid passing in the substance of the conductor.

If the conductor be good and of sufficient bigness, the fluid passes through it without hurting it. If otherwise, it is damaged or destroyed.

All metals, and water, are good conductors. Other bodies may become conductors by having some quantity of water in them, as wood, and other materials used in building, but not having much water in them, they are not good conductors, and therefore are often damaged in the operation.

Glass, wax, silk, wool, hair; feathers, and even wood, perfectly dry are non-conductors: that is, they resist instead of facilitating the passage of this subtle fluid.

When this fluid has an opportunity of passing through two conductors, one good, and sufficient, as of metal, the other not so good, it passes in the best, and will follow it in any direction.

The distance at which a body charged with this fluid will discharge itself suddenly, striking through the air into another body that is not charged, or not so highly charg'd, is different according to the quantity of the fluid, the dimensions and form of the bodies themselves, and the state of the air between them. This distance, whatever it happens to be between any two bodies, is called their *striking distance,* as till they come within that distance of each other, no stroke will be made.

The clouds have often more of this fluid in proportion than the earth; in which case as soon as they come near enough (that is, within the striking distance) or meet with a conductor, the fluid quits them and strikes into the earth. A cloud fully charged with this fluid, if so high as to be beyond the striking distance from the earth, passes quietly without making noise or giving light; unless it meets with other clouds that have less.

Tall trees, and lofty buildings, as the towers and spires of churches, become sometimes conductors between the clouds and the earth; but not being good ones, that is, not conveying the fluid freely, they are often damaged.

Buildings that have their roofs covered with lead, or other metal, and spouts of metal continued from the roof into the ground to carry off the water, are never hurt by lightning, as whenever it falls on such a building, it passes in the metals and not in the walls.

When other buildings happen to be within the striking distance from such clouds, the fluid passes in the walls whether of wood, brick or stone, quitting the walls only when it can find better conductors near them, as metal rods, bolts, and hinges of windows or doors, gilding on wainscot, or frames of pictures; the silvering on the backs of looking-glasses; the wires for bells; and the bodies of animals, as containing watry fluids. And in passing thro' the house it follows the direction of these conductors, taking as many in it's way as can assist it in its passage, whether in a strait or crooked line, leaping from one to the other, if not far distant from each other, only rending the wall in the spaces where these partial good conductors are too distant from each other.

An iron rod being placed on the outside of a building, from the highest part continued down into the moist earth, in any direction strait or crooked, following the form of the roof or other parts of the building, will receive the lightning at its upper end, attracting it so as to prevent its striking any other part; and, affording it a good conveyance into the earth, will prevent its damaging any part of the building.

A small quantity of metal is found able to conduct a great quantity of this fluid. A wire no bigger than a goose quill, has been known to conduct (with safety to the building as far as the wire was continued) a quantity of lightning that did prodigious damage both above and below it; and probably larger rods are not necessary, tho' it is common in America, to make them of half an inch, some of three quarters, or an inch diameter.

The rod may be fastened to the wall, chimney, &c. with staples of iron. The lightning will not leave the rod (a good conductor) to pass into the wall (a bad conductor), through those staples. It would rather, if any were in the wall, pass out of it into the rod to get more readily by that conductor into the earth.

If the building be very large and extensive, two or more rods may be placed at different parts, for greater security.

Small ragged parts of clouds suspended in the air between the great body of clouds and the earth (like leaf gold in electrical experiments), often serve as partial conductors for the lightning, which proceeds from one of them to another, and by their help comes within the striking distance to the earth or a building. It therefore strikes through those conductors a building that would otherwise be out of the striking distance.

Long sharp points communicating with the earth, and presented to such parts of clouds, drawing silently from them the fluid they are charged with, they are then attracted to the cloud, and may leave the distance so great as to be beyond the reach of striking.

It is therefore that we elevate the upper end of the rod six or eight feet above the highest part of the building, tapering it gradually to a fine sharp point, which is gilt to prevent its rusting.

Thus the pointed rod either prevents a stroke from the cloud, or, if a stroke is made, conducts it to the earth with safety to the building.

The lower end of the rod should enter the earth so deep as to come at the moist part, perhaps two or three feet; and if bent when under the surface so as to go in a horizontal line six or eight feet from the wall, and then bent again downwards three or four feet, it will prevent damage to any of the stones of the foundation.

A person apprehensive of danger from lightning, happening during the time of thunder to be in a house not so secured, will do well to avoid sitting near the chimney, near a looking glass, or any gilt pictures or wainscot; the safest place is in the middle of the room, (so it be not under a metal lustre suspended by a chain) sitting in one chair and laying the feet up in another. It is still safer to bring two or three mattrasses or beds into the middle of the room, and folding them up double, place the chair upon them; for they not being so good conductors as the walls, the lightning will not chuse an interrupted course through the air of the room and the bedding, when it can go thro' a continued better conductor the wall. But where it can be had, a hamock or swinging bed, suspended by silk cords equally distant from the walls on every side, and from the cieling and floor above and below, affords the safest situation a person can have in any room whatever; and what indeed may be deemed quite free from danger of any stroke by lightning.   B.F.

To Peter Collinson, 1753

Philadelphia, September 1753.
In my former Paper on this Subject, wrote first in 1747, enlarged and sent to England in 1749, I considered the Sea as the grand source of Lightning, imagining its luminous Appearance to be owing to Electric Fire, produced by Friction between the Particles of Water and those of Salt. Living far from the Sea I had then no opportunity of making Experiments on the Sea Water: And so embraced this opinion too hastily.

For in 1750 and 1751, being occasionally on the Sea Coast, I found, by Experiments, that Sea Water in a Bottle, tho' at first it would by Agitation appear luminous, yet in a few hours it lost that Virtue; hence, and from this, that I could not by agitating a Solution of Sea Salt in Water produce any Light, I first began to doubt of my former Hypothesis, and to suspect that the luminous appearance in Sea Water must be owing to some other Principle.

I then considered whether it were not possible, that the Particles of Air, being Electrics per se, might, in hard Gales of Wind, by their Friction against Trees, Hills, Buildings, &c. as so many minute electric Globes, rubbing against non-electric Cushions, draw the electric Fire from the Earth; and that the rising Vapours might receive that fire from the Air, and by such means the Clouds become electrified.

If this were so, I imagined that by forcing a constant violent Stream of Air against my Prime Conductor, by Bellows, I should electrify it *negatively,* the rubbing Particles of Air, drawing from it part of its natural Quantity of the electric Fluid. I accordingly made the Experiment, but it did not succeed.

In September 1752, I erected an Iron Rod to draw the Lightning down into my House, in order to make some Experiments on it, with two Bells to give Notice when the Rod should be electrified. A Contrivance obvious to every Electrician.

I found the Bells rang sometimes when there was no Lightning or Thunder, but only a dark Cloud over the Rod; that sometimes after a Flash of Lightning they would suddenly stop; and at other times, when they had not rang before, they would, after a Flash, suddenly begin to ring; that the Electricity was sometimes very faint, so that when a small Spark was obtained, another could not be got for sometime after; at other times the Sparks would follow extremely quick, and once I had a continual Stream from Bell to Bell, the size of a Crow-Quill. Even during the same Gust there were considerable variations.

In the Winter following I conceived an Experiment, to try whether the Clouds were electrified *positively*, or *negatively:* but my pointed Rod, with its Apparatus, becoming out of Order, I did not refit it 'till towards the Spring, when I expected the warm Weather would bring on more frequent Thunder Clouds.

The Experiment was this: To take two Vials, charge one of them with Lightning from the Iron Rod, and give the other an equal Charge by the electric Glass Globe thro' the prime Conductor: When charged, to place them on a Table within three or four Inches of each other, a small cork Ball being suspended by a fine Silk Thread from the Cieling, so as it might play between the Wires. If both Bottles then were electrify'd *positively,* the Ball being attracted and repelled by one, must be also repelled by the other. If the one *positively,* and the other *negatively;* then the Ball would be attracted and repelled alternately by each, and continue to play between them as long as any considerable Charge remained.

Being very intent on making this Experiment, it was no small Mortification to me, that I happened to be abroad during two of the greatest Thunder Storms we had early in the Spring; and tho' I had given orders in my Family that if the Bells rang when I was from home, they should catch some of the Lightning for me in electrical Vials, and they did so, yet it was mostly dissipated before my Return; and in some of the other Gusts, the Quantity of Lightning I was able to obtain, was so small, and the Charge so weak, that I could not satisfy myself: yet I sometimes saw what heighten'd my Suspicions and inflam'd my Curiosity.

At last, on the 12th. of April 1753, there being a smart Gust of some Continuance, I charged one Vial pretty well with Lightning, and the other equally, as near as I could judge, with Electricity from my Glass Globe; and having placed them properly, I beheld, with great surprize and pleasure, the Cork Ball play briskly between them; and was convinced that one Bottle was electrised *negatively.*

I repeated this Experiment several times during that and in eight succeeding Gusts, always with the same Success: And being of Opinion (for Reasons I formerly gave in my Letter to Mr. Kinnersley, since printed in London) that the Glass Globe electrises *positively;* I concluded that the Clouds are *always* electrised *negatively,* or have always in them less than their natural Quantity of the electric Fluid. [Ebenezer Kinnersley had assisted Franklin in early experiments and gave traveling lectures and exhibitions of electrical phenomena.]

Yet notwithstanding so many Experiments, it seems I concluded too soon; for at last, June the 6th. in a Gust which continued from five a Clock, P.M. to 7, I met with one Cloud that was electrised positively, tho' several that passed over my Rod before, during the same Gust, were in the negative State.

This was thus discovered:

I had another concurring Experiment which I often repeated, to prove the negative State of the Clouds, viz. While the Bells were ringing, I took the Vial charged from the Glass Globe, and applied its Wire to the erected Rod. Considering That if the Clouds were electrised *positively,* the Rod, which received its Electricity from them, must be so too; and then the additional *positive* Electricity of the Vial would make the Bells ring faster: But, if the Clouds were in a *negative* State, they must exhaust the Electrical Fluid from my Rod, and bring that into the same negative State with themselves; and then the Wire of a positively charged Vial, supplying the Rod with what it wanted (which it was obliged otherwise to draw from the Earth by means of the pendulous brass Ball playing between the two Bells) the Ringing would cease 'till the Bottle was discharged.

In this manner I quite discharged into the Rod several Vials, that were charged from the Glass Globe, the electric Fluid streaming from the Wire to the Rod, till the Wire would receive no Spark from the Finger; and during this Supply to the Rod from the Vial, the Bells stopt ringing; but by continuing the Application of the Vial Wire to the Rod, I exhausted the natural Quantity from the inside Surface of the same Vials, or, as I call it, charged them *negatively.*

At length, while I was charging a Vial by my Glass Globe, to repeat this Experiment, my Bells, of themselves, stopt ringing, and after some pause began to ring again. But now when I approached the Wire of the charged

Vial to the Rod, instead of the usual Stream that I expected from the Wire to the Rod, there was no Spark, not even when I brought the Wire and the Rod to touch; yet the Bells continued ringing vigorously; which proved to me, that the Rod was then *positively* electrify'd, as well as the Wire of the Vial, and equally so; and consequently, that the particular Cloud then over the Rod was in the same positive State. This was near the End of the Gust.

But this was a single Experiment; which however destroys my first too general Conclusion, and reduces me to this, That the Clouds of a Thunder Gust are *most commonly* in a negative State of Electricity, but *sometimes* in a positive State.

The latter I believe is rare; for tho' I soon after the last Experiment set out on a Journey to Boston, and was from home most part of the Summer, which prevented my making farther Trials and Observations; yet Mr. Kinnersley returning from the Islands just as I left home, pursued the Experiments during my Absence, and informs me, that he always found the Clouds in the *negative* State.

So that for the most part in Thunder Strokes, *'tis the Earth that strikes into the Clouds,* and not the Clouds that strike into the Earth.

Those who are versed in electrical Experiments, will easily conceive that the Effects and Appearances must be nearly the same in either case; the same Explosion, and the same Flash between one Cloud and another, and between the Clouds and Mountains, &c. the same rending of Trees, Walls, &c. which the electric Fluid meets with in its Passage, and the same fatal Shock to animal Bodies; and that pointed Rods fixt on Buildings or Masts of Ships, and communicating with the Earth, or Sea, must be of the same Service in restoring the Equilibrium silently between the Earth and Clouds, or in conducting a Flash or Stroke, if one should be, so as to save harmless the House or Vessel: For Points have equal Power to *throw off,* as to *draw on* the electric Fire, and Rods will conduct up as well as down.

But tho' the Light gained from these Experiments makes no Alteration in the Practice, it makes a considerable one in the Theory. And now we as much need an Hypothesis to explain by what means the Clouds become *negatively,* as before to show how they became *positively* electrify'd.

I cannot forbear venturing some few Conjectures on this Occasion; They are what occur to me at present; and tho' future Discoveries should prove them not wholly right, yet they may in the mean time be of some use, by stirring up the Curious to make more Experiments and occasion more exact Disquisitions.

I conceive then, that this Globe of Earth and Water, with its Plants, Animals and Buildings, have, diffused thro'out their Substance, a Quantity of the Electric Fluid, just as much as they can contain, which I call the *natural Quantity*.

That this natural Quantity is not the same in all kinds of common Matter under the same Dimensions, nor in the same kind of common Matter in all Circumstances; but a solid Foot, for instance, of one kind of common Matter may contain more of the Electric Fluid than a solid Foot of some other kind of common Matter; and a pound weight of the same kind of common Matter, may, when in a rarer State, contain more of the electric Fluid than when in a denser State.

For the electric Fluid, being attracted by any Portion of common Matter, the Parts of that Fluid, (which have among themselves a mutual Repulsion) are brought so near to each other by the Attraction of the common Matter that absorbs them, as that their Repulsion is equal to the condensing Power of Attraction in common Matter, and then such Portion of common Matter will absorb no more.

Bodies of different kinds having thus attracted and absorbed what I call their *natural Quantity*, i.e., just as much of the electric Fluid as is suited to their Circumstances of Density, Rarity, and Power of Attracting, do not then show any Signs of Electricity among each other.

And if more electric Fluid be added to one of these bodies, it does not enter, but spreads on the Surface, forming an Atmosphere, and then such Body shows Signs of Electricity.

I have in a former Paper compared common Matter to a Sponge, and the electric Fluid to Water: I beg leave once more to make use of the same Comparison to illustrate farther my Meaning in this particular.

When a Sponge is somewhat condensed by being squeezed between the Fingers, it will not receive and retain so much Water as when in its more loose and open State.

If *more* squeezed and condensed, some of the Water will come out of its inner Parts and flow on the Surface.

If the Pressure of the Fingers be intirely removed, the Sponge will not only resume what was lately forced out, but attract an additional Quantity.

As the Sponge in its rarer State will *naturally* attract and absorb *more* Water, and in its denser State will *naturally* attract and absorb *less* Water; we may call the Quantity it attracts and absorbs in either State, its *natural Quantity*, the State being considered.

Now what the Sponge is to Water, the same is Water to the Electric Fluid.

When a Portion of Water is in its common dense State, it can hold no more electric Fluid than it has; if any be added, it spreads on the Surface.

When the same Portion of Water is rarified into Vapour, and forms a Cloud, it is then capable of receiving and absorbing a much greater Quantity; there is room for each particle to have an electric Atmosphere.

Thus Water in its rarified state, or in the form of a Cloud, will be in a negative State of Electricity; it will have less than its *natural Quantity;* that is, less than it is naturally capable of attracting and absorbing in that State.

Such a Cloud, then, coming so near the Earth as to be within the striking Distance, will receive from the Earth a Flash of the Electric Fluid; which Flash, to supply a great extent of Cloud, must sometimes contain a very great Quantity of that Fluid.

Or such a Cloud, passing over Woods of tall Trees, may from the Points and sharp edges of their moist Top Leaves receive silently some Supply.

A Cloud being by any means supplied from the Earth may strike into other Clouds that have not been supplied, or not so much supply'd; and those to others, till an Equilibrium is produced among all the Clouds that are within striking Distance of each other.

The Cloud thus supplied, having parted with much of what it first received, may require and receive a fresh Supply from the Earth, or from some other Cloud, which by the wind is brought into such a Situation as to receive it more readily from the Earth.

Hence repeated and continual Strokes and Flashes 'till the Clouds have all got nearly their natural Quantity as Clouds; or 'till they have descended in Showers, and are united again with this terraqueous Globe, their Original.

Thus Thunder Clouds are generally in a negative State of Electricity compared with the Earth, agreeable to most of our Experiments; yet as by one Experiment we found a Cloud electrised positively, I conjecture that, in that Case, such Cloud after having received what was, in its rare State, only its natural Quantity, became compressed by the driving Winds, or some other means, so that part of what it had absorbed was forced out, and formed an electric Atmosphere around it in its denser State. Hence it was capable of communicating positive Electricity to my Rod.

To show that a Body in different Circumstances of Dilatation and Contraction is capable of receiving and retaining more or less of the Electric Fluid on its Surface, I would relate the following Experiment. I placed a clean Wine Glass on the Floor, and on it a small silver Cann. In the Cann I put about 3 yards of brass Chain, to one End of which I fastened a Silk Thread which went right up to the Cieling where it passed over a Pully, and came down again to my hand, that I might at Pleasure draw the Chain up out of the Cann, extending it 'till within a Foot of the Cieling and let it gradually sink into the Cann again. From the Cieling by another Thread of fine raw Silk, I suspended a small light Lock of Cotton, so as that when it hung perpendicularly, it came in Contact with the Side of the Cann. Then approaching the Wire of a charged Vial to the Cann, I gave it a Spark which flowed round it in an electric Atmosphere; and the Lock of Cotton was repelled from the Side of the Cann to the distance of about 9 or 10 Inches. The Cann would not then receive another Spark from the Wire of the Vial; but as I gradually drew up the Chain, the Atmosphere of the Cann diminished by flowing over the rising Chain, and the Lock of Cotton accordingly drew nearer and nearer to the Cann; and then, if I again brought the Vial Wire near the Cann, it would receive another Spark and the Cotton fly off again to its first Distance; and thus, as the Chain was drawn higher, the Cann would receive more Sparks; because the Cann and extended Chain were capable of supporting a greater Atmosphere than the Cann with the Chain gathered up into its Belly. And that the Atmosphere round the Cann was diminished by raising the Chain, and increased again by lowering it, is not only agreable to Reason, since the Atmosphere of the Chain must be drawn from that of the Cann, when it rose, and returned to it again, when it fell; but was also evident to the Eye, the Lock of Cotton always approaching the Cann, when the Chain was drawn up, and receding, when it was let down again.

Thus we see that Increase of Surface makes a Body capable of receiving a greater Electric Atmosphere: But this Experiment does not, I own, fully demonstrate my new Hypothesis; for the Brass and Silver still continue in their solid state, and are not rarify'd into Vapour, as the Water is in Clouds. Perhaps some future Experiments on vapouriz'd Water may set this Matter in a clearer Light.

One seemingly material Objection arises to the new Hypothesis, and it is this. If Water in its rarify'd State as a Cloud, requires and will absorb more of the electric Fluid than when in its dense State as Water, why does it not acquire from the Earth all it wants at the Instant of its leaving the Surface, while it is yet near, and but just rising in Vapour? To this Difficulty I own I cannot at present give a Solution satisfying to myself. I thought however that I ought to state it in its full Force, as I have done, and submit the whole to Examination.

And I would beg leave to recommend it to the Curious in this Branch of Natural Philosophy, to repeat with care and accurate Observation the Experiments I have reported in this and former Papers relating to *positive* and *negative* Electricity, with such other relative ones as shall occur to them, that it may be certainly known whether the Electricity communicated by a Glass Globe be *really positive*. And also I would request all who may have an Opportunity of observing the recent Effects of Lightning on Buildings, Trees, &c. that they would consider them particularly with a View to discover the Direction. But in these Examinations, this one thing is always to be understood, viz. That a Stream of the electric Fluid passing thro' Wood, Brick, Metal &c. while such Fluid passes in small Quantity, the mutually repulsive Power of its Parts is confined and overcome by the Cohesion of the Parts of the Body it passes through, so as to prevent an Explosion; but when the Fluid comes in a Quantity too great to be confined by such Cohesion, it explodes and rends or fuses the Body that endeavoured to confine it. If it be Wood, Brick, Stone, or the like, the Splinters will flie off on that Side where there is least Resistance. And thus when a Hole is struck thro' Paste board by the electrify'd Jar, if the Surfaces of the Paste board are not confin'd or compress'd, there will be a Bur raised all around the Hole on both Sides the Pasteboard; but if one side be confined, so that the Bur cannot be raised on that side, it will be all raised on the other, which way soever the Fluid was directed. For the Bur round the outside of the Hole, is the Effect of the Explosion every way from the Center of the Stream, and not an Effect of the Direction.

In every Stroke of Lightning, I am of Opinion that the Stream of the electric Fluid moving to restore the Equilibrium between the Cloud and the Earth, does always previously find its Passage and mark out as I may say its own Course, taking in its way all the Conductors it can find, such as Metals, damp Walls, moist Wood, &c. and will go considerably out of a direct Course for the sake of the Assistance of good Conductors; and that in this Course it is actually moving, tho' silently and imperceptibly, before the Explosion in and among the Conductors; which Explosion happens only when the Conductors cannot discharge it as fast as they receive it, by reason of their being incompleat, disunited, or not of the best Materials for Conducting. Metalline Rods, therefore, of Sufficient Thickness, and extending from the highest Part of an Edifice to the Ground, being of the best Materials and compleat Conductors, will, I think, secure the Building from Damage; either by restoring the Equilibrium so fast as to prevent a Stroke, or by conducting it in the Substance of the Rod as far as the Rod goes, so that there shall be no Explosion, but what is above its Point, between that and the Cloud.

If it be asked what Thickness of a Metalline Rod may be supposed sufficient? in answer I would remark, that 5 large glass Jarrs, such as I have described in my former Papers, discharge a very great Quantity of Electricity, which nevertheless will be all conducted round the corner of a Book by the fine Filleting of Gold on the Cover, it following the Gold, the farthest way about, rather than take the shorter Course thro the Cover, that not being so good a Conductor. Now in this Line of Gold the Metal is so extreamly thin as to be little more than the Colour of Gold, and on an 8 vo. [octavo] Book is not in the whole an Inch square and therefore not the 36th part of a Grain according to M. Reaumur [a French physician, naturalist, and physicist]; yet 'tis sufficient to conduct the Charge of 5 large Jarrs, and how many more I know not. Now I suppose a Wire of ¼ Inch Diameter to contain about 5000 times as much Metal as there is in that Gold Line, and if so, it will conduct the Charge of 25,000 such Glass Jarrs, which is a Quantity, I imagine far beyond what was ever contained in any one Stroke of natural Lightning. But a Rod of ½ Inch Diameter would conduct four times as much as one of ¼.

And with regard to Conducting; Tho' a certain Thickness of Metal be required to conduct a great Quantity of Electricity and at the same time keep its own Substance firm and inseparated; and a less Quantity, as a very small Wire for instance, will be destroy'd by the Explosion; yet such small Wire will have answered the end of conducting that Stroke, tho' it become incapable of conducting another. And considering the extream Rapidity with which the electric Fluid moves without exploding, when it has a free Passage, or compleat metal Communication, I should think a vast Quantity would be conducted in a short time, either to or from a Cloud, to restore its Equilibrium with the Earth, by Means of a very small Wire; and therefore thick Rods should seem not so necessary. However, as the Quantity of Lightning discharged in one Stroke cannot well be measur'd, and in different Strokes is certainly very various, in some much greater than in others; and as Iron (the best Metal for the Purpose, being least apt to fuse) is cheap; it may be well enough to provide a larger Canal to guide that impetuous Blast, than we imagine necessary: For though one middling Wire may be sufficient, two or three can do no harm. And Time, with careful Observations well compared, will at length point out the proper Size to greater Certainty.

Pointed Rods erected on Edifices may likewise often prevent a Stroke in the following manner. An Eye so situated as to view horizontally the under Side of a Thunder Cloud, will see it very ragged, with a Number of separate Fragments or petty Clouds one under another, the lowest sometimes not far from the Earth. These, as so many Stepping-Stones, assist in conducting a Stroke between the Cloud and a Building. To represent these by an Experiment. Take two or three Locks of fine loose Cotton, connect one of them with the Prime Conductor by a fine Thread of two Inches (which may be spun out of the same Lock by the Fingers) another to that, and the third to the second, by like Threads. Turn the Globe, and you will see these Locks extend themselves towards the Table (as the lower small Clouds do towards the Earth) being attracted by it: But on presenting a sharp Point erect under the lowest, it will shrink up to the second, the second to the first, and all together to the Prime Conductor, where they will continue as long as the Point continues under them. May not in like manner, the small electrised Clouds, whose Equilibrium with the Earth is soon restored by the Point, rise up to the main Body, and by that means occasion so large a Vacancy, as that the grand Cloud cannot strike in that Place?

These Thoughts, my dear Friend, are many of them crude and hasty, and if I were merely ambitious of acquiring some Reputation in Philosophy, I ought to keep them by me, 'till corrected and improved by Time and farther Experience. But since even short Hints, and imperfect Experiments in any new Branch of Science, being communicated, have oftentimes a good Effect, in exciting the attention of the Ingenious to the Subject, and so becoming the Occasion of more exact disquisitions (as I before observed) and more compleat Discoveries, you are at Liberty to communicate this Paper to whom you please; it being of more Importance that Knowledge should increase, than that your Friend should be thought an accurate Philosopher.

9 Geology and cosmology.

Although Franklin never placed a high value on suppositions that could not be verified by empirical observation or experiment, his thoughts were irresistibly prompted by things that *could* be observed. One of the puzzles for eighteenth-century naturalists was the presence of sea shells on mountains and the bones of tropical animals in northern climes. Franklin recorded his speculations prompted by these phenomena in a letter to the abbé Soulavie. Jean-Louis Giraud Soulavie was a learned French cleric whose specialty was natural history. In the letter Franklin apologized for speculations that could not be based on actual observation, and the apology, to a modern reader at least, was appropriate. His conjectures were plausible, in accordance with what could then be known, but far from what can now be known. Like later scientists Franklin was challenged to fit what was known into a larger unknown. In an attempt to put together what he had learned about earth, air, fire, and water, he devised a unified theory of the known and the unknown. He describes his favorite theory of a "universal fluid" in an essay he sent to David Rittenhouse, a Philadelphia astronomer. Self-taught, Rittenhouse became renowned in America for constructing an "orrery," a mechanism depicting the movements of the solar system.

What both these selections show is the limits imposed on Franklin's science by the basic scientific assumptions of the time. Franklin could ask questions about what he could see and hear, but he had to fit his answers into a paradigm of the physical world as made up of the four fundamental elements of earth, air, fire, and water. His observations and experiments with electricity were beginning to press beyond that view of the world, but he could not even have speculated how far beyond it his successors would reach.

Franklin's curiosity about the world and its wonders never ceased, and I have given only a sample of his work as a scientist. But he himself considered the people of the world and the laws they made for themselves to be more worthy of attention than the immutable laws that governed the world of nature. In 1750, as he was about to embark on his public career, he told a fellow devotee of science, Cadwallader Colden, who had held public office in New York, that Colden should not let science "have more than its due weight with you. Had Newton been Pilot but of a single common Ship, the finest of his Discoveries would scarce have excus'd or atton'd for his abandoning the Helm one Hour in Time of Danger; how much less if she had carried the Fate of the Commonwealth." Franklin was never quite at the helm of a commonwealth, but in Parts III and IV we will follow his dedication to serving one.

To the Abbé Soulavie, 1782

Sir   Passy. Sepr. 22d. 1782

I return the Papers with some corrections. I did not find Coal mines under the Calcareous rock in Derbyshire. I only remarked that at the lowest Part of that rocky Mountain which was in sight, there were Oyster Shells mixed with the Stone; & part of the high County of Derby being probably as much above the level of the Sea, as the Coal Mines of Whitehaven were below, it seemed a proof that there had been a great Bouleversement [overturning] in the Surface of that Island some part of it having been depressed under the Sea, & other Parts which had been under it being raised above it. Such Changes in the superficial Parts of the Globe seemed to me unlikely to happen if the Earth were solid to the Center. I therefore imagined that the internal parts might be a fluid more dense, & of greater specific gravity than any of the Solids we are acquainted with; which therefore might swim in or upon that Fluid. Thus the surface of the Globe would be a Shell, capable of being broken & disordered by the violent movements of the fluid on which it rested. And, as Air has been compressed by Art so as to be twice as dense as Water, in which case if such Air & Water could be contained in a strong glass Vessel, the Air would be seen to take the lowest place & the Water to float above & upon it; & as we know not yet the degree of Density to which Air may be compressed, & M. [Guillaume] Amontons [a physicist and fellow member of the Académie royale des sciences] calculated, that its Density encreasing as it approached the Center in the same proportion as above the Surface it would at the depth of [blank] Leagues be heavier than Gold, possibly the Dense Fluid occupying the internal Parts of the Globe might be Air compressed. And as the force of Expansion in dense Air when heated is in proportion to its density; this central air might afford another Agent to move the Surface; as well as be of use in keeping alive the central fires:— Tho' as you observe the sudden Rarefaction of Water coming into Contact with those fires, may be an Agent sufficiently strong for that purpose, when acting between the incumbent Earth & the fluid on which it rests.

If one might indulge Imagination in supposing how such a Globe was formed, I should conceive, that all the Elements in separate Particles being originally mixed in confusion & occupying a great Space they would as soon as the Almighty Fiat ordained Gravity or the mutual Attraction of certain Parts, & the mutual repulsion of other Parts to exist all move towards their common Center: That the Air being a fluid whose Parts repel each other, though drawn to the Common Center by their Gravity, would be densest towards the Center & rarer as more remote; consequently all Matter lighter than the central Parts of that Air, & immersed in it, would recede from the Center & rise till they arrived at the region of the Air which was of the same specific Gravity with themselves, where they would rest; while other Matter, mixed with the lighter Air would descend & the two meeting would form the Shell of the first Earth leaving the upper Atmosphere nearly clear. The original Movement of the Parts towards their common Center would form a Whirl there; which would continue in the turning of the new formed Globe upon its Axis & the greatest Diameter of the Shell would be in its Equator. If by any Accident afterwards the Axis should be changed, the dense internal Fluid by altering its form must burst the Shell & throw all its Substance into the confusion in which we find it. I will not trouble you at present with my fancies concerning the manner of forming the rest of our System. Superior Beings smile at our theories & at our presumption in making them. I will just mention that your observation on the Ferruginous Nature of the Lava which is thrown out from the Depths of our Volcanoes gave me great pleasure. It has long been a supposition of mine that the Iron contained in the substance of the Globe has made it capable of becoming, as it is, a Great Magnet. That the Fluid of magnetism exists perhaps in all space; so that there is a Magnetical North & South of the Universe as well as of this Globe, & that if it were possible for a man to fly from Star to Star he might govern his course by the Compass. That it was by the Power of this general Magnetism this Globe became a particular Magnet. In soft or hot Iron the fluid of Magnetism is naturally diffused equally—When within the influence of a Magnet, it is drawn to one end of the Iron, made denser there & rarer at the other. While the Iron continues soft & hot it is only a temporary Magnet: If it cools or grows hard in that situation, it becomes a permanent one, the Magnetic fluid not easily resuming its Equilibrium. Perhaps it may be owing to the permanent Magnetism of this Globe, which it had not at first, that its Axis is at the present kept parallel to itself, & not liable to the changes it formerly suffered, which occasioned the Rupture of its Shell, the submersion & Emersions of its Lands & the confusions of its Seasons. The present Polar & equatorial Diameters differing from each other near ten Leagues. It is easy to conceive in case some Power should shift the Axis gradually, & place it in the present Equator, & make the New Equator pass through the present Poles, what a sinking of the Waters would happen in the present equatorial regions, & what a rising in the present polar Regions; so that vast tracts would be discovered that now are under Water, & others covered that now are dry, the Water rising & sinking in the different Extreams near five Leagues. Such an operation as this, possibly, occasioned much of Europe, & among the rest this Mountain of Passy on which I live, & which is composed of Limestone Rock & Seashells, to be abandoned by the Sea & to change its antient Climate, which seems to have been a hot One. The Globe being now become a permanent Magnet we are perhaps safe from any future change of its Axis. But we are still subject to the Accidents on the

Surface which are occasioned by a Wave in the internal ponderous Fluid; & such a Wave is produced by the sudden violent Explosion you mention happening from the Junction of Water & fire under the Earth, which not only lifts the incumbent Earth that is over the Explosion, but impressing with the name force the fluid under it, creates a Wave that may run a thousand Leagues, lifting & thereby shaking successively all the countries under which it passes. I know not whether I have expressed myself so clearly, as not to get out of your Sight in these Reveries. — If they occasion any new enquiries & produce a better Hypothesis they will not be quite useless. You see I have given a loose to the Imagination, but I approve much more your Method of philosophizing, which proceeds upon actual Observation, makes a collection of facts, & concludes no farther than those facts will warrant. In my present circumstances, that mode of studying the Nature of the Globe is out of my Power & therefore I have permitted myself to wander a little in the wilds of fancy. With great Esteem I have the honor to be Sir &c,

B Franklin

PS. I have heard that Chemists can by their art decompose Stone & Wood, extracting a considerable Quantity of Water from the one & Air from the other. It seems natural to conclude from this that Water & Air were ingredients in the original Composition. For Men cannot make new Matter of any kind. In the same manner may we not suppose, that when we consume Combustibles of all kinds, & produce Heat or light, we do not create that Heat or light; we only decompose a Substance which received it originally as a part of its composition? Heat may thus be considered as originally in a fluid State but attracted by organized Bodies in their growth, becomes a part of the Solid. Besides this, I can conceive that in the first Assemblage of the Particles of which this Earth is composed, each brought its Portion of the loose heat that had been connected with it, & the whole when pressed together produced the Internal fire which still subsists.

[*In Franklin's hand:*] Letter to Abbé Soulavie occasioned by his sending me some Notes he had taken of what I had said to him in Conversation on the Theory of the Earth. I wrote it to set him right in some Points wherein he had mistaken my Meaning.

Loose Thoughts on a Universal Fluid, &c., 1784–88

For the Consideration of my Dear Friend David Rittenhouse Esqr

Universal Space, as far as we know of it, seems to be fill'd with a subtil Fluid, whose Motion, or Vibration, is called Light.

This Fluid may possibly be the same with that which being attracted by and entring into other more solid Matter, dilates the Substance, by separating the constituent Particles, and so rendering some Solids fluid, maintaining the Fluidity of others: of which Fluid when our Bodies are totally depriv'd, they are said to be frozen; when they have a proper Quantity, they are in Health and fit to perform all their Functions; it is then called natural Heat; when too much it is called Fever, and when forc'd into the Body in too great a Quantity from without, it gives Pain by separating and destroying the Flesh, and is then called burning; and the Fluid so entring and acting is called Fire.

While organiz'd Bodies, animal or vegetable, are augmenting in Growth, or are supplying their continual Waste, is not this done by attracting & consolidating this Fluid called Fire, so as to form of it a Part of their Substance; and is it not a Separation of the Parts of such Substance which dissolving its solid State, sets that subtil Fluid at Liberty, when it again makes its appearance as Fire.

For the Power of Man relative to Matter, seems limited to the dividing it or mixing the various kinds of it, or changing its Form and Appearance by different Compositions of it, but does not extend to the making or creating of new Matter, or annihilating the old: Thus if Fire be an original Element or kind of Matter, its Quantity is fix'd and permanent in the Universe. We cannot destroy any Part of it, or make addition to it. We can only separate it from that which confines it, and so set it at Liberty, as when we put Wood in a Situation to be burnt; or transfer it from one Solid to another, as when we make Lime by burning Stone, a Part of the Fire dislodg'd from the Wood being left in the Stone. May not this Fluid when at Liberty be capable of penetrating & entring into all Bodies, organiz'd or not: quitting easily in totality those not organiz'd, and quitting easily in part those which are; the part assum'd & fix'd remaining till the Body is dissolv'd.

Is it not this Fluid which keeps asunder the Particles of Air, permitting them to approach or separating them more in Proportion as its Quantity is diminish'd or augmented?

Is it not the greater Gravity of the Particles of Air, which forces the Particles of this Fluid to mount with the Matters to which it is attach'd as Smoke or Vapour?

Does it not seem to have a great Affinity with Water, since it will quit a Solid to unite with that Fluid, & go off with it in Vapour, leaving the Solid cold to the Touch, and the degree measurable by the Thermometer?

The Vapour rises attach'd to this Fluid, but at a certain height they separate, & the Vapour descends in Rain retaining but little of it, in Snow or Hail less. What becomes of that Fluid? Does it rise above our Atmosphere and mix with the universal Mass of the same kind?

Or does a Spherical Stratum of it, denser as less mix'd with Air attracted by this Globe, & repell'd or push'd up only to a certain height from its Surface by the greater Weight of Air, remain there surrounding the Globe and proceeding with it round the Sun.

In such case, as there may be a Continuity or Communication of this Fluid thro' the Air quite down to the Earth, is it not by the Vibrations given to it by the Sun that Light appears to us; and may it not be, that every one of the infinitely small Vibrations, striking common Matter with a certain Force, enters its Substance, is held there by Attraction, and augmented by succeeding Vibrations, till the Matter has receiv'd as much as their Force can drive into it?

Is it not thus that the Surface of this Globe is continually heated by such repeated Vibrations in the Day, and cool'd by the Escape of the Heat when those Vibrations are discontinu'd in the Night, or intercepted and reflected by Clouds?

Is it not thus that Fire is amass'd and makes the greatest Part of the Substance of combustible Bodies?

Perhaps when this Globe was first form'd and its original Particles took their Place at certain Distances from the Centre in proportion to their greater or less Gravity, the Fluid Fire attracted towards that Center might in great Part be oblig'd as lightest to take place above the rest, and thus form the Sphere of Fire above suppos'd; which would afterwards be continually diminishing by the Substance it afforded to organiz'd Bodies; and the Quantity restor'd to it again by the Burning or other Separating of the Parts of those Bodies?

Is not the natural Heat of Animals thus produc'd, by separating in digestion the Parts of Food, and setting their Fire at Liberty?

Is it not this Sphere of Fire which kindles the wandring Globes that sometimes pass thro' it in our Course round the Sun, have their Surface kindled by it, and burst when their included Air is greatly rarified by the Heat on their burning Surfaces?

May it not have been from such Considerations that the antient Philosophers suppos'd a Sphere of Fire to exist above the Air of our Atmosphere?

PART III

A continental vision.

A s Franklin told Joseph Huey (see chapter 4), he did not expect doing good to win him eternal salvation; and he had learned not to expect many earthly rewards from those he did good to. Virtue had to be its own reward. In the early years he found satisfaction in creating associations of his friends and neighbors for purposes that brought them all tangible benefits. As we have seen, he was not much of a talker. He liked working behind the scenes, getting other people to take the lead, and the credit, for doing things that he proposed anonymously in his newspaper: a fire company, an insurance company, a hospital, a library, an academy (which later became a university). And, perhaps most significant, in 1747 he organized a militia to defend the colony, threatened by the French and their Indian allies in the war that England was then waging against France and Spain (the War of the Austrian Succession). He kept his own role inconspicuous, serving as a common soldier in the militia he had created.

During these early years, while he was running the *Pennsylvania Gazette* Franklin was salting away the profits and using them to sponsor printers in other cities in return for a share of *their* profits. He could have gone on thus, accumulating capital and income until he had become one of the wealthiest men in the colonies. But by 1748, at age forty-two, he had acquired all he wanted or needed for himself. "I would rather have it said," he told his mother, "*he lived usefully,* than, *he died rich.*" He turned over the actual work of his Philadelphia print shop to his partner and retired from business, free now to devote full time to his electrical experiments and to the good works that were making life better for Philadelphians and Pennsylvanians generally.

For a couple of years Franklin carried on in this way, completing his electrical experiments and observations and describing them in the letters that Peter Collinson collected for publication in London in 1751 (see Part II). In that year, as he finished the establishment of his hospital and his academy, he began winding down his electrical research and started a new way of living usefully in which he could no longer gain his ends anonymously. In his *Almanack* for 1750 Poor Richard urged, "Hide not your Talents, they for Use were made / What's a Sun-Dial in the Shade!" And Franklin came out of the shade to serve as alderman in Philadelphia's governing council and as representative of the city in Pennsylvania's governing assembly. He was already the colony's best-known citizen, and his capacity for getting things done quickly made him a guiding figure in the assembly, to which he was reelected annually until he departed for England to serve Pennsylvania there. After 1751 he was never out of public office until the year before his death.

We have to ask what happened after he retired from business to turn him from anonymous social service and world-acclaimed scientific work to political action. The answer can be inferred from some of the things he wrote in 1751, a crucial year for him. It was then that he first set down in writing a vision of the American future that would give direction and purpose to the rest of his life. We will follow his pursuit of this vision from his first expression of it up to 1775, years when he was trying to get the British to see the magnificent opportunity it presented to them. After they proved blind to that opportunity, he devoted himself to its achievement in an independent America.

10 The colonies and the empire.

F ranklin is often described as a reluctant revolutionary because he tried for so long to keep the American colonies in the empire. But his attachment to the empire did not arise from any satisfaction with the status that British statesmen and politicians assigned the colonies. He spent the prime of his life—he was seventy in 1776—trying to persuade the British that the way to preserve the empire was to give the Americans their proper place in it. Before he explained what that place was, in the selections we will examine in the other chapters in this section, he made clear in one of his bitterest satires what that place was not.

Since 1718 the British government had used the colonies as a dumping ground for felons. An act of Parliament in that year offered convicted felons transportation to America (Australia had not yet been designated England's penal colony) as an alternative to hanging. The government paid English merchants to ship the felons and to sell their services to the highest bidders for terms of as much as fourteen years. Although for Virginia and Maryland tobacco planters, convicts were a bargain compared to slaves, to all the colonies they posed a danger. Not all convicts were villains or desperadoes, but many were hardened criminals, and Americans were being told that they must harbor them. When the colonies tried to prevent their importation by laws imposing heavy charges on such transactions, the British Board of Trade had these laws disallowed, including Pennsylvania's laws for that purpose in 1747. The reason given was particularly insulting: the laws against importing criminals, said the Board, would have prevented the much-desired "Improvement and well peopling of the Colonies."

The improvement that convicts brought to the colonies was exemplified in the continuing criminal careers of many of them, and Franklin gives his outraged reaction in the two items he placed in the *Pennsylvania Gazette* early in 1751. Britain continued to dump convicts and stifle American objections until the colonies broke away, and Franklin continued to denounce the practice. As we consider his attachment to the empire and his plans for its future, it will be well to remember his early and unalterable resentment of this imperial practice.

Convicts, of course, were not the only British export to the colonies. From the time of their founding in the seventeenth century, the colonies were viewed in the context of mercantilism, an economic doctrine that treated overseas possessions as sources of raw materials and captive markets for British manufactures. The colonists accepted without violent protest the acts of Parliament requiring them to play this role (the Navigation Acts), including the acts forbidding them to export woolen goods and penalizing the manufacture of hats from the American beaver pelts that British hatters coveted. To these acts in 1750 was added the Iron Act, which forbade Americans to manufacture hardware from the iron ores they themselves mined and smelted. Franklin found these acts a needless irritant, for few Americans found it worthwhile or profitable to engage in manufactures of any kind. Their labor was better used to clear and work the land. Such Parliamentary enactments merely served to remind them of their subjection to Britain, or rather to their fellow Britons.

He was thinking about this subjection and the inferiority implied in thrusting convicts upon the colonies when another upsetting development set him thinking about what Americans were and what they could be in an enlarged empire that acknowledged their proper role. In the summer of 1749 he watched 12,000 Germans step ashore in Philadelphia, a number about equal to the total existing population of the city. Was Pennsylvania about to become German? Although German immigrants were preferable to convicts and although they sought the religious freedom and economic opportunity that Franklin valued, their sudden influx raised disturbing questions about American identity, suggesting a new and unwelcome differentiation of Americans from British subjects in the homeland.

Franklin's thoughts on immigrants, on America's potential, and on the

British Empire were coming together in 1751. His first brief formulation of these ideas came in a letter to James Parker, a New York printer, in March, excerpted below. Sometime during the year he wrote them out at length in "Observations Concerning the Increase of Mankind." He showed this essay to selected friends but did not allow it to be published until 1755. It is the key, I believe, to the remainder of his long career. On its face it is an essay on demography, on the dramatic, exponential growth of population in new countries (America) and its relative stagnation in old countries (England). But it is at the same time a prophecy and a commitment, a prophecy of America's future and a commitment to the recognition of that future in the government and institutions of the continent. It betrays an ethnocentrism that will be examined more closely in the next chapter. But the point of the essay, shrouded in objective generalizations about economics and demography, is America's irresistible growth and Britain's inescapable limitations. As Franklin later put it more plainly to his friend Lord Kames, a Scots jurist, "I have long been of Opinion that the Foundations of the future Grandeur of the British Empire lie in America; and tho' like other Foundations, they are low and little seen, they are nevertheless, broad and Strong enough to support the greatest Political Structure Human Wisdom ever yet erected."

In reading the "Observations," one has to consider what else Franklin was thinking at the time and what he is celebrating when he rhapsodizes over America's contribution to the empire: "What an Accession of Power to the British Empire by Sea as well as Land! What Increase of Trade and Navigation! What Numbers of Ships and Seamen! We have been here but little more than 100 Years, and yet the Force of our Privateers in the late War [War of the Austrian Succession, 1740–48], united, was greater, both in Men and Guns than that of the whole British Navy in Queen Elizabeth's Time." Is there more than a hint in Franklin's celebration of empire that it might be a good idea not to antagonize a people who could already mount a battle fleet as large as the one that defeated the Spanish Armada? Was it a good idea to insult such a people by flooding their homeland with convicts in order to "improve" them? Was it a good idea to forbid them to do things they would be unlikely to do anyhow?

Much of the next twenty-five years of Franklin's life were spent trying to convince the British not to antagonize the Americans by reckless and counterproductive measures. He has begun here. The growth of population described in his pamphlet could be a cause for rejoicing, as he hoped, or an alarm bell, as he may also have hoped. After the quarrel between Britain and the colonies began in 1764 and Franklin emerged as the champion of the colonies, it was easy to conclude, as his opponents did, that it had always been his covert aim to move the headquarters of the empire to America and to place its control in American hands.

That was not Franklin's intention when he wrote the "Observations." All he wanted before 1775 was a recognition of America's present importance and future greatness within the empire. What he describes to Kames as "the greatest Political Structure Human Wisdom ever yet erected" could be a British institution—but need not be. The vision of that structure, with its foundations in America, would guide his activities in doing good and being useful for the rest of his life, whether as a British subject or an American statesman. The details would need working out, and human nature, including his own, would have to contend with human weakness, including his own. The rest of this book can be read as chapters in that contest.

On Transported Felons, 1751

From *Virginia* we hear, that six Convicts, who were transported for fourteen Years, and shipp'd at *Liverpool*, rose at Sea, shot the Captain, overcame and confin'd the Seamen, and kept Possession of the Vessel 19 Days; that coming in Sight of *Cape Hatteras*, they hoisted out the Boat to go on shore; when a Vessel passing by, a Boy they had not confin'd, hail'd her, and attempted to tell their Condition, but was prevented; and then the Villains drove a Spike up thro' his under and upper Jaws, and wound Spunyarn round the End that came out near his Nose, to prevent his getting it out: They then cut away the Sails from the Yards, left the Ship, and went ashore. But a *New-England* Sloop coming by soon after, and seeing a Ship driving in the Sea in that Manner, boarded her, found Things as above mentioned, and carried her into *North-Carolina;* from whence a Hue and Cry went after the Villains, who had stroll'd along to *Virginia;* they were taken at *Norfolk*, and one of them confess'd the Fact; upon which they were order'd up, about two Weeks since, to *Williamsburgh*, for Trial as Pyrates.

From *Maryland* we hear, that a Convict Servant, about three Weeks since, went into his Master's House, with an Ax in his Hand, determin'd to kill his Mistress; but changing his Purpose on seeing, as he expressed it, *how d——d innocent she look'd,* he laid his Left-hand on a Block, cut it off, and threw it at her, saying, *Now make me work, if you can.*

N. B. *'Tis said this desperate Villain is now begging in* Pennsylvania, *and 'tis thought has been seen in this City; he pretends to have lost his Hand by an Accident: The Publick are therefore caution'd to beware of him.*

From *Bucks* County we hear, that a Convict Servant, one *John McCaulefd,* imported here last Fall, has broke open and robb'd several Houses, of Goods to a considerable Value; but being apprehended at a Ferry, is committed to Prison.

Yesterday the Trial of *Samuel Saunders,* for the Murder of *Simon Girtie,* came on at the Supream Court, when the Jury return'd their Verdict *Manslaughter.*

"When we see our Papers fill'd continually with Accounts of the most audacious Robberies, the most cruel Murders, and infinite other Villainies perpetrated by Convicts transported from *Europe,* what melancholly, what terrible Reflections must it occasion! What will become of our Posterity!— These are some of thy Favours, BRITAIN! Thou art called our MOTHER COUNTRY; but what good *Mother* ever sent *Thieves* and *Villains* to accompany her *Children;* to corrupt some with their infectious Vices, and murder the rest? What *Father* ever endeavour'd to spread the *Plague* in his Family! —We do not ask Fish, but thou givest us *Serpents,* and worse than Serpents! —In what can *Britain* show a more Sovereign Contempt for us, than by emptying their *Jails* into our Settlements; unless they would likewise empty their *Jakes* [privies] on our Tables?—What must we think of that B——d, which has advis'd the Repeal of every Law we have hitherto made to prevent this Deluge of Wickedness overwhelming us; and with this *cruel* Sarcasm, *That these Laws were against the* Publick Utility, *for they tended to prevent the* IMPROVEMENT *and* WELL-PEOPLING *of the Colonies!*— And what must we think of those Merchants, who for the sake of a little paltry Gain, will be concern'd in importing and disposing of these abominable Cargoes?"

Felons and Rattlesnakes, 1751

To the Printers of the Gazette.

By a Passage in one of your late Papers, I understand that the Government at home will not suffer our mistaken Assemblies to make any Law for preventing or discouraging the Importation of Convicts from Great Britain, for this kind Reason, "*That such Laws are against the Publick Utility, as they tend to prevent the* IMPROVEMENT *and* WELL PEOPLING *of the Colonies.*"

Such a tender *parental* Concern in our *Mother Country* for the *Welfare* of her Children, calls aloud for the highest *Returns* of Gratitude and Duty. This every one must be sensible of: But 'tis said, that in our present Circumstances it is absolutely impossible for us to make *such* as are adequate to the Favour. I own it; but nevertheless let us do our Endeavour. 'Tis something to show a grateful Disposition.

In some of the uninhabited Parts of these Provinces, there are Numbers of these venomous Reptiles we call RATTLE-SNAKES; Felons-convict from the Beginning of the World: These, whenever we meet with them, we put to Death, by Virtue of an old Law, *Thou shalt bruise his Head.* But as this is a sanguinary Law, and may seem too cruel; and as however mischievous those Creatures are with us, they may possibly change their Natures, if they were to change the Climate; I would humbly propose, that this general Sentence of *Death* be changed for *Transportation.*

In the Spring of the Year, when they first creep out of their Holes, they are feeble, heavy, slow, and easily taken; and if a small Bounty were allow'd *per* Head, some Thousands might be collected annually, and *transported* to Britain. There I would propose to have them carefully distributed in St. James's Park, in the Spring-Gardens and other Places of Pleasure about London; in the Gardens of all the Nobility and Gentry throughout the Nation; but particularly in the Gardens of the *Prime Ministers,* the *Lords of Trade* and *Members of Parliament;* for to them we are *most particularly* obliged.

There is no human Scheme so perfect, but some Inconveniencies may be objected to it: Yet when the Conveniencies far exceed, the Scheme is judg'd rational, and fit to be executed. Thus Inconveniencies have been objected to that *good* and *wise* Act of Parliament, by virtue of which all the Newgates and Dungeons in Britain are emptied into the Colonies. It has been said, that these Thieves and Villains introduc'd among us, spoil the Morals of Youth in the Neighbourhoods that entertain them, and perpetrate many horrid Crimes: But let not *private Interests* obstruct *publick Utility.* Our *Mother* knows what is best for us. What is a little *Housebreaking, Shoplifting,* or *Highway Robbing;* what is a *Son* now and then *corrupted* and *hang'd,* a Daughter *debauch'd* and *pox'd,* a Wife *stabb'd,* a Husband's *Throat cut,* or a Child's *Brains beat out* with an Axe, compar'd with this "IMPROVEMENT and WELL PEOPLING of the Colonies!"

Thus it may perhaps be objected to my Scheme, that the *Rattle-Snake* is a mischievous Creature, and that his changing his Nature with the Clime is a mere Supposition, not yet confirm'd by sufficient Facts. What then? Is not Example more prevalent than Precept? And may not the honest rough British Gentry, by a Familiarity with these Reptiles, learn to *creep,* and to *insinuate,* and to *slaver,* and to *wriggle* into Place (and perhaps to *poison* such as stand in their Way) Qualities of no small Advantage to Courtiers! In comparison of which "*Improvement* and *Publick Utility,*" what is a *Child* now and then kill'd by their venomous Bite,—or even a favourite *Lap-Dog?*

I would only add, That this Exporting of Felons to the Colonies, may be consider'd as a *Trade,* as well as in the Light of a *Favour.* Now all Commerce implies *Returns:* Justice requires them: There can be no Trade without them. And *Rattle-Snakes* seem the most *suitable Returns* for the *Human Serpents* sent us by our *Mother* Country. In this, however, as in every other Branch of Trade, she will have the Advantage of us. She will reap *equal* Benefits without equal Risque of the Inconveniencies and Dangers. For the *Rattle-Snake* gives Warning before he attempts his Mischief; which the Convict does not. I am Yours, &c. Americanus

Thoughts on Immigrants, 1751

The Observation concerning the Importation of Germans in too great Numbers into Pennsylvania, is, I believe, a very just one. [Franklin refers to a proposal that barrier townships of Scots Highlanders and Germans be established on the frontiers.] This will in a few Years become a German Colony: Instead of their Learning our Language, we must learn their's, or live as in a foreign Country. Already the English begin to quit particular Neighbourhoods surrounded by Dutch, being made uneasy by the Dis-agreeableness of disonant Manners; and in Time, Numbers will probably quit the Province for the same Reason. Besides, the Dutch under-live, and are thereby enabled to under-work and under-sell the English; who are thereby extreamly incommoded, and consequently disgusted, so that there can be no cordial Affection or Unity between the two Nations. How good Subjects they may make, and how faithful to the British Interest, is a Question worth considering. And in my Opinion, equal Numbers might have been spared from the British Islands without being miss'd there, and on proper Encouragement would have come over: I say without being miss'd, perhaps I might say without lessening the Number of People at Home. I question indeed, whether there be a Man the less in Britain for the Establishment of the Colonies. An Island can support but a certain Number of People: When all Employments are full, Multitudes refrain Marriage, 'till they can see how to maintain a Family. The Number of Englishmen in England, cannot by their present common Increase be doubled in a Thou-sand Years; but if half of them were taken away and planted in America, where there is Room for them to encrease, and sufficient Employment and Subsistance; the Number of Englishmen would be doubled in *100 Years:* For those left at home, would multiply in that Time so as to fill up the Vacancy, and those here would at least keep Pace with them.

Observations Concerning the Increase of Mankind, *1751*

OBSERVATIONS concerning the Increase of Mankind, Peopling of Coun-tries, &c.

1. Tables of the Proportion of Marriage to Births, of Deaths to Births, of Marriages to the Numbers of Inhabitants, &c. form'd on Observations made upon the Bills of Mortality, Christnings, &c. of populous Cities, will not suit Countries; nor will Tables form'd on Observations made on full settled old Countries, as Europe, suit new Countries, as America.

2. For People increase in Proportion to the Number of Marriages, and that is greater in Proportion to the Ease and Convenience of supporting a Family. When Families can be easily supported, more Persons marry, and earlier in Life.

3. In Cities, where all Trades, Occupations and Offices are full, many delay marrying, till they can see how to bear the Charges of a Family; which Charges are greater in Cities, as Luxury is more common: many live single during Life, and continue Servants to Families, Journeymen to Trades, &c. hence Cities do not by natural Generation supply themselves with Inhabitants; the Deaths are more than the Births.

4. In Countries full settled, the Case must be nearly the same; all Lands being occupied and improved to the Heighth: those who cannot get Land, must Labour for others that have it; when Labourers are plenty, their Wages will be low; by low Wages a Family is supported with Difficulty; this Difficulty deters many from Marriage, who therefore long continue Servants and single. Only as the Cities take Supplies of People from the Country, and thereby make a little more Room in the Country; Marriage is a little more incourag'd there, and the Births exceed the Deaths.

5. Europe is generally full settled with Husbandmen, Manufacturers, &c. and therefore cannot now much increase in People: America is chiefly occupied by Indians, who subsist mostly by Hunting. But as the Hunter, of all Men, requires the greatest Quantity of Land from whence to draw his Subsistence, (the Husbandman subsisting on much less, the Gardner on still less, and the Manufacturer requiring least of all), The Europeans found America as fully settled as it well could be by Hunters; yet these having large Tracks, were easily prevail'd on to part with Portions of Territory to the new Comers, who did not much interfere with the Natives in Hunting, and furnish'd them with many Things they wanted.

6. Land being thus plenty in America, and so cheap as that a labouring Man, that understands Husbandry, can in a short Time save Money enough to purchase a Piece of new Land sufficient for a Plantation, whereon he may subsist a Family; such are not afraid to marry; for if they even look far enough forward to consider how their Children when grown up are to be provided for, they see that more Land is to be had at Rates equally easy, all Circumstances considered.

7. Hence Marriages in America are more general, and more generally early, than in Europe. And if it is reckoned there, that there is but one Marriage per Annum among 100 Persons, perhaps we may here reckon two; and if in Europe they have but 4 Births to a Marriage (many of their Marriages being late) we may here reckon 8, of which if one half grow up, and our Marriages are made, reckoning one with another at 20 Years of Age, our People must at least be doubled every 20 Years.

8. But notwithstanding this Increase, so vast is the Territory of North-America, that it will require many Ages to settle it fully; and till it is fully settled, Labour will never be cheap here, where no Man continues long a Labourer for others, but gets a Plantation of his own, no Man continues long a Journeyman to a Trade, but goes among those new Settlers, and sets up for himself, &c. Hence Labour is no cheaper now, in Pennsylvania, than it was 30 Years ago, tho' so many Thousand labouring People have been imported.

9. The Danger therefore of these Colonies interfering with their Mother Country in Trades that depend on Labour, Manufactures, &c. is too remote to require the Attention of Great-Britain.

10. But in Proportion to the Increase of the Colonies, a vast Demand is growing for British Manufactures, a glorious Market wholly in the Power of Britain, in which Foreigners cannot interfere, which will increase in a short Time even beyond her Power of supplying, tho' her whole Trade should be to her Colonies: Therefore Britain should not too much restrain Manufactures in her Colonies. A wise and good Mother will not do it. To distress, is to weaken, and weakening the Children, weakens the whole Family.

11. Besides if the Manufactures of Britain (by Reason of the American Demands) should rise too high in Price, Foreigners who can sell cheaper will drive her Merchants out of Foreign Markets; Foreign Manufactures will thereby be encouraged and increased, and consequently foreign Nations, perhaps her Rivals in Power, grow more populous and more powerful; while her own Colonies, kept too low, are unable to assist her, or add to her Strength.

12. 'Tis an ill-grounded Opinion that by the Labour of Slaves, America may possibly vie in Cheapness of Manufactures with Britain. The Labour of Slaves can never be so cheap here as the Labour of working Men is in

Britain. Any one may compute it. Interest of Money is in the Colonies from 6 to 10 per Cent. Slaves one with another cost £30 Sterling per Head. Reckon then the Interest of the first Purchase of a Slave, the Insurance or Risque on his Life, his Cloathing and Diet, Expences in his Sickness and Loss of Time, Loss by his Neglect of Business (Neglect is natural to the Man who is not to be benefited by his own Care or Diligence), Expence of a Driver to keep him at Work, and his Pilfering from Time to Time, almost every Slave being *by Nature* a Thief, and compare the whole Amount with the Wages of a Manufacturer of Iron or Wool in England, you will see that Labour is much cheaper there than it ever can be by Negroes here. Why then will Americans purchase Slaves? Because Slaves may be kept as long as a Man pleases, or has Occasion for their Labour; while hired Men are continually leaving their Master (often in the midst of his Business), and setting up for themselves. §8.

13. As the Increase of People depends on the Encouragement of Marriages, the following Things must diminish a Nation, viz. 1. The being conquered; for the Conquerors will engross as many Offices, and exact as much Tribute or Profit on the Labour of the conquered, as will maintain them in their new Establishment, and this diminishing the Subsistence of the Natives discourages their Marriages, and so gradually diminishes them, while the Foreigners increase. 2. Loss of Territory. Thus the Britons being driven into Wales, and crowded together in a barren Country insufficient to support such great Numbers, diminished 'till the People bore a Proportion to the Produce, while the Saxons increas'd on their abandoned Lands; 'till the Island became full of English. And were the English now driven into Wales by some foreign Nation, there would in a few Years be no more Englishmen in Britain, than there are now People in Wales. 3. Loss of Trade. Manufactures exported, draw Subsistence from Foreign Countries for Numbers; who are thereby enabled to marry and raise Families. If the Nation be deprived of any Branch of Trade, and no new Employment is found for the People occupy'd in that Branch, it will also be soon deprived of so many People. 4. Loss of Food. Suppose a Nation has a Fishery, which not only employs great Numbers, but makes the Food and Subsistence of the People cheaper; If another Nation becomes Master of the Seas, and prevents the Fishery, the People will diminish in Proportion as the Loss of

Employ, and Dearness of Provision, makes it more difficult to subsist a Family. 5. Bad Government and insecure Property. People not only leave such a Country, and settling Abroad incorporate with other Nations, lose their native Language, and become Foreigners; but the Industry of those that remain being discourag'd, the Quantity of Subsistence in the Country is lessen'd, and the Support of a Family becomes more difficult. So heavy Taxes tend to diminish a People. 6. The Introduction of Slaves. The Negroes brought into the English Sugar Islands, have greatly diminish'd the Whites there; the Poor are by this Means depriv'd of Employment, while a few Families acquire vast Estates; which they spend on Foreign Luxuries, and educating their Children in the Habit of those Luxuries; the same Income is needed for the Support of one that might have maintain'd 100. The Whites who have Slaves, not labouring, are enfeebled, and therefore not so generally prolific; the Slaves being work'd too hard, and ill fed, their Constitutions are broken, and the Deaths among them are more than the Births; so that a continual supply is needed from Africa. The Northern Colonies having few Slaves increase in Whites. Slaves also pejorate [cause to deteriorate] the Families that use them; the white Children become proud, disgusted with Labour, and being educated in Idleness, are rendered unfit to get a Living by Industry.

14. Hence the Prince that acquires new Territory, if he finds it vacant, or removes the Natives to give his own People Room; the Legislator that makes effectual Laws for promoting of Trade, increasing Employment, improving Land by more or better Tillage; providing more Food by Fisheries; securing Property, &c. and the Man that invents new Trades, Arts or Manufactures, or new Improvements in Husbandry, may be properly called *Fathers* of their Nation, as they are the Cause of the Generation of Multitudes, by the Encouragement they afford to Marriage.

15. As to Privileges granted to the married, (such as the *Jus trium Liberorum* ["right of three children": conferring privileges on mothers of three] among the Romans), they may hasten the filling of a Country that has been thinned by War or Pestilence, or that has otherwise vacant Territory; but cannot increase a People beyond the Means provided for their Subsistence.

16. Foreign Luxuries and needless Manufactures imported and used in a

Nation, do, by the same Reasoning, increase the People of the Nation that furnishes them, and diminish the People of the Nation that uses them. Laws therefore that prevent such Importations, and on the contrary promote the Exportation of Manufactures to be consumed in Foreign Countries, may be called (with Respect to the People that make them) *generative Laws,* as by increasing Subsistence they encourage Marriage. Such Laws likewise strengthen a Country, doubly, by increasing its own People and diminishing its Neighbours.

17. Some European Nations prudently refuse to consume the Manufactures of East-India. They should likewise forbid them to their Colonies; for the Gain to the Merchant, is not to be compar'd with the Loss by this Means of People to the Nation.

18. Home Luxury in the Great, increases the Nation's Manufacturers employ'd by it, who are many, and only tends to diminish the Families that indulge in it, who are few. The greater the common fashionable Expence of any Rank of People, the more cautious they are of Marriage. Therefore Luxury should never be suffer'd to become common.

19. The great Increase of Offspring in particular Families, is not always owing to greater Fecundity of Nature, but sometimes to Examples of Industry in the Heads, and industrious Education; by which the Children are enabled to provide better for themselves, and their marrying early, is encouraged from the Prospect of good Subsistence.

20. If there be a Sect therefore, in our Nation, that regard Frugality and Industry as religious Duties, and educate their Children therein, more than others commonly do; such Sect must consequently increase more by natural Generation, than any other Sect in Britain.

21. The Importation of Foreigners into a Country that has as many Inhabitants as the present Employments and Provisions for Subsistence will bear; will be in the End no Increase of People; unless the New Comers have more Industry and Frugality than the Natives, and then they will provide more Subsistence, and increase in the Country; but they will gradually eat the Natives out. Nor is it necessary to bring in Foreigners to fill up any occasional Vacancy in a Country; for such Vacancy (if the Laws are good, § 14, 16) will soon be filled by natural Generation. Who can now find the Vacancy made in Sweden, France or other Warlike Nations, by the Plague

of Heroism 40 Years ago; in France, by the Expulsion of the Protestants; in England, by the Settlement of her Colonies; or in Guinea, by 100 Years Exportation of Slaves, that has blacken'd half America? The thinness of Inhabitants in Spain is owing to National Pride and Idleness, and other Causes, rather than to the Expulsion of the Moors, or to the making of new Settlements.

22. There is in short, no Bound to the prolific Nature of Plants or Animals, but what is made by their crowding and interfering with each others Means of Subsistence. Was the Face of the Earth Vacant of other Plants, it might be gradually sowed and overspread with one Kind only; as, for Instance, with Fennel; and were it empty of other Inhabitants, it might in a few Ages be replenish'd from one Nation only; as, for Instance, with Englishmen. Thus there are suppos'd to be now upwards of One Million English Souls in North-America, (tho' 'tis thought scarce 80,000 have been brought over Sea) and yet perhaps there is not one the fewer in Britain, but rather many more, on Account of the Employment the Colonies afford to Manufacturers at Home. This Million doubling, suppose but once in 25 Years, will in another Century be more than the People of England, and the greatest Number of Englishmen will be on this Side the Water. What an Accession of Power to the British Empire by Sea as well as Land! What Increase of Trade and Navigation! What Numbers of Ships and Seamen! We have been here but little more than 100 Years, and yet the Force of our Privateers in the late War, united, was greater, both in Men and Guns, than that of the whole British Navy in Queen Elizabeth's Time. How important an Affair then to Britain, is the present Treaty [Treaty of Aix-la-Chapelle, 1748] for settling the Bounds between her Colonies and the French, and how careful should she be to secure Room enough, since on the Room depends so much the Increase of her People?

23. In fine, A Nation well regulated is like a Polypus [octopus]; take away a Limb, its Place is soon supply'd; cut it in two, and each deficient Part shall speedily grow out of the Part remaining. Thus if you have Room and Subsistence enough, as you may by dividing, make ten Polypes out of one, you may of one make ten Nations, equally populous and powerful; or rather, increase a Nation ten fold in Numbers and Strength.

And since Detachments of English from Britain sent to America, will have their Places at Home so soon supply'd and increase so largely here; why should the Palatine Boors [German peasants] be suffered to swarm into our Settlements, and by herding together establish their Language and Manners to the Exclusion of ours? Why should Pennsylvania, founded by the English, become a Colony of *Aliens,* who will shortly be so numerous as to Germanize us instead of our Anglifying them, and will never adopt our Language or Customs, any more than they can acquire our Complexion.

24. Which leads me to add one Remark: That the Number of purely white People in the World is proportionately very small. All Africa is black or tawny. Asia chiefly tawny. America (exclusive of the new Comers) wholly so. And in Europe, the Spaniards, Italians, French, Russians and Swedes, are generally of what we call a swarthy Complexion; as are the Germans also, the Saxons only excepted, who with the English, make the principal Body of White People on the Face of the Earth. I could wish their Numbers were increased. And while we are, as I may call it, *Scouring* our Planet, by clearing America of Woods, and so making this Side of our Globe reflect a brighter Light to the Eyes of Inhabitants in Mars or Venus, why should we in the Sight of Superior Beings, darken its People? why increase the Sons of Africa, by Planting them in America, where we have so fair an Opportunity, by excluding all Blacks and Tawneys, of increasing the lovely White and Red? But perhaps I am partial to the Complexion of my Country, for such Kind of Partiality is natural to Mankind.

11 Ethnic pride and prejudice.

Pennsylvania was the most ethnically diverse of England's colonies. It had taken on that character in Franklin's lifetime, and, as is evident in the "Observations," he was not happy about it. It would be fair to say, and he admits it, that he would have preferred an American continent peopled entirely by his own kind, Englishmen and their children. Before following the development of his later plans for the continent, we should consider the extent and limits of his early ethnocentrism, and look at whom he thought should be included in his great political structure. In a letter to Peter Collinson, he discloses a shallow understanding of the poverty of the poor and contempt for the intelligence of the Germans who were engulfing him and his kind in Pennsylvania. The same letter argues his view that the Indians are not really assimilable. Franklin's prejudices were already eroding, but they make a striking, though not wholly incompatible, contrast to the proposals we will later find him making for limiting accumulations of private property and reducing its influence in politics and government. Meanwhile, it will be worth thinking about his reaction to real poverty when he encountered it in England, as described in a letter to Joshua Babcock, an old friend he had often visited in Westerly, Rhode Island.

Franklin, however ethnocentric, seems to have been freer of overt racism than most of his contemporaries. While he believed the Indians must be either allies or enemies, rather than fellow citizens, he did not regard them as physically or intellectually inferior to whites. We have already seen his depiction of Indians as spokesmen for common sense in chapter 3. His view of Africans changed over time. He had at first no objection to slavery as a form of servitude and seems not to have thought about the injustice of enslaving Africans. In the course of his life before 1776 he held five slaves and took two of them to England in 1757 to serve in his household there. When or whether any of them became free is unclear. Initially he apparently accepted the prevailing racist view of Africans' intellectual capacities. But his letter to John Waring in 1763 suggests that he had learned better by then. Waring belonged to an association of Anglican clergymen, including William Sturgeon, referred to in the letter, which sponsored schools in America for African children. By the 1770s Franklin's Quaker friend Anthony Benezet was influential in prodding him into taking a stand, privately at least, against slavery, though it was not until 1789 that he joined in a petition to the first U.S. Congress to abolish it. When Congress predictably rejected the petition, Franklin wrote one of his most eloquent satirical pieces, the last publication in his lifetime. One of the problems that the new nation faced was the enslavement of its own citizens in the piratical states of North Africa. It was a regular practice for those states to prey on the ships that passed their shores and take as slaves all aboard whose governments did not pay tribute, as England and France did by treaty. After 1776 Americans no longer enjoyed the protection of the British flag, and many white Christian Americans now suffered in North Africa the same slavery that Africans suffered in the United States. Franklin took advantage of the irony to place in the mouth of an Algerian official, "Sidi Mehemet Ibrahim," the same arguments against freeing slaves that southern Congressmen had used against his petition.

The man who started out with all the prejudices of what we call a WASP, after cutting all his ties with his own kind in England, died with a multicultural view of the greatest political structure human wisdom could construct.

Indians and Germans, 1753

I have often observed with wonder, that Temper of the poor English Manufacturers and day Labourers which you mention, and acknowledge it to be pretty general. When any of them happen to come here, where Labour is much better paid than in England, their Industry seems to diminish in equal proportion. But it is not so with the German Labourers; They retain the habitual Industry and Frugality they bring with them, and now receiving higher Wages an accumulation arises that makes them all rich.

When I consider, that the English are the Offspring of Germans, that the Climate they live in is much of the same Temperature; when I can see nothing in Nature that should create this Difference, I am apt to suspect it must arise from Institution[s], and I have sometimes doubted, whether the Laws peculiar to England which compel the Rich to maintain the Poor, have not given the latter, a Dependance that very much lessens the care of providing against the wants of old Age.

I have heard it remarked that the Poor in Protestant Countries on the Continent of Europe, are generally more industrious than those of Popish Countries, may not the more numerous foundations in the latter for the relief of the poor have some effect towards rendering them less provident. To relieve the misfortunes of our fellow creatures is concurring with the Deity, 'tis Godlike, but if we provide encouragements for Laziness, and supports for Folly, may it not be found fighting against the order of God and Nature, which perhaps has appointed Want and Misery as the proper Punishments for, and Cautions against as well as necessary consequences of Idleness and Extravagancy.

Whenever we attempt to mend the scheme of Providence and to interfere in the Government of the World, we had need be very circumspect lest we do more harm than Good. In New England they once thought Black-birds useless and mischievous to their corn, they made [Laws] to destroy them, the consequence was, the Black-birds were diminished but a kind of Worms which devoured their Grass, and which the Black-birds had been used to feed on encreased prodigiously; Then finding their Loss in Grass much greater than their saving in corn they wished again for their Black-birds.

We had here some years since a Transylvanian Tartar, who had travelled much in the East, and came hither merely to see the West, intending to go home thro' the spanish West Indies, China &c. He asked me one day what I thought might be the Reason that so many and such numerous nations, as the Tartars in Europe and Asia, the Indians in America, and the Negroes in Africa, continued a wandring careless Life, and refused to live in Cities, and to cultivate the arts they saw practiced by the civilized part of Mankind.

While I was considering what answer to make him; I'll tell you, says he in his broken English, God make man for Paradise, he make him for to live lazy; man make God angry, God turn him out of Paradise, and bid him work; man no love work; he want to go to Paradise again, he want to live lazy; so all mankind love lazy. Howe'er this may be it seems certain, that the hope of becoming at some time of Life free from the necessity of care and Labour, together with fear of penury, are the mainsprings of most peoples industry.

To those indeed who have been educated in elegant plenty, even the provision made for the poor may appear misery, but to those who have scarce ever been better provided for, such provision may seem quite good and sufficient, these latter have then nothing to fear worse than their present Conditions, and scarce hope for any thing better than a Parish maintainance; so that there is only the difficulty of getting that maintainance allowed while they are able to work, or a little shame they suppose attending it, that can induce them to work at all, and what they do will only be from hand to mouth.

The proneness of human Nature to a life of ease, of freedom from care and labour appears strongly in the little success that has hitherto attended every attempt to civilize our American Indians, in their present way of living, almost all their Wants are supplied by the spontaneous Productions of Nature, with the addition of very little labour, if hunting and fishing may indeed be called labour when Game is so plenty, they visit us frequently, and see the advantages that Arts, Sciences, and compact Society procure us, they are not deficient in natural understanding and yet they have never shewn any Inclination to change their manner of life for ours, or to learn any of our Arts; When an Indian Child has been brought up among us, taught our language and habituated to our Customs, yet if he goes to see his relations and make one Indian Ramble with them, there is no perswading him ever to return, and that this is not natural [to them] merely as Indians, but as men, is plain from this, that when white persons of either sex have been taken prisoners young by the Indians, and lived a while among them, tho' ransomed by their Friends, and treated with all imaginable tenderness to prevail with them to stay among the English, yet in a Short time they become disgusted with our manner of life, and the care and pains that are necessary to support it, and take the first good Opportunity of escaping again into the Woods, from whence there is no reclaiming them. One instance I remember to have heard, where the person was brought home to possess a good Estate; but finding some care necessary to keep it together, he relinquished it to a younger Brother, reserving to himself nothing but a gun and a match-Coat, with which he took his way again to the Wilderness.

Though they have few but natural wants and those easily supplied. But with us are infinite Artificial wants, no less craving [demanding] than those of Nature, and much more difficult to satisfy; so that I am apt to imagine that close Societies subsisting by Labour and Arts, arose first not from choice, but from necessity: When numbers being driven by war from their hunting grounds and prevented by seas or by other nations were crowded together into some narrow Territories, which without labour would not afford them Food. However as matters [now] stand with us, care and industry seem absolutely necessary to our well being; they should therefore have every Encouragement we can invent, and not one Motive to diligence be subtracted, and the support of the Poor should not be by maintaining them in Idleness, But by employing them in some kind of labour suited to their Abilities of body &c. as I am informed of late begins to be the practice in many parts of England, where work houses are erected for that purpose. If these were general I should think the Poor would be more careful and work voluntarily and lay up something for themselves against a rainy day, rather than run the risque of being obliged to work at the pleasure of others for a bare subsistence and that too under confinement. . . .

I am perfectly of your mind, that measures of great Temper are necessary with the Germans: and am not without Apprehensions, that thro' their indiscretion or Ours, or both, great disorders and inconveniences may one day arise among us; Those who come hither are generally of the most ignorant Stupid Sort of their own Nation, and as Ignorance is often attended with Credulity when Knavery would mislead it, and with Suspicion when Honesty would set it right; and as few of the English understand the German Language, and so cannot address them either from the Press or Pulpit, 'tis almost impossible to remove any prejudices they once entertain.

Their own Clergy have very little influence over the people; who seem to take an uncommon pleasure in abusing and discharging the Minister on every trivial occasion. Not being used to Liberty, they know not how to make a modest use of it; and as Kolben says of the young Hottentots, that they are not esteemed men till they have shewn their manhood by beating their mothers, so these seem to think themselves not free, till they can feel their liberty in abusing and insulting their Teachers [Peter Kolben, *The Present State of the Cape of Good-Hope* (1731)]. Thus they are under no restraint of Ecclesiastical Government; They behave, however, submissively enough at present to the Civil Government which I wish they may continue to do: For I remember when they modestly declined intermeddling in our Elections, but now they come in droves, and carry all before them, except in one or two Counties; Few of their children in the Country learn English; they import many Books from Germany; and of the six printing houses in the Province, two are entirely German, two half German half English, and but two entirely English; They have one German Newspaper, and one half German. Advertisments intended to be general are now printed in Dutch and English; the Signs in our Streets have inscriptions in both languages, and in some places only German: They begin of late to make all their Bonds and other legal Writings in their own Language, which (though I think it ought not to be) are allowed good in our Courts, where the German Business so encreases that there is continual need of Interpreters; and I suppose in a few years they will be also necessary in the Assembly, to tell one half of our Legislators what the other half say; In short unless the stream of their importation could be turned from this to other Colonies, as you very judiciously propose, they will soon so out number us, that all the advantages we have will not in My Opinion be able to preserve our language, and even our Government will become precarious. . . . Yet I am not for refusing entirely to admit them into our Colonies: all that seems to be necessary is, to distribute them more equally, mix them with the English, establish English Schools where they are now too thick settled, and take some care to prevent the practice lately fallen into by some of the Ship Owners, of sweeping the German Goals [jails] to make up the number of their Passengers. I say I am not against the Admission of Germans in general, for they have their Virtues, their industry and frugality is exemplary; They are excellent husbandmen and contribute greatly to the improvement of a Country.

I pray God long to preserve to Great Britain the English Laws, Manners, Liberties and Religion notwithstanding the complaints so frequent in Your public papers, of the prevailing corruption and degeneracy of your People; I know you have a great deal of Virtue still subsisting among you, and I hope the Constitution is not so near a dissolution, as some seem to apprehend; I do not think you are generally become such Slaves to your Vices, as to draw down that *Justice* Milton speaks of when he says that

—sometimes Nations will descend so low
From reason, which is virtue, that no Wrong,
But Justice, and some fatal curse annex'd
Deprives them of their *outward* liberty,
Their *inward* lost.   Parad: lost. [12.97–101]
[The original reads: "Yet sometimes Nations will decline so low / From vertue, which is reason, that no wrong. . . ."]

In history we find that Piety, Public Spirit and military Prowess have their Flows, as well as their ebbs, in every nation, and that the Tide is never so low but it may rise again; But should this dreaded fatal change happen in my time, how should I even in the midst of the Affliction rejoice, if we have been able to preserve those invaluable treasures, and can invite the good among you to come and partake of them! O let not Britain seek to oppress us, but like an affectionate parent endeavour to secure freedom to her children; they may be able one day to assist her in defending her own— Whereas a Mortification begun in the Foot may spread upwards to the destruction of the nobler parts of the Body.

To Joshua Babcock, 1772

Dear Sir,   London, Jan. 13. 1772
It was with great Pleasure I learnt by Mr. Marchant, that you and Mrs. Babcock and all your good Family continue well and happy. I hope I shall find you all in the same State when I next come your Way, and take Shelter as often heretofore under your hospitable Roof. The Colonel [Babcock's

son], I am told, continues an active and able Farmer, the most honourable of all Employments, in my Opinion as being the most useful in itself, and rendring the Man most independent. My Namesake, his Son, will soon I hope be able to drive the Plough for him.

I have lately made a Tour thro' Ireland and Scotland. In these Countries a small Part of the Society are Landlords, great Noblemen and Gentlemen, extreamly opulent, living in the highest Affluence and Magnificence: The Bulk of the People Tenants, extreamly poor, living in the most sordid Wretchedness in dirty Hovels of Mud and Straw, and cloathed only in Rags. I thought often of the Happiness of New England, where every Man is a Freeholder, has a Vote in publick Affairs, lives in a tidy warm House, has plenty of good Food and Fewel, with whole Cloaths from Head to Foot, the Manufactury perhaps of his own Family. Long may they continue in this Situation! But if they should ever envy the *Trade* of these Countries, I can put them in a Way to obtain a Share of it. Let them with three fourths of the People of Ireland, live the Year round on Potatoes and Butter milk, without Shirts, then may their Merchants export Beef, Butter and Linnen. Let them with the Generality of the Common People of Scotland go Barefoot, then may they make large Exports in Shoes and Stockings: And if they will be content to wear Rags like the Spinners and Weavers of England, they may make Cloths and Stuffs for all Parts of the World. Farther, if my Countrymen should ever wish for the Honour of having among them a Gentry enormously wealthy, let them sell their Farms and pay rack'd Rents [rents raised beyond what tenants can reasonably be expected to pay]; the Scale of the Landlords will rise as that of the Tenants is depress'd who will soon become poor, tattered, dirty, and abject in Spirit. Had I never been in the American Colonies, but was to form my Judgment of Civil Society by what I have lately seen, I should never advise a Nation of Savages to admit of Civilisation: For I assure you, that in the Possession and Enjoyment of the various Comforts of Life, compar'd to these People every Indian is a Gentleman: And the Effect of this kind of Civil Society seems only to be, the depressing Multitudes below the Savage State that a few may be rais'd above it. My best Wishes attend you and yours, being ever with great Esteem, Dear Sir, Your most obedient and most humble Servant   B F

To John Waring, 1763

Reverend and dear Sir,   Philada. Dec. 17. 1763

. . . This is chiefly to acquaint you, that I have visited the Negro School here in Company with the Revd. Mr. Sturgeon and some others; and had the Children thoroughly examin'd. They appear'd all to have made considerable Progress in Reading for the Time they had respectively been in the School, and most of them answer'd readily and well the Questions of the Catechism; they behav'd very orderly, showd a proper Respect and ready Obedience to the Mistress, and seem'd very attentive to, and a good deal affected by, a serious Exhortation with which Mr. Sturgeon concluded our Visit. I was on the whole much pleas'd, and from what I then saw, have conceiv'd a higher Opinion of the natural Capacities of the black Race, than I had ever before entertained. Their Apprehension seems as quick, their Memory as strong, and their Docility in every Respect equal to that of white Children. You will wonder perhaps that I should ever doubt it, and I will not undertake to justify all my Prejudices, nor to account for them. . . . Be pleased to present my best Respects to the Associates, and believe me, with sincere Esteem Dear Sir, Your most obedient Servant   B FRANKLIN

The Speech of Sidi Mehemet Ibrahim, 1790

To the EDITOR *of the* FEDERAL GAZETTE.   March 23.
Sir,

READING last night in your excellent paper the speech of Mr. Jackson in Congress, against meddling with the affair of slavery, or attempting to mend the condition of slaves, it put me in mind of a similar one made about one hundred years since, by Sidi Mehemet Ibrahim, a member of the Divan of Algiers, which may be seen in *Martin's* account of his consulship, anno 1687. It was against granting the petition of the Sect called *Erika* or Purists, who prayed for the abolition of piracy and slavery, as being unjust.—Mr. Jackson does not quote it; perhaps he has not seen it.—If therefore some of its reasonings are to be found in his eloquent speech, it may only show that men's interests and intellects operate and are operated on with surprising similarity in all countries and climates, whenever they are under similar circumstances. — The African's speech, as translated, is as follows:

"*Allah Bismillah, &c. God is great, and Mahomet is his Prophet.*

"Have these *Erika* considered the consequences of granting their petition? If we cease our cruises against the christians, how shall we be furnished with the commodities their countries produce, and which are so necessary for us? If we forbear to make slaves of their people, who, in this hot climate, are to cultivate our lands? Who are to perform the common labours of our city, and in our families? Must we not then be our own slaves? And is there not more campassion and more favour due to us Mussulmen, than to these christian dogs? We have now above 50,000 slaves in and near Algiers. — This number, if not kept up by fresh supplies, will soon diminish, and be gradually annihilated. If then we cease taking and plundering the Infidel ships, and making slaves of the seamen and passengers, our lands will become of no value for want of cultivation; the rents of houses in the city will sink one half? and the revenues of government arising from its share of prizes must be totally destroyed. And for what? to gratify the whim of a whimsical sect! who would have us not only forbear making more slaves, but even to manumit those we have. — But who is to indemnify their masters for the loss? Will the state do it? Is our treasury sufficient? Will the *Erika* do it? Can they do it? Or would they, to do what they think justice to the slaves, do a greater injustice to the owners? And if we set our slaves free, what is to be done with them? Few of them will return to their countries, they know too well the greater hardships they must there be subject to: they will not embrace our holy religion: they will not adopt our manners: our people will not pollute themselves by intermarrying with them: must we maintain them as beggars in our streets; or suffer our properties to be the prey of their pillage; for men accostomed to slavery, will not work for a livelihood when not compelled. — And what is there so pitiable in their present condition? Were they not slaves in their own countries? Are not Spain, Portugal, France and the Italian states, governed by despots, who hold all their subjects in slavery, without exception? Even England treats its sailors as slaves, for they are, whenever the government pleases, seized and confined in ships of war, condemned not only to work but to fight for small wages or a mere subsistance, not better than our slaves are allowed by us. Is their condition then made worse by their falling into our hands? No, they have only exchanged one slavery for another: and I may say a better: for here they are brought into a land where the sun of Islamism gives forth its light, and shines in full splendor, and they have an opportunity of making themselves acquainted with the true doctrine, and thereby saving their immortal souls. Those who remain at home have not that happiness. Sending the slaves home then, would be sending them out of light into darkness.—I repeat the question, what is to be done with them? I have heard it suggested, that they may be planted in the wilderness, where there is plenty of land for them to subsist on, and where they may flourish as a free state;—but they are, I doubt, too little disposed to labour without compulsion, as well as too ignorant to establish a good government, and the wild Arabs would soon molest and destroy or again enslave them. While serving us, we take care to provide them with every thing; and they are treated with humanity. The labourers in their own countries, are, as I am well informed, worse fed, lodged and cloathed. The condition of most of them is therefore already mended, and requires no farther improvement. Here their lives are in safety. They are not liable to be impressed for soldiers, and forced to cut one another's christian throats, as in the wars of their own countries.—If some of the religious mad bigots who now teaze us with their silly petitions, have in a fit of blind zeal freed their slaves, it was not generosity, it was not humanity that moved them to the action; it was from the conscious burthen of a load of sins, and hope from the supposed merits of so good a work to be excused from damnation— How grosly are they mistaken in imagining slavery to be disallowed by the Alcoran! Are not the two precepts, to quote no more, *Masters treat your slaves with kindness: Slaves serve your masters with cheerfulness and fidelity,* clear proofs to the contrary? Nor can the plundering of infidels be in that sacred book forbidden, since it is well known from it, that God has given the world and all that it contains to his faithful Mussulmen, who are to enjoy it of right as fast as they can conquer it. Let us then hear no more of this detestable proposition, the manumission of christian slaves, the adoption of which would, by depreciating our lands and houses, and thereby depriving so many good citizens of their properties, create universal discontent, and provoke insurrections, to the endangering of government, and producing general confusion. I have therefore no doubt, but this wise Council will prefer the comfort and happiness of a whole nation of true believers, to the whim of a few *Erika,* and dismiss their petition."

The result was, as *Martin* tells us, that the Divan came to this resolution, "The doctrine that plundering and enslaving the Christians is unjust, is at best *problematical;* but that it is the interest of this state to continue the practice, is clear; therefore let the petition be rejected."

And it was rejected accordingly.

And since like motives are apt to produce in the minds of men like opinions and resolutions, may we not, Mr. Brown, venture to predict, from this account, that the petitions to the parliament of England for abolishing the slave trade, to say nothing of other legislatures, and the debates upon them, will have a similar conclusion.

I am, Sir, Your constant reader and humble servant

Historicus.

12 Join or die.

At the time when Franklin began to envision a future British American empire as "the greatest Political Structure Human Wisdom ever yet created," he could not have had any details of the structure in mind. But he knew that there was already a structure in place. It had come into existence haphazardly in the preceding century and a half and now contained the population whose exponential growth he had described in the "Observations." The old structure would have to be adapted, if not replaced, if it was to exhibit the greatness he confidently anticipated. Most obvious, its institutions would have to be conformed to the needs of what must, in the not-so-distant future, become the center of its population and power. Franklin had no doubt of what the first step should be. In a letter to Peter Collinson, with whom he had been corresponding (mainly about electricity) more frequently than with anyone else at the time, he gave a broad hint: "May I presume to whisper my Sentiments in a private letter? Britain and her Colonies should be considered as one Whole, and not as different States with separate Interests."

He was writing in May 1754, just before departing from Philadelphia for Albany on a mission of some urgency. The expansion of population in the English colonies was already coming up against the imperial ambitions of the French in Canada. France and its Indian allies were building forts in the Ohio valley, from which they raided the farms of English settlers pressing westward. The French were few in number, and not growing in numbers the way the English were; but their Indian allies were a potent threat, and the French monarchy was preparing to back them up with soldiers. The

Americans had always been able to hold their own against sporadic raids by small forces, but a concerted operation by the French was evidently in the offing. There was no machinery for a common defense by the colonies, for they had no formal connection with one another except through the colonial bureaucracy in London.

Franklin had been thinking for some time of an intercolonial union, and in 1751 he had outlined a plan for one in a passage of the same letter to James Parker where he had presented his preliminary views on German immigration and American population growth. The juxtaposition is not, I think, a coincidence. Consider the sequence. On March 10, 1751, he shared his views on population growth and continental union with Parker; on April 11 he denounced the exportation of convicts to America; on May 9 he published the satire proposing the exchange of rattlesnakes for felons; and sometime during the year he expanded his views on American growth in the "Observations." This progression shows that Franklin was already thinking continentally, in American terms, when the prospect of open war with France made a continental union in arms imperative. On May 9, 1754, reporting a gruesome French and Indian raid on frontier settlements, he had his partner, David Hall, print one of the first cartoons to appear in an American newspaper, the famous "Join or Die" depiction of a dismembered snake.

Meanwhile, the British government had called a meeting at Albany to concoct a plan of defense. Franklin was present as a Pennsylvania delegate when the congress, as it was called, began its sessions on June 19. He had more on his mind than warfare when he presented the members with a plan of union, basically the one he had outlined to Parker, that would define the relations of the colonies both with one another and with Britain. It could have been a preliminary step to a reorganization of the empire. If Britain and the colonies were to be "one Whole," as he had whispered to Collinson, the colonies might first have to consider themselves an American whole. To Franklin's mind the purpose of this proposed union was not merely instrumental, not merely a way of coordinating defense in the face of a particular threat. He believed, as he told another English friend, "that the colonies would by this connection learn to consider themselves, not as so many independent states, but as members of the same body."

The words "independent states" did not carry the same meaning in 1754 that they would twenty years later. Franklin doubtless meant independence of one another rather than independence from the home country. But to the British, if not to Franklin, the very idea of an American union held inescapable connotations of a bid for freedom from British rule. Even before the founding of Virginia in 1607 it had been widely assumed by proponents of colonization that at some distant time overseas settlements would shake off their connection with the mother country. In the eighteenth century, as the colonies came to play a significant role in the British economy, that possibility became a little more likely to the British, and a lot less desirable. And it was probable that union would be the way the colonists would try to bring it about, for a single colony could scarcely have succeeded in standing against British might.

Franklin's Plan of Union at Albany carried no implication of independence. It was directed toward defending Britain's empire against Britain's traditional enemies, the detested French. Whereas Franklin had originally told Parker that the colonies must initiate an agreement for mutual defense, the Plan of Union was to be effected by an act of Parliament. However, the plan would have created a Grand Council with power not only to raise troops and build warships but also to purchase lands from the Indians and to create and govern new settlements. New settlements there must be, to hold the burgeoning Americans, and Franklin's plan would have placed them under the control of an American council. Its acts would have been subject to British approval, but its powers would have been larger—it could levy taxes—than those the Continental Congress exercised before and after declaring independence twenty-two years later.

In 1754 the Plan of Union did not fly. The commissioners from the other colonies, after a few minor revisions, approved it unanimously, but their constituents in their respective colonial assemblies unanimously rejected it as an encroachment on their own authority. It was never presented to Parliament because the colonial ministers who called the Albany meeting had grave second thoughts concerning the "ill consequences to be apprehended from uniting too closely the northern colonies with each other, an Independency upon this country to be feared from such an union." There is nothing in the plan or in any of Franklin's correspondence to suggest that he desired or foresaw any such consequence, and upon reviewing the document in 1789 he concluded that it might have prevented the Revolution. But if he abhorred the thought of independence in 1754, he was not happy with the idea of dependence, then or ever. If there was to be any dependence in his great political structure, it would be a happy dependence of the British on their ever-growing American cousins. And his vision of a brilliant American future grew even grander during the war that was beginning even as the Albany Congress deliberated.

Franklin played an active role in securing Pennsylvania's support of the British army in the early stages of the war. But by the time British victory was assured with the capture of Montreal in 1760, he was in London. There the authorities deliberated about how much of what they had captured they could afford to keep. Canada was weighed in the balance against the French sugar islands in the West Indies, the value of whose exports far exceeded Canada's. The question was widely debated in the English press, and Franklin contributed a lengthy pamphlet on the necessity of holding onto Canada. He envisaged Canada as forming a vital part of the broader empire he contemplated. Below we reprint passages from the Canada pamphlet, in which he writes as though he were an Englishman disputing opposing arguments by "the Remarker."

One of those arguments was that retaining Canada would remove the French menace to the colonies, freeing them from the need for British protection and thus tempting the Americans to unite in a bid for independence.

The failure of the Plan of Union now became an argument for the improbability of any such move. But Franklin did not hesitate to disclose his plans for American expansion and added a warning note that "grievous tyranny and oppression" could overcome the obstacles to Americans' uniting to throw off their subjection to Britain. In testimony to his confidence in a British American empire, he appended to the pamphlet a copy of his "Observations Concerning the Increase of Mankind."

To James Parker, 1751

Dear Mr. Parker,   Philadelphia, March 20, 1751

I have, as you desire, read the Manuscript you sent me [by Archibald Kennedy, printed as *The Importance of Gaining and Preserving the Friendship of the Indians to the British Interest, Considered* (1751)]; and am of Opinion, with the publick-spirited Author, that securing the Friendship of the Indians is of the greatest Consequence to these Colonies; and that the surest Means of doing it, are, to regulate the Indian Trade, so as to convince them, by Experience, that they may have the best and cheapest Goods, and the fairest Dealing from the English; and to unite the several Governments, so as to form a Strength that the Indians may depend on for Protection, in Case of a Rupture with the French; or apprehend great Danger from, if they should break with us.

This Union of the Colonies, however necessary, I apprehend is not to be brought about by the Means that have hitherto been used for that Purpose. A Governor of one Colony, who happens from some Circumstances in his own Government, to see the Necessity of such an Union, writes his Sentiments of the Matter to the other Governors, and desires them to recommend it to their respective Assemblies. They accordingly lay the Letters before those Assemblies, and perhaps recommend the Proposal in general Words. But Governors are often on ill Terms with their Assemblies, and seldom are the Men that have the most Influence among them. And perhaps some Governors, tho' they openly recommend the Scheme, may privately throw cold Water on it, as thinking additional publick Charges will make their People less able, or less willing to give to them. Or perhaps they do not clearly see the Necessity of it, and therefore do not very earnestly press the Consideration of it: And no one being present that has the Affair at Heart, to back it, to answer and remove Objections, &c. 'tis easily dropt, and nothing is done. Such an Union is certainly necessary to us all, but more immediately so to your Government [New York]. Now, if you were to pick out half a Dozen Men of good Understanding and Address, and furnish them with a reasonable Scheme and proper Instructions, and send them in the Nature of Ambassadors to the other Colonies, where they might apply particularly to all the leading Men, and by proper Management get them to engage in promoting the Scheme; where, by being present, they would have the Opportunity of pressing the Affair both in publick and private, obviating Difficulties as they arise, answering Objections as soon as they are made, before they spread and gather Strength in the Minds of the People, &c. &c. I imagine such an Union might thereby be made and established: For reasonable sensible Men, can always make a reasonable Scheme appear such to other reasonable Men, if they take Pains, and have Time and Opportunity for it; unless from some Circumstances their Honesty and good Intentions are suspected. A voluntary Union entered into by the Colonies themselves, I think, would be preferable to one impos'd by Parliament; for it would be perhaps not much more difficult to procure, and more easy to alter and improve, as Circumstances should require, and Experience direct. It would be a very strange Thing, if six Nations of ignorant Savages should be capable of forming a Scheme for such an Union [the Iroquois Confederacy], and be able to execute it in such a Manner, as that it has subsisted Ages, and appears indissoluble; and yet that a like Union should be impracticable for ten or a Dozen English Colonies, to whom it is more necessary, and must be more advantageous; and who cannot be supposed to want an equal Understanding of their Interests.

Were there a general Council form'd by all the Colonies, and a general Governor appointed by the Crown to preside in that Council, or in some Manner to concur with and confirm their Acts, and take Care of the Execution; every Thing relating to Indian Affairs and the Defence of the Colonies, might be properly put under their Management. Each Colony should be represented by as many Members as it pays Sums of [blank] Hundred Pounds into the common Treasury for the common Expence; which Treasury would perhaps be best and most equitably supply'd, by an equal

Excise on strong Liquors in all the Colonies, the Produce never to be apply'd to the private Use of any Colony, but to the general Service. Perhaps if the Council were to meet successively at the Capitals of the several Colonies, they might thereby become better acquainted with the Circumstances, Interests, Strength or Weakness, &c. of all, and thence be able to judge better of Measures propos'd from time to time: At least it might be more satisfactory to the Colonies, if this were propos'd as a Part of the Scheme; for a Preference might create Jealousy and Dislike.

. . .

I wish I could offer any Thing for the Improvement of the Author's Piece, but I have little Knowledge, and less Experience in these Matters. I think it ought to be printed; and should be glad there were a more general Communication of the Sentiments of judicious Men, on Subjects so generally interesting; it would certainly produce good Effects. Please to present my Respects to the Gentleman, and thank him for the Perusal of his Manuscript. I am, Yours affectionately.

The Albany Plan of Union, 1754

PLAN of a Proposed Union of the Several Colonies of Masachusets-bay, New Hampshire, Coneticut, Rhode Island, New York, New Jerseys, Pensilvania, Maryland, Virginia, North Carolina, and South Carolina, For their Mutual Defence and Security, and for Extending the British Settlements in North America.

THAT humble Application be made for an Act of the Parliament of Great Britain, by Virtue of which, one General Government may be formed in America, including all the said Colonies, within and under which Government, each Colony may retain its present Constitution, except in the Particulars wherein a Change may be directed by the said Act, as hereafter follows.

President General.   That the said General Government be administred by a President General, To be appointed and Supported by the Crown, and a Grand Council to be Chosen by the Representatives of the People of the Several Colonies, met in their respective Assemblies.

Grand Council.

That within [blank] Months after the passing of such Act, The House of Representatives in the Several Assemblies, that Happen to be Sitting within that time or that shall be Specially for that purpose Convened, may and Shall Choose Members for the Grand Council in the following Proportions, that is to say.

Election of Members.

Masachusets-Bay. . . . . 7.
New Hampshire . . . . 2.
Conecticut . . . . 5.
Rhode-Island . . . . 2.
New-York . . . . 4.
New-Jerseys . . . . 3.
Pensilvania. . . . . 6.
Maryland. . . . . 4.
Virginia . . . . 7.
North-Carolina . . . . 4.
South-Carolina . . . . <u>4.</u>
48.

Place of first meeting.

Who shall meet for the first time at the City of Philadelphia, in Pensilvania, being called by the President General as soon as conveniently may be, after his Appointment.

New Election.

That there shall be a New Election of Members for the Grand Council every three years; And on the Death or Resignation of any Member his Place shall be Supplyed by a New Choice at the next Sitting of the Assembly of the Colony he represented.

Proportion of Members after first 3 years.

That after the first three years, when the Proportion of Money arising out of each Colony to the General Treasury can be known, The Number of Members to be Chosen, for each Colony shall from time to time in all ensuing Elections be regulated by that proportion (yet so as that the Number to be Chosen by any one Province be not more than Seven nor less than Two).

That the Grand Council shall meet once in every

Meetings of Grand Council. Year, and oftner if Occasion require, at such Time and place as they shall adjourn to at the last preceeding meeting, or as they shall be called to meet at by

Call. the President General, on any Emergency, he having first obtained in Writing the Consent of seven of the Members to such call, and sent due and timely Notice to the whole.

That the Grand Council have Power to Chuse

Speaker. their Speaker, and shall neither be Dissolved, prorogued nor Continue Sitting longer than Six Weeks at

Continuance. one Time without their own Consent, or the Special Command of the Crown.

That the Members of the Grand Council shall be

Member's Allowed for their Service ten shillings Sterling per

Allowance. Diem, during their Sessions or Journey to and from the Place of Meeting; Twenty miles to be reckoned a days Journey.

Assent of President That the Assent of the President General be requi-

General. site, to all Acts of the Grand Council, and that it be

His Duty. His Office, and Duty to cause them to be carried into Execution.

That the President General with the Advice of the

Power of President Grand Council, hold or Direct all Indian Treaties

and Grand Council. in which the General Interest or Welfare of the

Peace and War. Colony's may be Concerned; And make Peace or Declare War with the Indian Nations. That they make such Laws as they Judge Necessary for regulat-

Indian ing all Indian Trade. That they make all Purchases

Purchases. from Indians for the Crown, of Lands not within the Bounds of Particular Colonies, or that shall not be within their Bounds when some of them are reduced to more Convenient Dimensions. That they make

New Settlements. New Settlements on such Purchases, by Granting Lands in the Kings Name, reserving a Quit Rent to

the Crown, for the use of the General Treasury. That
they make Laws for regulating and Governing such
new Settlements, till the Crown shall think fit to form
them into Particular Governments.

That they raise and pay Soldiers, and build Forts
for the Defence of any of the Colonies, and equip
Vessels of Force to Guard the Coasts and Protect the
Trade on the Ocean, Lakes, or Great Rivers; But they
shall not Impress Men in any Colonies, without the
Consent of its Legislature. That for these purposes
they have Power to make Laws And lay and Levy
such General Duties, Imposts, or Taxes, as to them
shall appear most equal and Just, Considering the
Ability and other Circumstances of the Inhabitants in
the Several Colonies, and such as may be Collected
with the least Inconvenience to the People, rather
discouraging Luxury, than Loading Industry with
unnecessary Burthens. That they may Appoint a
General Treasurer and a Particular Treasurer in each
Government, when Necessary, And from Time to
Time may Order the Sums in the Treasuries of each
Government, into the General Treasury, or draw on
them for Special payments as they find most Convenient; Yet no money to Issue, but by joint Orders
of the President General and Grand Council Except
where Sums have been Appropriated to particular
Purposes, And the President General is previously
impowered By an Act to draw for such Sums.

That the General Accounts shall be yearly Settled
and Reported to the Several Assembly's.

That a Quorum of the Grand Council impower'd
to Act with the President General, do consist of
Twenty-five Members, among whom there shall be
one, or more from a Majority of the Colonies. That
the Laws made by them for the Purposes aforesaid,

Side notes (left margin):

Laws to
Govern them.

Raise Soldiers
&c.
Lakes.

Not to Impress.

Power to make
Laws Duties &c.

Treasurer.

Money how
to Issue.

Accounts.

Quorum.

Laws to be
Transmitted.

shall not be repugnant but as near as may be agreeable to the Laws of England, and Shall be transmitted to the King in Council for Approbation, as Soon as may be after their Passing and if not disapproved within Three years after Presentation to remain in Force.

Death of President
General.

That in case of the Death of the President General The Speaker of the Grand Council for the Time Being shall Succeed, and be Vested with the Same Powers, and Authority, to Continue until the King's Pleasure be known.

Officers how
Appointed.

That all Military Commission Officers Whether for Land or Sea Service, to Act under this General Constitution, shall be Nominated by the President General But the Approbation of the Grand Council, is to be Obtained before they receive their Commissions, And all Civil Officers are to be Nominated, by the Grand Council, and to receive the President General's Approbation, before they Officiate; But in Case

Vacancies how
Supplied.

of Vacancy by Death or removal of any Officer Civil or Military under this Constitution, The Governor of the Province, in which such Vacancy happens, may Appoint till the Pleasure of the President General and Grand Council can be known. That the Particular Military as well as Civil Establishments in each Colony remain in their present State, this General

Each Colony may
defend itself
on Emergency.

Constitution Notwithstanding. And that on Sudden Emergencies any Colony may Defend itself, and lay the Accounts of Expence thence Arisen, before the President General and Grand Council, who may allow and order payment of the same As far as they Judge such Accounts Just and reasonable.

The Interest of Great Britain Considered [Canada Pamphlet], 1760

. . . With Canada in our possession, our people in America will increase amazingly. I know, that their common rate of increase, where they are not molested by the enemy, is doubling their numbers every twenty five years by natural generation only, exclusive of the accession of foreigners. I think this increase continuing, would probably in a century more, make the number of British subjects on that side the water more numerous than they now are on this; but I am far from entertaining on that account, any fears of their becoming either *useless* or *dangerous* to us; and I look on those fears, to be merely imaginary and without any probable foundation. The *remarker* is reserv'd in giving his reasons, as in his opinion this "is not a fit subject for discussion." I shall give mine, because I conceive it a subject necessary to be discuss'd; and the rather, as those fears how groundless and chimerical soever, may by possessing the multitude, possibly induce the ablest ministry to conform to them against their own judgment, and thereby prevent the assuring to the British name and nation a stability and permanency that no man acquainted with history durst have hoped for, 'till our American possessions opened the pleasing prospect.

The remarker thinks that our people in America, "finding no check from Canada would extend themselves almost without bounds into the inland parts, and increase infinitely from all causes." The very reason he assigns for their so extending, and which is indeed the true one, their being "invited to it by the pleasantness, fertility and plenty of the country," may satisfy us, that this extension will continue to proceed as long as there remains any pleasant fertile country within their reach. And if we even suppose them confin'd by the waters of the Mississipi westward, and by those of St. Laurence and the lakes to the northward, yet still we shall leave them room enough to increase even in the *sparse* manner of settling now practis'd there, till they amount to perhaps a hundred millions of souls. This must take some centuries to fulfil, and in the mean time, this nation must necessarily supply them with the manufactures they consume, because the new settlers will be employ'd in agriculture, and the new settlements will so continually draw off the spare hands from the old, that our present colonies will not, during the period we have mention'd find themselves in a condition to manufacture even for their own inhabitants, to any considerable degree, much less for those who are settling behind them. Thus our *trade* must, till that country becomes as fully peopled as England, that is for centuries to come, be continually increasing, and with it our naval power; because the ocean is between us and them, and our ships and seamen must increase as that trade increases.

. . .

Thus much as to the apprehension of our colonies becoming *useless* to us. I shall next consider the other supposition, that their growth may render them *dangerous*. Of this I own, I have not the least conception, when I consider that we have already fourteen separate governments on the maritime coast of the continent [Nova Scotia was the fourteenth], and if we extend our settlements shall probably have as many more behind them on the inland side. Those we now have, are not only under different governors, but have different forms of government, different laws, different interests, and some of them different religious persuasions and different manners. Their jealousy of each other is so great that however necessary an union of the colonies has long been, for their common defence and security against their enemies, and how sensible soever each colony has been of that necessity, yet they have never been able to effect such an union among themselves, nor even to agree in requesting the mother country to establish it for them. Nothing but the immediate command of the crown has been able to produce even the imperfect union but lately seen there, of the forces of some colonies. If they could not agree to unite for their defence against the French and Indians, who were perpetually harassing their settlements, burning their villages, and murdering their people; can it reasonably be supposed there is any danger of their uniting against their own nation, which protects and encourages them, with which they have so many connections and ties of blood, interest and affection, and which 'tis well known they all love much more than they love one another? In short, there are so many causes that must operate to prevent it, that I will venture to say, an union amongst them for such a purpose is not merely improbable, it is impossible; and if the union of the whole is impossible, the attempt of a part must be madness: as those colonies that did not join the rebellion, would join the mother country in suppressing it.

When I say such an union is impossible, I mean without the most grievous tyranny and oppression. People who have property in a country which they may lose, and privileges which they may endanger; are generally dispos'd to be quiet; and even to bear much, rather than hazard all. While the government is mild and just, while important civil and religious rights are secure, such subjects will be dutiful and obedient. The waves do not rise, but when the winds blow. . . .

But what is the prudent policy inculcated by the *remarker*, to obtain this end, security of dominion over our colonies: It is, to leave the French in Canada, to "*check*" their growth, for otherwise our people may "increase infinitely from all causes." We have already seen in what manner the French and their Indians *check the growth* of our colonies. 'Tis a modest word, this, *check*, for massacring men, women and children. The writer would, if he could, hide from himself as well as from the public, the horror arising from such a proposal, by couching it in general terms: 'tis no wonder he thought it a "subject not fit for discussion" in his letter, tho' he recommends it as "a point that should be the constant object of the minister's attention!" But if Canada is restored on this principle, will not Britain be guilty of all the blood to be shed, all the murders to be committed in order to check this dreaded growth of our own people? Will not this be telling the French in plain terms, that the horrid barbarities they perpetrate with their Indians on our colonists, are agreeable to us; and that they need not apprehend the resentment of a government with whose views they so happily concur? Will not the colonies view it in this light? Will they have reason to consider themselves any longer as subjects and children, when they find their cruel enemies halloo'd upon them by the country from whence they sprung, the government that owes them protection as it requires their obedience? Is not this the most likely means of driving them into the arms of the French, who can invite them by an offer of that security their own government chuses not to afford them? I would not be thought to insinuate that the *remarker* wants humanity. I know how little many good-natured persons are affected by the distresses of people at a distance and whom they do not know. There are even those, who, being present, can sympathize sincerely with the grief of a lady on the sudden death of her favourite bird, and yet can read of the sinking of a city in Syria with very little concern. If it be, after all, thought necessary to *check* the growth of our colonies, give me leave to propose a method less cruel. It is a method of which we have an example in scripture. The murder of husbands, of wives, of brothers, sisters, and children whose pleasing society has been for some time enjoyed, affects deeply the respective surviving relations: but grief for the death of a child just born is short and easily supported. The method I mean is that which was dictated by the Egyptian policy, when the "infinite increase" of the children of Israel was apprehended as dangerous to the state. Let an act of parliament, then be made, enjoining the colony mid-wives to stifle in the birth every third or fourth child. By this means you may keep the colonies to their present size. And if they were under the hard alternative of submitting to one or the other of these schemes for *checking* their growth, I dare answer for them, they would prefer the latter.

. . .

The objection I have often heard, that if we had Canada, we could not people it, without draining Britain of its inhabitants, is founded on igno-rance of the nature of population in new countries. When we first began to colonize in America, it was necessary to send people, and to send seed-corn; but it is not now necessary that we should furnish, for a new colony, either one or the other. The annual increment alone of our present colo-nies, without diminishing their numbers, or requiring a man from hence, is sufficient in ten years to fill Canada with double the number of English that it now has of French inhabitants. . . .

13 The vision challenged.

When Franklin wrote the Canada Pamphlet in 1760 he had been in England for three years as agent of the Pennsylvania Assembly. He returned to Philadelphia in 1762 but was back in England by the end of 1764 and remained there until 1775. During these years Franklin never lost sight of his larger vision, but he had to occupy himself more and more in trying simply to hold the empire together until it could be reorganized to fulfill its promise. His purpose in crossing the ocean had been to reduce and ultimately remove the authority of the Penn family over the government of Pennsylvania. In that mission he failed almost completely, despite his own ardent (and unwise) commitment to it. His first years in England were nevertheless a time of fulfillment for him. He loved the English. Writing to Polly Stevenson during his two-year stay back in Philadelphia he had to admit it: "Of all the enviable Things England has, I envy it most its People. Why should that petty Island, which compar'd to America is but like a stepping Stone in a Brook, scarce enough of it above Water to keep one's Shoes dry; why I say should that little Island, enjoy in almost every Neighbourhood, more sensible, virtuous and elegant Minds than we can collect in ranging 100 Leagues of our vast Forests."

Because of the fame his electrical experiments had brought him, Franklin had an entrée, from the time he arrived, to the circle of Britain's most elegant minds. He had already been elected to membership in the Royal Society, an honor reserved for the most distinguished contributors to scientific advancement. He had made friends by mail with a variety of important people: Peter Collinson, of course; John Fothergill, a leading London physician, who with Collinson arranged for the publication of Franklin's *Experiments and Observations on Electricity;* William Strahan, publisher of the *London Chronicle;* Richard Jackson, a London barrister famed for his "omniscience." And he rapidly made many more friends in high places, including the Scots jurist Lord Kames and Sir John Pringle, who became the queen's personal physician.

Franklin's social success may have given him an exaggerated view of his influence in the circles where policy was made. In 1762 the ministry had taken notice of him by appointing his son William royal governor of New Jersey. Britain had kept Canada, as Franklin advised, in the treaty that ended the Seven Years' War in 1763. But it was not actually his advice that tipped the balance in favor of Canada over the sugar islands, for the men who decided these things gave little attention to the public debate on the question. And while he could rejoice in William's preferment, he got nowhere in his effort to displace the Penn family. Moreover, he soon found himself on the losing end of a policy decision that threatened the future of the empire, as he saw it, far more than the Penns ever had.

In 1764 the king's ministry, led by George Grenville, persuaded Parliament to impose new taxes on American trade. These were faintly disguised as regulations. But Grenville let it be known that he had a direct tax, the Stamp Act, drawn up and ready to present to Parliament in 1765. Franklin joined with other colonial agents in a fruitless attempt to dissuade him. Franklin knew that Americans would regard a direct tax as an unprecedented violation of their right to be taxed solely by their own representatives. For his part Franklin was less concerned with rights on either side than he was with keeping the empire running smoothly until it could be made into the great political structure he envisaged. Without American representatives, Parliament was ill equipped to make wise decisions about America. When rumors of the coming tax measures reached him, his first reaction, as he told Collinson, was to think that Parliament would not do anything so foolish. When Parliament went ahead with the measures, he began at once to work to have them repealed or suspended, but he expected the Americans to buckle down and make the best of it until the members of Parliament came to their senses. He even accepted George Grenville's gesture of goodwill in letting him name Pennsylvania's collector of the obnoxious Stamp Tax.

Confounding Franklin's sanguine expectations, Americans were not prepared to make the best of it. In their colonial assemblies and an inter-colonial congress they passed resolutions denouncing the Stamp Act as a violation of their natural rights and their rights as British subjects. In towns and cities they took to the streets to threaten the men appointed to collect the tax, including Franklin's friend John Hughes, for whom Franklin had secured the appointment. By November, when the act was scheduled to take effect, all the appointed collectors, from New Hampshire to Georgia, had been forced to resign or agree not to exercise their powers under it.

With his eye on a larger future Franklin regretted the elevation of a misguided measure into a conflict over basic rights. But when he learned of the all but unanimous colonial resistance to taxation, he recognized it as a fact that would not go away and as a challenge to a Parliament whose members considered their authority unlimited. His task in the coming years would be to persuade the British that the authority of Parliament did not extend to America and to persuade Americans to avoid confrontations that would needlessly antagonize the British, in an attempt to avert a possibly fatal collision.

The Stamp Act was the first testing ground. In a conversation with Lord Dartmouth, which he reported to his son William, he offered a typically Franklinian solution: let the act die by not enforcing it. When a change in the ministry made repeal of the act a possibility, he opened a campaign in the London newspapers with his usual weapon of satire, proclaiming, "Peace is sought by war [*Pax quaeritur Bello*]." At the same time he worked behind the scenes for a change in British policy, much aided by his large circle of influential friends and allies. His friends in the House of Commons arranged for him to appear for an interview there, where his testimony helped to secure repeal of the act. The later publication of that testimony enhanced his reputation both in London and in the colonies as the voice of America. The few short passages reprinted below will show why: many of the questions were clearly planted by well-wishers to give Franklin the chance to make his most telling points.

To Peter Collinson, 1764

Dear Friend,   Philada. April 30. 1764

. . .

I suppose by this Time the Wisdom of your Parliament has determin'd in the Points you mention, of Trade, Duties, Troops and Fortifications in America. Our Opinions or Inclinations, if they had been known, would perhaps have weigh'd but little among you. We are in your Hands as Clay in the Hands of the Potter; and so in one more Particular than is generally consider'd: for as the Potter cannot waste or spoil his Clay without injuring himself; so I think there is scarce anything you can do that may be hurtful to us, but what will be as much or more so to you. This must be our chief Security; for Interest with you we have but little: The West Indians vastly outweigh us of the Northern Colonies. What we get above a Subsistence, we lay out with you for your Manufactures. Therefore what you get from us in Taxes you must lose in Trade. The Cat can yield but her Skin. And as you must have the whole Hide, if you first cut Thongs out of it, 'tis at your own Expence. The same in regard to our Trade with the foreign West India Islands: If you restrain it in any Degree, you restrain in the same Proportion our Power of making Remittances to you, and of course our Demand for your Goods; for you will not clothe us out of Charity, tho' to receive 100 per Cent for it, in Heaven. In time perhaps Mankind may be wise enough to let Trade take its own Course, find its own Channels, and regulate its own Proportions, &c. At present, most of the Edicts of Princes, Placaerts [Placets], Laws and Ordinances of Kingdoms and States, for that purpose, prove political Blunders. The Advantages they produce not being *general* for the Commonwealth; but *particular,* to private Persons or Bodies in the State who procur'd them, and *at the Expence of the rest of the People.* Does no body see, that if you confine us in America to your own Sugar Islands for that Commodity, it must raise the Price of it upon you in England? Just so much as the Price advances, so much is every Englishman tax'd to the West Indians. Apropos. Now we are on the Subject of Trade and Manufactures, let me tell you a Piece of News, that though it might displease a very respectable Body among you, the Button-makers, will be agreable to yourself as a Virtuoso [man of learning]; It is, that we have discover'd a Beach in a Bay several Miles round, the Pebbles of which are all in the Form of Buttons, whence it is called *Button-mold Bay;* where thousands of Tons may be had for fetching; and as the Sea washes down the slaty Cliff, more are continually manufacturing out of the Fragments by the Surge. I send you a Specimen of Coat, Wastecoat and Sleeve Buttons; just as Nature has turn'd them. But I think I must not mention the Place, lest some Englishman get a Patent for this *Button-mine,* as one did for the *Coal mine* at Louisburgh, and by neither suffering others to work it, nor working it himself, deprive us of the Advantage God and Nature seems to have intended us. As we have now got Buttons, 'tis something towards our Cloathing; and who knows but in time we may find out where to get Cloth? for as to our being always supply'd by you, 'tis a Folly to expect it. Only consider *the Rate of our Increase,* and tell me if you can increase your Wooll in that Proportion, and where, in your little Island you can feed the Sheep. Nature has put Bounds to your Abilities, tho' none to your Desires. Britain would, if she could, manufacture and trade for all the World; England for all Britain; London for all England; and every Londoner for all London. So selfish is the human Mind! But 'tis well there is One above that rules these Matters with a more equal Hand. He that is pleas'd to feed the Ravens, will undoubtedly take care to prevent a Monopoly of the Carrion. Adieu, my dear Friend, and believe me ever Yours most affectionately

B Franklin

To William Franklin, 1765

London, Novr. 9, 1765

Mr. [Grey] Cooper, Secretary of the Treasury, is our old Acquaintance, and expresses a hearty Friendship for us both. Enclosed I send you his Billet proposing to make me acquainted with Lord Rockingham [who succeeded George Grenville as first lord of the Treasury on July 10, 1765]. I dine with his Lordship To-morrow.

I had a long Audience on Wednesday with Lord Dartmouth [president of the Board of Trade]. He was highly recommended to me by Lords Grantham and Bessborough [the joint postmasters general], as a young Man of excellent Understanding and the most amiable Dispositions. They seem'd extremely intent on bringing us together. I had been to pay my Respects to his Lordship on his Appointment to preside at the Board of Trade; but during the Summer he has been much out of Town, so that I had not till now the Opportunity of conversing with him. I found him all they said of him. He even exceeded the Expectations they had raised in me. If he continues in that Department, I foresee much Happiness from it to American Affairs. He enquired kindly after you, and spoke of you handsomely.

I gave it him as my Opinion, that the general Execution of the Stamp Act would be impracticable without occasioning more Mischief than it was worth, by totally alienating the Affections of the Americans from this Country, and thereby lessening its Commerce. I therefore wish'd that Advantage might be taken of the Address [a petition from the Stamp Act Congress] expected over (if express'd, as I hop'd it would be, in humble and dutiful Terms) to suspend the Execution of the Act for a Term of Years, till the Colonies should be more clear of Debt, and better able to bear it, and then drop it on some other decent Pretence, without ever bringing the Question of Right to a Decision. And I strongly recommended either a thorough Union with America, or that Government here would proceed in the old Method of Requisition, by which I was confident more would be obtained in the Way of voluntary Grant, than could probably be got by compulsory Taxes laid by Parliament. That particular Colonies might at Times be backward, but at other Times, when in better Temper, they would make up for that Backwardness, so that on the whole it would be nearly equal. That to send Armies and Fleets to enforce the Act, would not, in my Opinion, answer any good End; That the Inhabitants would probably take every Method to encourage the Soldiers to desert, to which the high Price of Labour would contribute, and the Chance of being never apprehended in so extensive a Country, where the Want of Hands, as well as the Desire of wasting the Strength of an Army come to oppress, would encline every one to conceal Deserters, so that the Officers would probably soon be left alone. That Fleets might indeed easily obstruct their Trade, but withal must ruin great Part of the Trade of Britain; as the Properties of American and British or London Merchants were mix'd in the same Vessels, and no Remittances could be receiv'd here; besides the Danger, by mutual Violences, Excesses and Severities, of creating a deep-rooted Aversion between the two Countries, and laying the Foundation of a future total Separation. I added, that notwithstanding the present Discontents, there still remain'd so much Respect in America for this Country, that Wisdom would do more towards reducing Things to order, than all our Force; And that, if the Address expected from the Congress of the Colonies should be unhappily such as could not be made the Foundation of a Suspension of the Act, in that Case three or four wise and good Men, Personages of some Rank and Dignity, should be sent over to America, with a Royal Commission to enquire into Grievances, hear Complaints, learn the true State of Affairs, giving Expectations of Redress where they found the People really aggriev'd, and endeavouring to convince and reclaim them by Reason, where they found them in the Wrong. That such an Instance of the Considerateness, Moderation and Justice of this Country towards its remote Subjects would contribute more towards securing and perpetuating the Dominion, than all its Force, and be much cheaper. A great deal more I said on our American Affairs; too much to write. His Lordship heard all with great Attention and Patience. As to the Address expected from the Congress, he doubted some Difficulty would arise about receiving it, as it was an irregular Meeting, unauthoriz'd by any American Constitution. I said, I hoped Government here would not be too nice on that Head; That the Mode was indeed new, but to the People there it seem'd necessary, their separate Petitions last Year being rejected. And to refuse hearing Complaints and Redressing Grievances, from Punctilios about Form, had always an ill Effect, and gave great Handle to those turbulent factious Spirits who are ever ready to blow the Coals of Dissension. He thank'd me politely for the Visit, and desired to see me often.

It is true that Inconveniences may arise to Government here by a Repeal of the Act, as it will be deem'd a tacit giving up the Sovereignty of Parliament: And yet I think the Inconveniences of persisting much greater, as I have said above. The present Ministry are truely perplex'd how to act on the Occasion: as, if they relax, their Predecessors will reproach them with giving up the Honour, Dignity, and Power of this Nation. And yet even they, I am told, think they have carry'd Things too far; So that if it were indeed true that I had plann'd the Act (as you say it is reported with you) I believe we should soon hear some of them exculpating themselves by saying I had misled them. I need not tell you that I had not the least Concern in it. It was all cut and dry'd, and every Resolve fram'd at the Treasury ready for the House, before I arriv'd in England, or knew any thing of the Matter; so that if they had given me a Pension on that Account (as is said by some, I am told) it would have been very dishonest in me to accept of it.

. . .

Peace Is Sought by War, *1766*

To the Printer of the Public Advertiser.   Jan. 23, 1766.

Pax quaeritur Bello.

Sir,

The very important Controversy being next Tuesday to be finally determined between the Mother Country and their rebellious American Children, I shall think myself happy if I can furnish any Hints that may be of public Utility.

There are some Persons besides the Americans so amazingly stupid, as to distinguish in this Dispute between *Power* and *Right,* as tho' the former did not always imply the latter. The Right of Conquest invests the Conqueror with Authority to establish what Laws he pleases, however contrary to the Laws of Nature, and the common Rights of Mankind. Examine every Form of Government at this Day subsisting on the Face of the Globe, from the absolute Despotism of the Grand Sultan to the Democratic Government of the City of Geneva, and it will be found that the Exertion of Power in those Hands with whom it is lodged, however unconstitutional, is always justified. The Reign of the Stuarts might serve to exemplify this Observation. Happy it was for the Nation that, upon Trial, the superior Power was found to be in the People. The American Plea of *Right,* their Appeal to Magna Charta, must of course be set aside; and I make no Doubt but the Grand Council of the Nation will at all Hazards insist upon an absolute Submission to the Tax imposed upon them. But that they will comply without coercive Measures, is to me a Matter of very great Doubt: For when we consider, that these People, especially the more Northern Colonies, are the Descendants of your Pymms, Hampdens [John Pym and John Hampden, heroes of Parliament's resistance to Charles I], and others of the like Stamp, those outrageous Assertors of Civil and Religious Liberties; that they have been nursed up in the same Old English Principles; that a little more than a Century ago their Forefathers, many of them of Family and Fortune, left their native Land, and endured all the Distresses and Hardships which are the necessary Consequences of an Establishment in a new uncultivated Country, surrounded with a cruel Blood-thirsty Enemy, oftentimes severely pinched with Cold and Hunger; and all this to enjoy unmolested that Liberty which they thought was infringed: I say, however these People may be mistaken, they will not tamely give up what they call their natural, their constitutional Rights. Force must therefore be made use of.

Now in order to bring these People to a proper Temper, I have a Plan to propose, which I think cannot fail, and which will be entirely consistent with the Oeconomy at present so much in Vogue. It is so cheap a Way of going to work, that even Mr. G— G— [George Grenville], that great Oeconomist, could have no reasonable Objection to it.

Let Directions be given, that Two Thousand Highlanders be immediately raised, under proper Officers of their own. It ought to be no Objection, that they were in the Rebellion in Forty-five: If Roman Catholics, the better. The C—l [Colonel] at present in the P—ze [Portuguese] Service may be at their Head [probably a reference to Francis Mclean, an officer who had been sent to Portugal in 1762 to organize Portuguese defenses]. Transport them early in the Spring to Quebec: They with the Canadians, natural Enemies to our Colonists, who would voluntarily engage, might make a Body of Five or Six Thousand Men; and I doubt not, by artful Management, and the Value of two or three Thousand Pounds in Presents, with the Hopes of Plunder, as likewise a Gratuity for every Scalp, the Savages on the Frontiers might be engaged to join, at least they would make a Diversion, which could not fail of being useful. I could point out a very proper General [General James Murray, governor of Quebec] to command the Expedition; he is of a very sanguine Disposition, and has an inordinate Thirst for Fame, and besides has the Hearts of the Canadians. He might march from Canada, cross the Lakes, and fall upon these People without their expecting or being prepared for him, and with very little Difficulty over-run the whole Country.

The Business might be done without employing any of the Regular

Troops quartered in the Country, and I think it would be best they should remain neuter, as it is to be feared they would be rather backward in embruing their Hands in the Blood of their Brethren and Fellow Subjects.

I would propose, that all the Capitals of the several Provinces should be burnt to the Ground, and that they cut the Throats of all the Inhabitants, Men, Women, and Children, and scalp them, to serve as an Example; that all the Shipping should be destroyed, which will effectually prevent Smuggling, and save the Expence of Guarda Costas.

No Man in his Wits, after such terrible Military Execution, will refuse to purchase stamp'd Paper. If any one should hesitate, five or six Hundred Lashes in a cold frosty Morning would soon bring him to Reason.

If the Massacre should be objected to, as it would too much depopulate the Country, it may be replied, that the Interruption this Method would occasion to Commerce, would cause so many Bankruptcies, such Numbers of Manufacturers and Labourers would be unemployed, that, together with the Felons from our Gaols, we should soon be enabled to transport such Numbers to repeople the Colonies, as to make up for any Deficiency which Example made it Necessary to sacrifice for the Public Good. Great Britain might then reign over a loyal and submissive People, and be morally certain, that no Act of Parliament would ever after be disputed. Your's,   Pacificus.

Franklin's Examination Before the Committee of the House of Commons, 1766

The EXAMINATION of Doctor BENJAMIN FRANKLIN, before an August Assembly, relating to the Repeal of the STAMP-ACT, &c.

Q. What is your name, and place of abode?
A. Franklin, of Philadelphia.

. . .

Q. What was the temper of America towards Great-Britain before the year 1763?
A. The best in the world. They submitted willingly to the government of the Crown, and paid, in all their courts, obedience to acts of parliament.

Numerous as the people are in the several old provinces, they cost you nothing in forts, citadels, garrisons or armies, to keep them in subjection. They were governed by this country at the expence only of a little pen, ink and paper. They were led by a thread. They had not only a respect, but an affection, for Great-Britain, for its laws, its customs and manners, and even a fondness for its fashions, that greatly increased the commerce. Natives of Britain were always treated with particular regard; to be an Old England-man was, of itself, a character of some respect, and gave a kind of rank among us.

Q. And what is their temper now?

A. O, very much altered.

Q. Did you ever hear the authority of parliament to make laws for America questioned till lately?

A. The authority of parliament was allowed to be valid in all laws, except such as should lay internal taxes. It was never disputed in laying duties to regulate commerce.

Q. In what proportion hath population increased in America?

A. I think the inhabitants of all the provinces together, taken at a medium, double in about 25 years. But their demand for British manufactures increases much faster, as the consumption is not merely in proportion to their numbers, but grows with the growing abilities of the same numbers to pay for them. In 1723, the whole importation from Britain to Pennsylvania, was but about 15,000 Pounds Sterling; it is now near Half a Million.

Q. In what light did the people of America use to consider the parliament of Great-Britain?

A. They considered the parliament as the great bulwark and security of their liberties and privileges, and always spoke of it with the utmost respect and veneration. Arbitrary ministers, they thought, might possibly, at times, attempt to oppress them; but they relied on it, that the parliament, on application, would always give redress. They remembered, with gratitude, a strong instance of this, when a bill was brought into parliament, with a clause to make royal instructions laws in the Colonies, which the house of commons would not pass, and it was thrown out.

Q. And have they not still the same respect for parliament?

A. No; it is greatly lessened.

Q. To what causes is that owing?

A. To a concurrence of causes; the restraints lately laid on their trade, by which the bringing of foreign gold and silver into the Colonies was prevented; the prohibition of making paper money among themselves; and then demanding a new and heavy tax by stamps; taking away, at the same time, trials by juries, and refusing to receive and hear their humble petitions.

Q. Don't you think they would submit to the stamp-act, if it was modified, the obnoxious parts taken out, and the duty reduced to some particulars, of small moment?

A. No; they will never submit to it.

. . .

Q. Can any thing less than a military force carry the stamp-act into execution?

A. I do not see how a military force can be applied to that purpose.

Q. Why may it not?

A. Suppose a military force sent into America, they will find nobody in arms; what are they then to do? They cannot force a man to take stamps who chooses to do without them. They will not find a rebellion; they may indeed make one.

Q. If the act is not repealed, what do you think will be the consequences?

A. A total loss of the respect and affection the people of America bear to this country, and of all the commerce that depends on that respect and affection.

Q. How can the commerce be affected?

A. You will find, that if the act is not repealed, they will take very little of your manufactures in a short time.

Q. Is it in their power to do without them?

A. I think they may very well do without them.

Q. Is it their interest not to take them?

A. The goods they take from Britain are either necessaries, mere conveniences, or superfluities. The first, as cloth, &c. with a little industry they can make at home; the second they can do without, till they are able to provide them among themselves; and the last, which are much the greatest part, they will strike off immediately. They are mere articles of fashion, purchased and consumed, because the fashion in a respected country, but will now be detested and rejected. The people have already struck off, by general agreement, the use of all goods fashionable in mournings, and many thousand pounds worth are sent back as unsaleable.

Q. Is it their interest to make cloth at home?

A. I think they may at present get it cheaper from Britain, I mean of the same fineness and neatness of workmanship; but when one considers other circumstances, the restraints on their trade, and the difficulty of making remittances, it is their interest to make every thing.

Q. Suppose an act of internal regulations, connected with a tax, how would they receive it?

A. I think it would be objected to.

Q. Then no regulation with a tax would be submitted to?

A. Their opinion is, that when aids to the Crown are wanted, they are to be asked of the several assemblies, according to the old established usage, who will, as they always have done, grant them freely. And that their money ought not to be given away without their consent, by persons at a distance, unacquainted with their circumstances and abilities. The granting aids to the Crown, is the only means they have of recommending themselves to their sovereign, and they think it extremely hard and unjust, that a body of men, in which they have no representatives, should make a merit to itself of giving and granting what is not its own, but theirs, and deprive them of a right they esteem of the utmost value and importance, as it is the security of all their other rights.

. . .

Q. Are they acquainted with the declaration of rights? And do they know that, by that statute, money is not to be raised on the subject but by consent of parliament?

A. They are very well acquainted with it.

Q. How then can they think they have a right to levy money for the Crown, or for any other than local purposes?

A. They understand that clause to relate to subjects only within the realm; that no money can be levied on them for the Crown, but by consent of parliament. The Colonies are not supposed to be within the realm; they have assemblies of their own, which are their parliaments, and they are in that respect, in the same situation with Ireland. When money is to be raised for the Crown upon the subject in Ireland, or in the Colonies, the consent is given in the parliament of Ireland, or in the assemblies of the Colonies. They think the parliament of Great-Britain cannot properly give that consent till it has representatives from America; for the petition of right expressly says, it is to be by common consent in parliament, and the people of America have no representatives in parliament, to make a part of that common consent.

. . .

Q. Suppose the King should require the colonies to grant a revenue, and the parliament should be against their doing it, do they think they can grant a revenue to the King, without the consent of the parliament of G. Britain?

A. That is a deep question. As to my own opinion, I should think myself at liberty to do it, and should do it, if I liked the occasion.

Q. When money has been raised in the Colonies, upon requisitions, has it not been granted to the King?

A. Yes, always; but the requisitions have generally been for some service expressed, as to raise, clothe and pay troops, and not for money only.

. . .

14 The empire at risk.

With the Stamp Act repealed, Franklin had high hopes for the future of the empire. For the next nine years he clung to them even as they gradually eroded. These were some of the most active years of his public life, as he tried to persuade three different sets of people to do what was best; the Americans, the British people, and the British Parliament, each seemingly impervious to the views of the other two. After repeal, his first message to his countrymen was that they should recognize that Parliament had shown good sense in the end. Be patient and grateful, as he advised his Philadelphia business partner, David Hall.

With the two sides seemingly reconciled, now might be the moment for a sweeping institutional change that would keep Parliament better informed in the future. At the Albany Congress he had proposed an intercolonial congress operating in tandem with Parliament. When that was rejected by both sides, he thought of persuading Parliament to admit representatives from the colonies in a union like that which England had made with Scotland in 1707. He had proposed this in a letter to Governor Shirley of Massachusetts in 1754, which he now had printed in the *London Chronicle*. Franklin continued to toy with the idea for several years without much hope of its success, and in a letter to Lord Kames in 1767 (excerpted as "On the Disputes with America") he predicted trouble ahead, repeating what was now a warning about America's growth and Britain's limitations.

The trouble came in a new set of taxes on British exports to the colonies, the so-called Townshend duties of 1767. When the Americans responded with nonimportation agreements, Franklin's first reaction was that they would produce more anti-American feeling in England. But by early in 1769 he had decided that "nothing will bring a Change of Measures here but our unanimous Resolution to consume no more of their goods." It was apparent where American growth and British failure to recognize it were leading. In England he was doing his best to wake up the public and the government to the facts, in meetings with ministers and in pleas, polemics, and satires in the newspapers. One of his gentler pieces was a set of modern fables, printed in the *Public Advertiser.*

Nonimportation did help pressure Parliament to repeal the Townshend duties in 1770, but in an all too typical piece of folly Parliament insisted upon retaining the duty on one product, East India tea, to demonstrate its power over the colonies. By the end of the year three colonies besides Pennsylvania —Massachusetts, New Jersey, and Georgia—had made Franklin their agent, and from that time onward he advised them to stand firm against any Parliamentary pretensions to authority in the colonies. His letter to Samuel Cooper, a Boston minister active in politics, makes the point.

Franklin was still trying to laugh the English out of the policies that resulted six years later in the Declaration of Independence. In 1773 he dedicated to the secretary of state for the colonies a pamphlet he entitled "Rules by Which a Great Empire May Be Reduced to a Small One." In the same year he published one of his more plausible hoaxes. The English had justified their policies on the ground that Englishmen had settled North America a century and a half earlier, making the colonies subject to the mother country's regulation for all time. It was well known, or at least commonly believed, that England itself had been anciently settled by colonists from the German forests. In "An Edict by the King of Prussia," British readers could find applied to themselves restrictions identical to those they had placed on the American colonies with no sounder justification. Franklin gives the hoax further credibility by citing Prussia's assistance in England's most recent war with France, for which Prussia had "not yet received adequate compensation." The measures he depicts Prussia as imposing on England are taken, often word for word, from the Iron Act, the Woollen Act, the Hat Act, and other restrictions on colonial manufactures and commerce. The emptying of Prussian jails into England reflects Franklin's longstanding anger at the transportation of convicts. Even during his flush of good feeling after repeal of the Stamp Act, he had drafted a petition for repeal of the act for transporting felons to America. Though his friend, Richard Jackson, a member of Parliament, dissuaded him from presenting it, he had continued to denounce the practice in conversation and in print.

By the time he published "An Edict by the King of Prussia," in September 1773, Franklin knew that both sides in the contest were moving toward a showdown. The preceding May, Parliament had passed an act that precipitated the final confrontation. The Tea Act of 1773 sought to rescue the East India Company from bankruptcy by measures that enabled the company to sell tea cheaply in the colonies while retaining the tax. It seemed, as it may well have been, an attempt to buy or bribe colonial acquiescence to taxation. The colonists certainly regarded it as a snare and showed their resentment in the famous Boston Tea Party of December 1773, which was only the most violent of colonial responses.

When the British answered by closing the port of Boston and altering the Massachusetts government, the other colonies united in defying these "Intolerable Acts" by forming the Continental Congress of 1774. Franklin all but abandoned his wish for the union with Britain that he had so long advocated. By 1775 England could have retained the colonies, as he explained to Admiral Lord Richard Howe, but only by disclaiming any Parliamentary control over them. When Franklin's friend Joseph Galloway proposed to the Continental Congress a union patterned on Franklin's Albany Plan, Congress rejected it, and so, when he heard of the Galloway proposal, did Franklin. Arriving back in Philadelphia in May 1775, with war already under way in Massachusetts, Franklin wrote his epitaph for British-American union while reaffirming his prediction for America's destiny in a letter to David Hartley, his English friend, who would later take part in the peace negotiations of 1782.

To David Hall, 1766

Dear Mr. Hall,   London, Feb. 24. 1766

The House of Commons after a long Debate, which lasted from Friday 3 aClock to 2 the next Morning, came to a Resolution to *repeal* the Stamp Act, 275 to 167, the Minority being for *explaining and amending*. The Party of the late Ministry will give the Bill all the Obstruction and Delay possible, but there is reason now to believe it will pass both Houses which has long been rather doubtful. The present Ministry, who have been true Freinds to America in this Affair, purpose also to review the Acts of Trade, and give us every farther Relief that is reasonable. I hope therefore that Harmony between the two Countries will be restor'd, and all Mobs and Riots on our Side the Water totally cease. It will certainly become us on this Occasion to behave decently and respectfully with regard to Government here, that we may not disgrace our Friends who have in a manner engag'd their Credit for us on that head. We now see that tho' the Parliament may sometimes possibly thro' Misinformation be mislead to do a wrong Thing towards America, yet as soon as they are rightly inform'd, they will immediately rectify it, which ought to confirm our Veneration for that most august Body, and Confidence in its Justice and Equity. . . . I am, as ever, yours affectionately   B Franklin

To William Shirley, 1754

Sir,   Boston, Dec. 22, 1754

Since the conversation your Excellency was pleased to honour me with, on the subject of uniting the Colonies more intimately with Great Britain, by allowing them Representatives in Parliament, I have something further considered that matter, and am of opinion, that such an Union would be very acceptable to the Colonies, provided they had a reasonable number of Representatives allowed them; and that all the old Acts of Parliament restraining the trade or cramping the manufactures of the Colonies, be at the same time repealed, and the British Subjects on this side the water put, in those respects, on the same footing with those in Great Britain, 'till the new Parliament, representing the whole, shall think it for the interest of the whole to re-enact some or all of them: It is not that I imagine so many Representatives will be allowed the Colonies, as to have any great weight by their numbers; but I think there might be sufficient to occasion those laws to be better and more impartially considered, and perhaps to over-come the private interest of a petty corporation, or of any particular set of artificers or traders in England, who heretofore seem, in some instances, to have been more regarded than all the Colonies, or than was consistent with the general interest, or best national good. I think too, that the government of the Colonies by a Parliament, in which they are fairly represented, would be vastly more agreeable to the people, than the method lately attempted to be introduced by Royal Instructions [bills introduced in the House of Commons in 1744 and 1749 which would have made royal instructions to the governors binding in the colonies; neither measure passed], as well as more agreeable to the nature of an English Constitution, and to English Liberty; and that such laws as now seem to bear hard on the Colonies, would (when judged by such a Parliament for the best interest of the whole) be more chearfully submitted to, and more easily executed.

I should hope too, that by such an union, the people of Great Britain and the people of the Colonies would learn to consider themselves, not as belonging to different Communities with different Interests, but to one Community with one Interest, which I imagine would contribute to strengthen the whole and greatly lessen the danger of future separations.

It is, I suppose, agreed to be the general interest of any state, that it's people be numerous and rich; men enow to fight in its defence, and enow to pay sufficient taxes to defray the charge; for these circumstances tend to the security of the state, and its protection from foreign power: But it seems not of so much importance whether the fighting be done by John or Thomas, or the tax paid by William or Charles: The iron manufacture employs and enriches British Subjects, but is it of any importance to the state, whether the manufacturers live at Birmingham or Sheffield, or both, since they are still within its bounds, and their wealth and persons at its command? Could the Goodwin Sands [a line of shoals at the eastern entrance to the Strait of Dover] be laid dry by banks, and land equal to a large country thereby gain'd to England, and presently filled with English Inhabitants, would it be right to deprive such Inhabitants of the common privileges enjoyed by other Englishmen, the right of vending their produce in the same ports, or of making their own shoes, because a merchant, or a shoemaker, living on the old land, might fancy it more for his advantage to trade or make shoes for them? Would this be right, even if the land were gained at the expence of the state? And would it not seem less right, if the charge and labour of gaining the additional territory to Britain had been borne by the settlers themselves? And would not the hardship appear yet greater, if the people of the new country should be allowed no Representatives in the Parliament enacting such impositions? Now I look on the Colonies as so many Counties gained to Great Britain, and more advantageous to it than if they had been gained out of the sea around its coasts, and joined to its land: For being in different climates, they afford greater variety of produce, and materials for more manufactures; and being separated by the ocean, they increase much more its shipping and seamen; and since they are all included in the British Empire, which has only extended itself by their means; and the strength and wealth of the parts is the strength and wealth of the whole; what imports it to the general state, whether a merchant, a smith, or a hatter, grow rich in *Old* or *New* England? And if, through increase of people, two smiths are wanted for one employed before, why may not the *new* smith be allowed to live and thrive in the *new Country*, as well as the *old* one in the *Old?* In fine, why should the countenance of a state be *partially* afforded to its people, unless it be most in favour of those, who have most merit? and if there be any difference, those, who have most contributed to enlarge Britain's empire and commerce, encrease her strength, her wealth, and the numbers of her people, at the risque of their own lives and private fortunes in new and strange countries, methinks ought rather to expect some preference.

With the greatest respect and esteem I have the honour to be Your Excellency's most obedient and most humble servant.

On the Disputes with America, *1767*

I am fully persuaded . . . that a consolidating Union, by a fair and equal Representation of all the Parts of this Empire in Parliament, is the only firm Basis on which its political Grandeur and Stability can be founded. Ireland once wish'd it, but now rejects it. The Time has been when the Colonies might have been pleas'd with it; they are now indifferent about it; and, if 'tis much longer delay'd, they too will refuse it. But the *Pride* of *this People* cannot bear the Thoughts of it. Every Man in England seems to consider himself as a Piece of a Sovereign over America; seems to jostle himself into the Throne with the King, and talks of OUR *Subjects in the Colonies.* The

Parliament cannot well and wisely make Laws suited to the Colonies, without being properly and truly informed of their Circumstances, Abilities, Temper, &c. This it cannot be without Representatives from thence. And yet it is fond of this Power, and averse to the only Means of duly acquiring the necessary Knowledge for exercising it, which is desiring to be *omnipotent* without being *omniscient*.

. . .

It is a common but mistaken Notion here, that the Colonies were planted at the Expence of Parliament, and that therefore the Parliament has a Right to tax them, &c. The Truth is, they were planted at the Expence of private Adventurers, who went over there to settle with Leave of the King given by Charter. On receiving this Leave and these Charters, the Adventurers voluntarily engag'd to remain the King's Subjects, though in a foreign Country, a Country which had not been conquer'd by either King or Parliament, but was possess'd by a free People. When our Planters arriv'd, they purchas'd the Lands of the Natives without putting King or Parliament to any Expence. Parliament had no hand in their Settlement, was never so much as consulted about their Constitution, and took no kind of Notice of them till many Years after they were established; never attempted to meddle with the Government of them, till that Period when it destroy'd the Constitution of all Parts of the Empire, and usurp'd a Power over Scotland, Ireland, Lords and King. I except only the two modern Colonies, or rather Attempts to make Colonies, (for they succeed but poorly, and as yet hardly deserve the Name of Colonies) I mean Georgia and Nova Scotia, which have been hitherto little better than Parliamentary Jobbs. Thus all the Colonies acknowledge the King as their Sovereign: His Governors there represent his Person. Laws are made by their Assemblies or little Parliaments, with the Governor's Assent, subject still to the King's Pleasure to confirm or annul them. Suits arising in the Colonies, and Differences between Colony and Colony, are not brought before your Lords of Parliament, as those within the Realm, but determined by the King in Council. In this View they seem so many separate little States, subject to the same Prince. The Sovereignty of the King is therefore easily understood. But nothing is more common here than to talk of the *Sovereignty of Parliament*, and the *Sovereignty of this Nation* over the Colonies; a kind of Sovereignty the Idea of which is not so clear, nor does it clearly appear on what Foundations it is established. On the other hand it seems necessary for the common Good of the Empire, that a Power be lodg'd somewhere to regulate its general Commerce; this, as Things are at present circumstanc'd, can be plac'd no where so properly as in the Parliament of Great Britain; and therefore tho' that Power has in some Instances been executed with great partiality to Britain and Prejudice to the Colonies, they have nevertheless always submitted to it. Customhouses are established in all of them by Virtue of Laws made here, and the Duties constantly paid, except by a few Smugglers, such as are here and in all Countries; but internal Taxes laid on them by Parliament are and ever will be objected to, for the Reasons . . . mentioned [in his examination before the House of Commons].

Upon the whole, I have lived so great a Part of my Life in Britain, and have formed so many Friendships in it, that I love it and wish its Prosperity, and therefore wish to see that Union on which alone I think it can be secur'd and establish'd. As to America, the Advantages of such an Union to her are not so apparent. She may suffer at present under the arbitrary Power of this Country; she may suffer for a while in a Separation from it; but these are temporary Evils that she will outgrow. Scotland and Ireland are differently circumstanc'd. Confin'd by the Sea, they can scarcely increase in Numbers, Wealth and Strength so as to overbalance England. But America, an immense Territory, favour'd by Nature with all Advantages of Climate, Soil, great navigable Rivers and Lakes, &c. must become a great Country, populous and mighty; and will in a less time than is generally conceiv'd be able to shake off any Shackles that may be impos'd on her, and perhaps place them on the Imposers. In the mean time, every Act of Oppression will sour their Tempers, lessen greatly if not annihilate the Profits of [Britain's] Commerce with them, and hasten their final Revolt: For the Seeds of Liberty are universally sown there, and nothing can eradicate them. And yet there remains among that People so much Respect, Veneration and Affection for Britain, that, if cultivated prudently, with kind Usage and Tenderness for their Privileges, they might be easily govern'd still for Ages, without Force or any considerable Expence. But I do not see here a sufficient Quantity of the Wisdom that is necessary to produce such a Conduct, and I lament the Want of it.

New Fables, 1770

NEW FABLES, *humbly inscribed to the S[ecretar]y of St[at]e for the* American Department.

FABLE I.

A Herd of Cows had long afforded Plenty of Milk, Butter, and Cheese to an avaricious Farmer, who grudged them the Grass they subsisted on, and at length mowed it to make Money of the Hay, leaving them to *shift for Food* as they could, and yet still expected to *milk them* as before; but the Cows, offended with his Unreasonableness, resolved for the future *to suckle one another.*

FABLE II.

An Eagle, King of Birds, sailing on his Wings aloft over a Farmer's Yard, saw a Cat there basking in the Sun, *mistook it for a Rabbit,* stoop'd, seized it, and carried it up into the Air, *intending to prey on it.* The Cat turning, set her Claws into the Eagle's Breast; who, finding his Mistake, opened his Talons, and would have let her drop; but Puss, unwilling to fall so far, held faster; and the Eagle, to get rid of the Inconvenience, found it necessary to *set her down where he took her up.*

FABLE III.

A Lion's Whelp was put on board a Guinea Ship bound to America as a Present to a Friend in that Country: It was tame and harmless as a Kitten, and therefore not confined, but suffered to walk about the Ship at Pleasure. A stately, full-grown English Mastiff, belonging to the Captain, despising the Weakness of the young Lion, frequently took it's *Food* by Force, and often turned it out of it's Lodging Box, when he had a Mind to repose therein himself. The young Lion nevertheless grew daily in Size and Strength, and the Voyage being long, he became at last a more equal Match for the Mastiff; who continuing his Insults, received a stunning Blow from the Lion's Paw that fetched his Skin over his Ears, and deterred him from any future Contest with such growing Strength; regretting that he had not rather secured it's Friendship than provoked it's Enmity.

To Samuel Cooper, 1770

Dear Sir,   London, June 8. 1770

. . . The Repeal of the whole late Act would undoubtedly have been a prudent Measure, and I have reason to believe that Lord North was for it, but some of the other Ministers could not be brought to agree to it. So the Duty on Tea, with that obnoxious Preamble, remains to continue the Dispute. But I think the next Session will hardly pass over without repealing them; for the Parliament must finally comply with the Sense of the Nation. As to the Standing Army kept up among us in time of Peace, without the Consent of our Assemblies, I am clearly of Opinion that it is not agreable to the Constitution. Should the King by the Aid of his Parliaments in Ireland and the Colonies, raise an Army and bring it into England, quartering it here in time of Peace without the Consent of the Parliament of Great Britain, I am persuaded he would soon be told that he had no Right so to do, and the Nation would ring with Clamours against it. I own that I see no Difference in the Cases. And while we continue so many distinct and separate States, our having the same Head or Sovereign, the King, will not justify such an Invasion of the separate Right of each State to be consulted on the Establishment of whatever Force is proposed to be kept up within its Limits, and to give or refuse its Consent as shall appear most for the Public Good of that State. That the Colonies originally were constituted distinct States, and intended to be continued such, is clear to me from a thorough Consideration of their original Charters, and the whole Conduct of the Crown and Nation towards them until the Restoration. Since that Period, the Parliament here has usurp'd an Authority of making Laws for them, which before it had not. We have for some time submitted to that Usurpation, partly thro' Ignorance and Inattention, and partly from our Weakness and Inability to contend. I hope when our Rights are better understood here, we shall, by a prudent and proper Conduct be able to obtain from the Equity of this Nation a Restoration of them. And in the mean time I could wish that such Expressions as, *The supreme Authority of Parliament; The Subordinacy of our Assemblies to the Parliament* and the like (which in Reality mean nothing if our Assemblies with the King have a true Legislative Authority) I say, I could wish that such Expressions were no more seen in our publick Pieces. They are too strong for Compliment, and tend to confirm a Claim [of] Subjects in one Part of the King's Dominions to be Sovereigns over their Fellow-Subjects in another Part of his Dominions; when [in] truth they have no such Right, and their Claim is founded only on Usurpation, the several States having equal Rights and Liberties, and being only connected, as England and Scotland were before the Union, by having one common Sovereign, the King. This kind of Doctrine the Lords and Commons here would deem little less than Treason against what they think their Share of the Sovereignty over the Colonies. To me those Bodies seem to have been long encroaching on the Rights of their and our Sovereign, assuming too much of his Authority, and betraying his Interests. By our Constitutions he is, with [his] Plantation Parliaments, the sole Legislator of his American Subjects, and in that Capacity is and ought to be free to exercise his own Judgment unrestrain'd and unlimited by his Parliament here. And our Parliaments have Right to grant him Aids without the Consent of this Parliament, a Circumstance which, by the [way] begins to give it some Jealousy. Let us therefore hold fast [our] Loyalty to our King (who has the best Disposition towards us, and has a Family-Interest in our Prosperity) as that steady Loyalty is the most probable Means of securing us from the arbitrary Power of a corrupt Parliament, that does not like us, and conceives itself to have an Interest in keeping us down and fleecing us. If they should urge the *Inconvenience* of an Empire's being divided into so many separate States, and from thence conclude that we are not so divided; I would answer, that an Inconvenience proves nothing but itself. England and Scotland were once separate States, under the same King. The Inconvenience found in their being separate States, did not prove that the Parliament of England had a Right to govern Scotland. A formal Union was thought necessary, and England was an hundred Years soliciting it, before she could bring it about. If Great Britain now thinks such an Union necessary with us, let her propose her Terms, and we may consider of them. Were the general Sentiments of this Nation to be consulted in the Case, I should hope the Terms, whether practicable or not, would at least be equitable: for I think that except among those with whom the Spirit of Toryism prevails, the popular Inclination here is, to wish us well, and that we may preserve our Liberties.

I unbosom my self thus to you in Confidence of your Prudence, and wishing to have your Sentiments on the Subject in Return.

. . . With sincerest Esteem and Affection, I am, Dear Sir, Your most obedient and most humble Servant   B Franklin

An Edict by the King of Prussia, 1773

For the Public Advertiser.
The SUBJECT of the following Article of FOREIGN INTELLIGENCE being exceeding EXTRAORDINARY, is the Reason of its being separated from the usual Articles of *Foreign News.*

Dantzick, September 5.

WE have long wondered here at the Supineness of the English Nation, under the Prussian Impositions upon its Trade entering our Port. We did not till lately know the *Claims,* antient and modern, that hang over that Nation, and therefore could not suspect that it might submit to those Impositions from a Sense of *Duty,* or from Principles of *Equity.* The following *Edict,* just made public, may, if serious, throw some Light upon this Matter.

"FREDERICK, by the Grace of God, King of Prussia, &c. &c. &c. to all present and to come, HEALTH. The Peace now enjoyed throughout our Dominions, having afforded us Leisure to apply ourselves to the Regulation of Commerce, the Improvement of our Finances, and at the same Time the easing our *Domestic Subjects* in their Taxes: For these Causes, and other good Considerations us thereunto moving, We hereby make known, that after having deliberated these Affairs in our Council, present our dear Brothers, and other great Officers of the State, Members of the same, WE, of our certain Knowledge, full Power and Authority Royal, have made and isued this present Edict, viz.

WHEREAS it is well known to all the World, that the first German Settlements made in the Island of Britain, were by Colonies of People, Subjects to our renowned Ducal Ancestors, and drawn from *their* Dominions, under the Conduct of Hengist, Horsa, Hella, Uffa, Cerdicus, Ida, and others; and that the said Colonies have flourished under the Protection of our august House, for Ages past, have never been *emancipated* therefrom, and yet have hitherto yielded little Profit to the same. And whereas We Ourself have in the last War fought for and defended the said Colonies against the Power of France, and thereby enabled them to make Conquests from the said Power in America, for which we have not yet received adequate Compensation. And whereas it is just and expedient that a Revenue should be raised from the said Colonies in Britain towards our Indemnification; and that those who are Descendants of our antient Subjects, and thence still owe us due Obedience, should contribute to the replenishing of our Royal Coffers, as they must have done had their Ancestors remained in the Territories now to us appertaining: WE do therefore hereby ordain and command, That from and after the Date of these Presents, there shall be levied and paid to our Officers of the Customs, on all Goods, Wares and Merchandizes, and on all Grain and other Produce of the Earth exported from the said Island of Britain, and on all Goods of whatever Kind imported into the same, a *Duty* of *Four and an Half* per Cent. *ad Valorem,* for the Use of us and our Successors. And that the said Duty may more effectually be collected, We do hereby ordain, that all Ships or Vessels bound from Great Britain to any other Part of the World, or from any other Part of the World to Great Britain, shall in their respective Voyages touch at our Port of KONINGSBERG, there to be unladen, searched, and charged with the said Duties.

AND WHEREAS there have been from Time to Time discovered in the said Island of Great Britain by our Colonists there, many Mines or Beds of Iron Stone; and sundry Subjects of our antient Dominion, skilful in converting the said Stone into Metal, have in Times past transported themselves thither, carrying with them and communicating that Art; and the Inhabitants of the said Island, *presuming* that they had a natural Right to make the best Use they could of the natural Productions of their Country for their own Benefit, have not only built Furnaces for smelting the said Stone into Iron, but have erected Plating Forges, Slitting Mills, and Steel Furnaces, for the more convenient manufacturing of the same, thereby endangering a Diminution of the said Manufacture in our antient Dominion. WE *do therefore* hereby farther ordain, that from and after the Date hereof, no Mill or other Engine for Slitting or Rolling of Iron, or any Plating Forge to work with a Tilt-Hammer, or any Furnace for making

Steel, shall be erected or continued in the said Island of Great Britain: And the Lord Lieutenant of every County in the said Island is hereby commanded, on Information of any such Erection within his County, to order and by Force to cause the same to be abated and destroyed, as he shall answer the Neglect thereof to Us at his Peril. But We are nevertheless graciously pleased to permit the Inhabitants of the said Island to transport their Iron into Prussia, there to be manufactured, and to them returned, they paying our Prussian Subjects for the Workmanship, with all the Costs of Commission, Freight and Risque coming and returning, any Thing herein contained to the contrary notwithstanding.

WE do not however think fit to extend this our Indulgence to the Article of *Wool*, but meaning to encourage not only the manufacturing of woollen Cloth, but also the raising of Wool in our antient Dominions, and to prevent *both*, as much as may be, in our said Island, We do hereby absolutely forbid the Transportation of Wool from thence even to the Mother Country Prussia; and that those Islanders may be farther and more effectually restrained in making any Advantage of their own Wool in the Way of Manufacture, We command that none shall be carried *out of one County into another*, nor shall any Worsted-Bay, or Woollen-Yarn, Cloth, Says, Bays, Kerseys, Serges, Frizes, Druggets, Cloth-Serges, Shalloons, or any other Drapery Stuffs, or Woollen Manufactures whatsoever, made up or mixt with Wool in any of the said Counties, be carried into any other County, or be Water-borne even across the smallest River or Creek, on Penalty of Forfeiture of the same, together with the Boats, Carriages, Horses, &c. that shall be employed in removing them. *Nevertheless* Our loving Subjects there are hereby permitted, (if they think proper) to use all their Wool as *Manure for the Improvement of their Lands.*

AND WHEREAS the Art and Mystery of making *Hats* hath arrived at great Perfection in Prussia, and the making of Hats by our remote Subjects ought to be as much as possible restrained. And forasmuch as the Islanders before-mentioned, being in Possession of Wool, Beaver, and other Furs, have *presumptuously* conceived they had a Right to make some Advantage thereof, by manufacturing the same into Hats, to the Prejudice of our domestic Manufacture, WE do therefore hereby strictly command and ordain, that no Hats or Felts whatsoever, dyed or undyed, finished or unfinished, shall be loaden or put into or upon any Vessel, Cart, Carriage or Horse, to be transported or conveyed *out of one County* in the said Island *into another County,* or to *any other Place whatsoever,* by any Person or Persons whatsoever, on Pain of forfeiting the same, with a Penalty of *Five Hundred Pounds* Sterling for every Offence. Nor shall any Hat-maker in any of the said Counties employ more than two Apprentices, on Penalty of *Five Pounds* Sterling per Month: We intending hereby that such Hat-makers, being so restrained both in the Production and Sale of their Commodity, may find no Advantage in continuing their Business. But lest the said Islanders should suffer Inconveniency by the Want of Hats, We are farther graciously pleased to permit them to send their Beaver Furs to Prussia; and We also permit Hats made thereof to be exported from Prussia to Britain, the People thus favoured to pay all Costs and Charges of Manufacturing, Interest, Commission to Our Merchants, Insurance and Freight going and returning, as in the Case of Iron.

And lastly, Being willing farther to favour Our said Colonies in Britain, We do hereby also ordain and command, that all the Thieves, Highway and Street-Robbers, House-breakers, Forgerers, Murderers, So[domi]tes, and Villains of every Denomination, who have forfeited their Lives to the Law in Prussia, but whom We, in Our great Clemency, do not think fit here to hang, shall be emptied out of our Gaols into the said Island of Great Britain *for the* BETTER PEOPLING *of that Country.*

We flatter Ourselves that these Our Royal Regulations and Commands will be thought *just* and *reasonable* by Our much-favoured Colonists in England, the said Regulations being copied from their own Statutes of 10 and 11 Will. III. C. 10, 5 Geo. II. C. 22, 23 Geo. II. C. 29, 4 Geo. I. C. 11, and from other equitable Laws made by their Parliaments, or from Instructions given by their Princes, or from Resolutions of both Houses entered into for the GOOD *Government* of their own Colonies in Ireland and America.

And all Persons in the said Island are hereby cautioned not to oppose in any wise the Execution of this Our Edict, or any Part thereof, such Opposition being HIGH TREASON, of which all who are *suspected* shall be transported in Fetters from Britain to Prussia, there to be tried and executed according to the *Prussian Law.*

Such is our Pleasure.

Given at Potsdam this twenty-fifth Day of the Month of August, One
Thousand Seven Hundred and Seventy-three, and in the Thirty-third
year of our Reign.

By the KING in his Council   RECHTMAESSIG, *Secr.*"

Some take this Edict to be merely one of the King's *Jeux d'Esprit:* Others
suppose it serious, and that he means a Quarrel with England: But all here
think the Assertion it concludes with, "that these Regulations are copied
from Acts of the English Parliament respecting their Colonies," a very
injurious one: it being impossible to believe, that a People distinguish'd for
their *Love of Liberty,* a Nation so *wise,* so *liberal in its Sentiments,* so *just and
equitable* towards its *Neighbours,* should, from mean and *injudicious* Views
of *petty immediate Profit,* treat *its own Children* in a Manner so *arbitrary* and
TYRANNICAL!

To Joseph Galloway, *1775*

Dear Friend,   London, Feb. 25. 1775

In my last ... I mention'd to you my showing your Plan of Union to Lords
Chatham [William Pitt] and Camden [the Lord Chancellor]. I now hear that
you had sent it to Lord Dartmouth [president of the Board of Trade]. Lord
Gower [president of the Privy Council] I believe alluded to it, when in the
House he censur'd the Congress severely as first resolving to receive a Plan
for Uniting the Colonies to the Mother Country, and afterwards rejecting it,
and ordering their first Resolution to be eras'd out of their Minutes. ...

I have not heard what Objections were made to the Plan in the Congress,
nor would I make more than this one, that when I consider the extream
Corruption prevalent among all Orders of Men in this old rotten State, and
the glorious publick Virtue so predominant in our rising Country, I cannot
but apprehend more Mischief than Benefit from a closer Union. I fear They
will drag us after them in all the plundering Wars their desperate Circumstances, Injustice and Rapacity, may prompt them to undertake; and their
wide-wasting Prodigality and Profusion a Gulph that will swallow up
every Aid we may distress ourselves to afford them. Here Numberless and
needless Places, enormous Salaries, Pensions, Perquisites, Bribes, ground-

less Quarrels, foolish Expeditions, false Accompts or no Accompts, Contracts and Jobbs devour all Revenue, and produce continual Necessity in the Midst of natural Plenty. I apprehend therefore that To unite us intimately, will only be to corrupt and poison us also. It seems like Mezentius's coupling and binding together the dead and the living,

> Tormenti genus! et sanie taboque fluentis
> Complexu in misero, longa sic morte necabat.
> ["Truly torture: as they floated in the poisonous, putrid blood in vile
> embrace, he slew them with a lingering death." Vergil, *Aeneid*, 8: 487–
> 88. Mezentius or Medzentius was a mythological Etruscan king.]

However I would try any thing, and bear any thing that can be borne with Safety to our just Liberties rather than engage in a War with such near Relations, unless compelled to it by dire Necessity in our own Defence.

But should that Plan be again brought forward, I imagine that before establishing the Union, it would be necessary to agree on the following preliminary Articles.

1. The Declaratory Act of Parliament to be repeal'd.

2. All Acts of Parliament or Parts of Acts, laying Duties on the Colonies, to be repeal'd.

3. All Acts of Parliament altering the Charters or Constitutions or Laws, of any Colony to be repeal'd.

4. All Acts of Parliament restraining Manufactures in the Colonies, to be repeal'd.

5. Those Parts of the Navigation Acts, which are for the Good of the whole Empire, such as require that Ships in the Trade should be British or Plantation built, and navigated by ¾ British Subjects; with the Duties necessary for regulating Commerce to be re-enacted by both Parliaments.

6. Then to induce the Americans to see the regulating Acts faithfully executed, it would be well to give the Duties collected in each Colony to the Treasury of that Colony, and let the Governor and Assembly appoint the Officers to collect them, and proportion their Salaries. Thus the Business will be cheaper and better done, and the Misunderstandings between the two Countries now created and fomented by the unprincipled Wretches generally appointed from England, be entirely prevented.

These are hasty Thoughts, submitted to your Consideration.

You will see the new Proposal of Lord North made on Monday last, which I have sent to the Committee [a motion in Parliament to forbear taxing any colony that would tax itself in an unspecified amount, subject to parliamentary approval. The colonial assemblies all treated it with the same contempt that Franklin expressed here.]. Those in Administration who are for violent Measures, are said to dislike it. The others rely upon it as a means of *dividing* and by that means subduing us. But I cannot conceive that any Colony will undertake to grant a Revenue, to a Government that holds a Sword over their Heads, with a Threat to strike the moment they cease to give or do not give so much as it is pleas'd to expect. In such a Situation, where is the Right of giving our own Property freely? or the Right to judge of our own Ability to give? It seems to me the Language of a Highwayman, who with a Pistol in your Face says, Give me your Purse, and then I will not put my Hand into your Pocket. But give me all your Money or I'll shoot you thro' the Head. With great and sincere Esteem, I am ever, my dear Friend Your most obedient and most humble Servant B F.

To David Hartley, 1775

Philadelphia, Oct. 3, 1775.

I wish as ardently as you can do for peace, and should rejoice exceedingly in co-operating with you to that end. But every ship from Britain brings some intelligence of new measures that tend more and more to exasperate; and it seems to me that until you have found by dear experience the reducing us by force impracticable, you will think of nothing fair and reasonable. We have as yet resolved only on defensive measures. If you would recall your forces and stay at home, we should meditate nothing to injure you. A little time so given for cooling on both sides would have excellent effects. But you will goad and provoke us. You despise us too much; and you are insensible of the Italian adage, that *there is no little enemy.* I am persuaded the body of the British people are our friends; but they are changeable, and by your lying Gazettes may soon be made our enemies. Our respect for them will proportionally diminish; and I see clearly we are on the high road to mutual enmity, hatred, and detestation.

A separation will of course be inevitable. 'Tis a million of pities so fair a plan as we have hitherto been engaged in for increasing strength and empire with *public felicity*, should be destroyed by the mangling hands of a few blundering ministers. It will not be destroyed: God will protect and prosper it: You will only exclude yourselves from any share in it. We hear that more ships and troops are coming out. We know you may do us a great deal of mischief, but we are determined to bear it patiently as long as we can; but if you flatter yourselves with beating us into submission, you know neither the people nor the *country.* . . .

PART IV War, peace, and humanity.

When Franklin left England for the last time, in 1775, he had fifteen of the busiest years of his life ahead of him: organizing the war that had already started, getting help from France to sustain a country that could not yet sustain itself, negotiating the treaty that put an end to British interference. Interference was what he had been resisting since 1764, interference with Americans in the exercise of the autonomy within the empire that they had previously enjoyed. Until 1775 he would have been willing to settle for the same degree of autonomy, but he had long been convinced that American growth would ultimately require a far greater freedom and exercise of power. British intransigence settled the question for him: by 1776 he knew that Americans could not realize their potential within the British Empire. He now engaged himself with an energy beyond his years in the immediate tasks, military and diplomatic, of winning independence against tremendous odds.

Franklin's dealings with George Washington on a committee to organize the Continental Army left him in no doubt that the military was in good hands. His happy relations with the general were in stark contrast to the difficulties and exasperations of dealing with his American colleagues in diplomacy. Arriving in Paris to negotiate for loans and other assistance, he was soon embroiled in sorting out the suspicions and rivalries of a delegation rife with conflict. But the short-sightedness of those he had to work with did not blur his vision of what his country could become. The grandeur of the vision is apparent in his negotiating propositions for peace with Britain. And he expressed his ideas about what "human wisdom" might invent for America in proposals for structuring society and government, proposals that showed more confidence in ordinary human beings than other American leaders shared. In the selections that follow, from his last, highly productive years, his comfort with common people translates into a belief in democracy, or perhaps something like socialism. He was the oldest of the founding fathers. Was he in everything but years the youngest?

15 Independence.

Franklin came ashore in Philadelphia on May 5, 1775. Sixteen days earlier, while he was still at sea, war with England had begun at Lexington and Concord. On his arrival the Pennsylvania Assembly immediately elected him to the Second Continental Congress, which met on May 10. For the next eighteen months, until Congress sent him to France, he was immersed in its activities. It would be more than a year before his colleagues were ready to vote for independence; Franklin himself was probably ready for it by the time he left England. He continued to hope for reconciliation, but only on terms that he never expected the British ministry to accept. And he was willing to wait for his colleagues to catch up, sustained by his confidence in his country's growing strength and future greatness.

Congress made use of his talents and experience in many ways: in organizing the Continental Army, in appealing to the Canadians to join the cause (involving a fruitless overland journey to Quebec that would have exhausted a much younger man), and finally in going to France for men and money. But the record of what he had to say to his countrymen in the year and a half he spent with them is not large. We know that he sat on the committee that drafted the Declaration of Independence, but of course it was Thomas Jefferson who wrote most of it. Franklin's principal contribution may have been to change Jefferson's "We hold these truths to be sacred and undeniable" to "We hold these truths to be self-evident," a by no means trivial improvement. But we learn what he was thinking in this period mainly from letters to old friends in England who had supported his efforts to prevent the ministry's alienation of the Americans. In a letter to Jonathan Shipley, who had published a forceful pamphlet against ministerial policies, Franklin summed up what had happened in his first two months at home. He never despaired of America's ultimate triumph, as he told another friend, Joseph Priestley.

Before Franklin left England, Lord Richard Howe, hoping to avert the war that both of them expected, had engaged him in unofficial discussions under the guise of social calls on Howe's sister. Franklin had no authority to negotiate but nevertheless suggested the terms he thought Americans might accept. Howe carried them to the ministry and brought back the ministry's blunt rejection. A few days after Congress declared independence, Admiral Lord Howe arrived off Staten Island in command of a large fleet. His brother, General Sir William Howe, had already landed nearly 24,000 British troops there in June. Admiral Howe was still reluctant to force the issue to a state of open war. From his flagship he dispatched a letter to Franklin with what he must have known was a futile offer of pardon to penitent rebels. Franklin's unrepentant reply is one of the most eloquent statements he ever penned, and it reveals the depth of his understanding of human conflicts: victims may forgive and forget an injury, but they can never be forgiven by those who have injured them.

In spite of these developments Franklin struggled to devise a peaceful settlement on terms that would fulfill his original vision of empire. Sometime before departing on his mission to France, he wrote a new proposal for reconciliation ("Sketch of Propositions for a Peace"), but again there is no evidence that he ever presented it. Nevertheless, it gives us a hint of his deep reluctance to settle differences by war, anticipating the view he later expressed that war was a costly and wasteful business whose purposes could always be achieved at less cost by a proper use of money. Like other Americans before 1776, Franklin called the conflict a "ministerial war," and he may have been thinking that the king's ministers, however impervious to reason, were perfectly comfortable in a culture that centered on bribery and jobbery, with money changing hands to influence political outcomes.

Franklin had no doubt of American victory in the field, though he expected the war to last longer than his lifetime. He did not want his country to seek assistance from France, however willing France might be to grant it. He evidently expressed this view in Congress, but again the records are silent about it. We know about his reluctance only from a passage in a letter to Arthur Lee of March 21, 1777, in which he wrote, "I have never yet changed the Opinion I gave in Congress, that a Virgin State should preserve the Virgin Character, and not go about suitering for Alliances, but wait with decent dignity for the applications of others. I was over-ruld, perhaps for the best." He was not only overruled but sent on the mission that he did not approve, to solicit men, money, and arms from France. He left Philadelphia on October 27, 1776, and landed in France on December 3.

To Jonathan Shipley, 1775

Philada July 7. 1775

I received with great Pleasure my dear Friends very kind Letter of April 19, as it informed me of his Welfare, and that of the amiable Family in Jermyn Street. I am much obliged by the Information of what pass'd in Parliament after my departure; in return I will endeavor to give you a short Sketch of the State of Affairs here.

I found at my arrival all America from one End of the 12 united Provinces [Georgia did not become the thirteenth until July 20] to the other, busily employed in learning the Use of Arms. The Attack upon the Country People near Boston by the Army had rous'd every Body, and exasperated the whole Continent; The Tradesmen of this City, were in the Field twice a day, at 5 in the Morning, and Six in the Afternoon, disciplining with the utmost Diligence, all being Volunteers. We have now three Battalions, a Troop of Light Horse, and a Company of Artillery, who have made surprizing Progress. The same Spirit appears every where and the Unanimity is amazing.

The day after my Arrival, I was unanimously chosen by our Assembly, then sitting, an additional Delegate to the Congress, which met the next Week. The numerous Visits of old Friends, and the publick Business has since devoured all my time: for We meet at nine in the Morning, and often sit 'till four. I am also upon a Committee of Safety appointed by the Assembly, which meets at Six, and sits 'til near nine. The Members attend closely without being bribed to it, by either Salary, Place or Pension, or the hopes of any; which I mention for your Reflection on the difference, between a new virtuous People, who have publick Spirit, and an old corrupt one, who have not so much as an Idea that such a thing exists in Nature. There has not been a dissenting Voice among us in any Resolution for Defence, and our Army which is already formed, will soon consist of above 20,000 Men.

You will have heard before this reaches you of the Defeat the Ministerial Troops met with in their first *Sortie* [Lexington and Concord]; the several small Advantages we have since had of them [the capture in May of Ticonderoga, Crown Point, and St. Johns], and the more considerable Affair of the 17th. [Bunker Hill] when after two severe Repulses, they carry'd the unfinished Trenches of the Post we had just taken on a Hill near Charlestown. They suffered greatly however, and I believe are convinc'd by this time, that they have Men to deal with, tho' unexperienced, and not yet well arm'd. In their way to this Action, without the least Necessity, they barbarously plundered and burnt a fine, undefended Town, opposite to Boston, called Charlestown, consisting of about 400 Houses, many of them elegantly built; some sick, aged, and decrepit poor Persons, who could not be carried off in time perish'd in the Flames. In all our Wars, from our first settlement in America, to the present time, we never received so much damage from the Indian *Savages*, as in this one day from these. Perhaps Ministers may think this a Means of disposing us to Reconciliation. I feel and see every where the Reverse. Most of the little Property I have, consists of Houses in the Seaport Towns, which I suppose may all soon be destroyed in the same way, and yet I think I am not half so reconcileable now, as I was a Month ago.

The Congress will send one more Petition to the King, which I suppose will be treated as the former was, and therefore will probably be the last; for tho' this may afford Britain one chance more of recovering our Affections and retaining the Connection, I think she has neither Temper nor Wisdom enough to seize the Golden Opportunity. When I look forward to the Consequences, I see an End to all Commerce between us: on our Sea Coasts She may hold some fortified Places as the Spaniards do on the Coast of Africa, but can penetrate as little into the Country. A very numerous

Fleet extending 1500 Miles at an immense Expense may prevent other Nations trading with us: but as we have or may have within ourselves every thing necessary to the Comfort of Life, and generally import only Luxuries and Superfluities, her preventing our doing that, will in some Respects contribute to our Prosperity. By the present Stoppage of our Trade we save between four and five Millions per Annum which will do something towards the Expence of the War. What *she* will get by it, I must leave to be computed by her own political Arithmeticians. These are some of my present Ideas which I throw out to you in the Freedom of Friendship. Perhaps I am too sanguine in my opinion of our Abilities for the Defence of our Country after we shall have given up our Seaports to Destruction: but a little time will shew.

General Gage we understand enter'd into a Treaty with the Inhabitants of Boston, whom he had confin'd by his Works, in which Treaty it was agreed that if they delivered their Arms to the Select Men, their own Magistrates, they were to be permitted to go out with their *Effects*. As soon as they had so delivered their Arms, he seiz'd them, and then cavil'd about the meaning of the word *Effects* which he said was only wearing Apparel and Household Furniture, and not Merchandize or Shop Goods which he therefore detains: And the continual Injuries and Insults they met with from the Soldiery, made them glad to get out by relinquishing all that kind of Property. How much those People have suffered, and are now suffering rather than submit to what they think unconstitutional Acts of Parliament is really amazing. Two or three Letters I send you inclosed may give you some, tho' a faint Idea of it. Gage's Perfidy has now made him universally detested. When I consider that all this Mischief is done my Country, by Englishmen and Protestant Christians, of a Nation among whom I have so many personal Friends, I am ashamed to feel any Consolation in a prospect of Revenge; I chuse to draw it rather from a Confidence that we shall sooner or later obtain Reparation; I have proposed therefore to our People that they keep just Accounts and never resume the Commerce or the Union, 'till Satisfaction is made. If it is refused for 20 Years, I think we shall then be able to take it with Interest.

Your excellent Advice was, that if we must have a War, let it be carried on as between Nations who had once been Friends, and wish to be so again.

In this ministerial War against us, all Europe is conjur'd not to sell us Arms or Amunition, that we may be found defenceless, and more easily murdered. The humane Sir W: Draper, who had been hospitably entertain'd in every one of our Colonies, proposes, in his Papers call'd the Traveller [*Thoughts of a Traveller upon Our American Disputes* (1774)] to excite the Domestic Slaves, you have sold us, to cut their Master's Throats. Dr. [Samuel] Johnson a Court Pensioner, in his *Taxation no Tyranny* adopts and recommends that Measure, together with another of hiring the Indian savages to assassinate our Planters in the Back-Settlements. They are the poorest and most innocent of all People; and the Indian manner is to murder and scalp Men, Women and Children. His Book I heard applauded by Lord Sandwich [First Lord of the Admiralty, in charge of the Royal Navy] in Parliament, and all the ministerial People recommended it. Lord Dunmore and Governor Martin [governors, respectively, of Virginia and North Carolina], have already, we are told, taken some Steps towards carrying one part of the Project into Execution, by exciting an Insurrection among the Blacks. And Governor Carleton [governor of Canada], we have certain Accounts, has been very industrious in engaging the Indians to begin their horrid Work. This is making War like Nations who never had been Friends, and never wish to be such while the World stands. You see I am warm: and if a Temper naturally cool and phlegmatic can, in old age, which often cools the warmest, be thus heated, you will judge by that of the general Temper here, which is now little short of Madness. We have however as yet ask'd no foreign Power to assist us, nor made any Offer of our Commerce to other Nations for their Friendship. What another year's Persecution may drive us to, is yet uncertain. I drop this disagreeable Subject; and will take up one, that I know must afford you and the good Family, as my Friends, some Pleasure. It is the State of my own Family, which I found in good Health; my Children affectionately dutifull and attentive to every thing that can be agreeable to me; with three very promising Grandsons, in whom I take great Delight. So that were it not for our publick Troubles, and the being absent from so many that I love in England, my present Felicity would be as perfect, as in this World one could well expect it. I enjoy however, what there is of it while it lasts, mindfull at the same time that its Continuance is like other earthly Goods, uncertain. Adieu my dear Friend, and believe me ever, with sincere and great Esteem Yours most Affectionately   B Franklin

To Joseph Priestley, *1775*

Dear Sir,   Philadelphia, 3d Octob. 1775.

I am to set out to-morrow for [Washington's] camp, and having but just heard of this opportunity, can only write a line to say that I am well and hearty. Tell our dear good friend . . . , [Richard Price, a prominent nonconformist clergyman who favored the American cause] who sometimes has his doubts and despondencies about our firmness, that America is determined and unanimous; a very few tories and placemen excepted, who will probably soon export themselves. Britain, at the expence of three millions, has killed 150 Yankies this campaign, which is £20,000 a head; and at Bunker's Hill she gained a mile of ground, half of which she lost again by our taking post on Ploughed Hill. During the same time 60,000 children have been born in America. From these *data* his mathematical head will easily calculate the time and expence necessary to kill us all, and conquer our whole territory. My sincere respects to . . . , and to the club of honest whigs at. . . . [the London Coffeehouse] Adieu. I am ever Yours most affectionately,   B. F.

To Admiral Lord Howe, *1776*

My Lord,   Philada. July 20th. 1776.

I received safe the Letters your Lordship so kindly forwarded to me, and beg you to accept my Thanks.

The Official Dispatches to which you refer me, contain nothing more than what we had seen in the Act of Parliament, viz. Offers of Pardon upon Submission; which I was sorry to find, as it must give your Lordship Pain to be sent so far on so hopeless a Business.

Directing Pardons to be offered the Colonies, who are the very Parties injured, expresses indeed that Opinion of our Ignorance, Baseness, and Insensibility which your uninform'd and proud Nation has long been pleased to entertain of us; but it can have no other Effect than that of increasing our

Resentment. It is impossible we should think of Submission to a Government, that has with the most wanton Barbarity and Cruelty, burnt our defenceless Towns in the midst of Winter, excited the Savages to massacre our Farmers, and our Slaves to murder their Masters, and is even now bringing foreign Mercenaries to deluge our Settlements with Blood. These atrocious Injuries have extinguished every remaining Spark of Affection for that Parent Country we once held so dear: But were it possible for *us* to forget and forgive them, it is not possible for *you* (I mean the British Nation) to forgive the People you have so heavily injured; you can never confide again in those as Fellow Subjects, and permit them to enjoy equal Freedom, to whom you know you have given such just Cause of lasting Enmity. And this must impel you, were we again under your Government, to endeavour the breaking our Spirit by the severest Tyranny, and obstructing by every means in your Power our growing Strength and Prosperity.

But your Lordship mentions "the Kings paternal Solicitude for promoting the Establishment of lasting *Peace* and Union with the Colonies." If by *Peace* is here meant, a Peace to be entered into between Britain and America as distinct States now at War, and his Majesty has given your Lordship Powers to treat with us of such a Peace, I may venture to say, tho' without Authority, that I think a Treaty for that purpose not yet quite impracticable, before we enter into Foreign Alliances. But I am persuaded you have no such Powers. Your Nation, tho' by punishing those American Governors who have created and fomented the Discord, rebuilding our burnt Towns, and repairing as far as possible the Mischiefs done us, She might yet recover a great Share of our Regard and the greatest part of our growing Commerce, with all the Advantage of that additional Strength to be derived from a Friendship with us; I know too well her abounding Pride and deficient Wisdom, to believe she will ever take such Salutary Measures. Her Fondness for Conquest as a Warlike Nation, her Lust of Dominion as an Ambitious one, and her Thirst for a gainful Monopoly as a Commercial one, (none of them legitimate Causes of War) will all join to hide from her Eyes every View of her true Interests; and continually goad her on in these ruinous distant Expeditions, so destructive both of Lives and Treasure, that must prove as pernicious to her in the End as the Croisades formerly were to most of the Nations of Europe.

I have not the Vanity, my Lord, to think of intimidating by thus predicting the Effects of this War; for I know it will in England have the Fate of all my former Predictions, not to be believed till the Event shall verify it.

Long did I endeavour with unfeigned and unwearied Zeal, to preserve from breaking, that fine and noble China Vase the British Empire: for I knew that being once broken, the separate Parts could not retain even their Share of the Strength or Value that existed in the Whole, and that a perfect Re-Union of those Parts could scarce even be hoped for. Your Lordship may possibly remember the Tears of Joy that wet my Cheek, when, at your good Sister's in London, you once gave me Expectations that a Reconciliation might soon take place. I had the Misfortune to find those Expectations disappointed, and to be treated as the Cause of the Mischief I was labouring to prevent. My Consolation under that groundless and malevolent Treatment was, that I retained the Friendship of many Wise and Good Men in that Country, and among the rest some Share in the Regard of Lord Howe.

The well founded Esteem, and permit me to say Affection, which I shall always have for your Lordship, makes it painful to me to see you engag'd in conducting a War, the great Ground of which, as expressed in your Letter, is, "the Necessity of preventing the American Trade from passing into foreign Channels." To me it seems that neither the obtaining or retaining of any Trade, how valuable soever, is an Object for which Men may justly Spill each others Blood; that the true and sure means of extending and securing Commerce is the goodness and cheapness of Commodities; and that the profits of no Trade can ever be equal to the Expence of compelling it, and of holding it, by Fleets and Armies. I consider this War against us therefore, as both unjust, and unwise; and I am persuaded cool dispassionate Posterity will condemn to Infamy those who advised it; and that even Success will not save from some degree of Dishonour, those who voluntarily engag'd to conduct it. I know your great Motive in coming hither was the Hope of being instrumental in a Reconciliation; and I believe when you find *that* impossible on any Terms given you to propose, you will relinquish so odious a Command, and return to a more honourable private Station. With the greatest and most sincere Respect I have the honour to be, My Lord your Lordships most obedient humble Servant   B Franklin

Sketch of Propositions for a Peace, 1776

Sketch of Propositions for a peace 1776.

There shall be a perpetual peace between Great Britain and the United States of America on the following conditions.

Great Britain shall renounce and disclaim all pretence of right or authority to govern in any of the United States of America.

To prevent those occasions of misunderstanding which are apt to arise where the territories of different powers border on each other through the bad conduct of frontier inhabitants on both sides, Britain shall cede to the United states the provinces or Colonies of Quebec, St. John's, Nova Scotia, Bermuda, East and West Florida, and the Bahama islands, with all their adjoining and intermediate territories now claimed by her.

In return for this Cession, the United States shall pay to Great Britain the sum of [*blank*] Sterling in annual payments that is to say [*blank*] per annum for and during the term of [*blank*] years.

And shall moreover grant a free trade to all British subjects throughout the United States and the ceeded Colonies And shall guarantee to Great Britain the Possession of her islands in the West Indies.

Motives for proposing a peace at this time.

1. The having such propositions in charge, will by the Law of nations be some protection to the Commissioners or Ambassadors if they should be taken.

2. As the news of our declared independence will tend to unite in Britain all parties against us; so our offering peace with commerce and payments of money, will tend to divide them again. For peace is as necessary to them as to us: our commerce is wanted by their merchants and manufacturers, who will therefore incline to the accommodation, even though the monopoly is not continued, since it can be easily made appear their *share* of our growing trade, will soon be greater than the *whole* has been heretofore. Then for the landed interest, who wish an alleviation of taxes, it is demonstrable by figures that if we should agree to pay suppose ten millions in one hundred years, viz. £100,000 per annum for that term, it would being faithfully employed [as] a sinking fund more than pay off all their present national debt. It is besides a prevailing opinion in England, that they must in the

nature of things sooner or later lose the Colonies, and may think they had better be without the government of them, so that the Proposition will on that account have more supporters and fewer opposers.

3. As the having such propositions to make; or any powers to treat of peace, will furnish a pretence for BF's going to England, where he has many friends and acquaintance, particularly among the best writers and ablest speakers in both Houses of Parliament, he thinks he shall be able when there if the terms are not accepted, to work up such a division of sentiments in the nation as greatly to weaken its exertions against the United States and lessen its credit in foreign countries.

4. The knowledge of there being powers given to the Commissioners [not yet appointed] to treat with England, may have some effect in facilitating and expediting the proposed treaty with France.

5. It is worth our while to offer such a sum for the countries to be ceded, since the vacant lands will in time sell for a great part of what we shall give, if not more; and if we are to obtain them by conquest, after perhaps a long war, they will probably cost us more than that sum. It is absolutely necessary for us to have them for our own security, and though the sum may seem large to the present generation, in less than half the term, it will be to the whole United States, a mere trifle.

16 Poor richard's diplomacy.

F ranklin arrived in France to discover himself a celebrity of greater renown than he had ever experienced at home or in England. In 1772 he had been named to the Académie royale des sciences, an honor rarely conferred on anyone outside France. Intellectual distinction probably counted for more in eighteenth-century France than in England, but Franklin could scarcely have been prepared for the public adulation that greeted him. His image soon stared at him from such a multitude of prints, medallions, and busts that, as he told his sister Jane Mecom, "my Face is now almost as well known as that of the Moon." His popularity extended to the fashionable ladies of Paris, who practiced flirtation on a grand scale. We have already seen a sample of this in his letter to Madame Brillon in chapter 2. His letters to her and the others are all in the same vein.

Franklin did not mistake popularity for power, but his fame must have given an added charge to the case he could present to the French foreign minister for funds, comparing the respective credit risks posed by Great Britain and the United States. Not least among his arguments were those he had used in 1751 predicting America's future strength and Britain's present and future limits. He was not entirely a novice in diplomacy, for his dealings with the English ministry had resembled, in English eyes, those of a foreign supplicant. As a supplicant in France he was far more success-ful than he had been in Britain, but he was hampered by two quarrel-ing colleagues. Congress had appointed Arthur Lee of Virginia and Silas Deane of Connecticut to act with him in soliciting treaties of alliance and commerce with France. Lee, a certifiable paranoiac, accorded the French,

Franklin, and Deane equal measures of suspicion. In spite of his obstructionism the French signed the treaties Franklin sought, in which France gave up any claim to the American continent. The United States had not succeeded, despite Franklin's personal efforts, in winning over Canada for the union, but the treaty would prevent any attempt by France to recover its former colony. If wrested from Britain in the war, Canada could still become a part of Franklin's America. Once the continent was free from British or French control, the population expanding from the United States would see to that.

The Spanish presence on the Mississippi was a different matter, but Franklin had expectations in that quarter too. In 1780, when congressional delegate John Jay was in Madrid, seeking to bring Spain into support of the American cause, Franklin urged him not to offer concessions that might impair the future he envisaged. "Poor as we are," he told Jay, "yet as I know we shall be rich, I would rather agree with them to buy at a great price the whole of their right on the Mississippi than sell a drop of its waters. A neighbor might as well ask me to sell my street door." It may be worth noting that he says "street door," not "back door."

After the French treaties were signed, Lee's poisonous letters persuaded Congress to recall Deane from the French mission. From then on, Congress was split into pro-Deane and anti-Deane parties, a division that continued even after Deane was driven by congressional neglect or hostility to abandon the American cause, a complicated story that we need not deal with. In 1778 the anti-Deane party appointed John Adams to succeed Deane. When Adams arrived in Paris, with the treaties of alliance and commerce already signed, he proved as suspicious of the French and of Franklin as Lee had been. Adams recorded in his diary his view of the way Franklin did business:

> I found that the Business of our Commission would never be done unless I did it. My two colleagues [Lee and Franklin] would agree on nothing. The life of Dr. Franklin was a Scene of continual Discipation. I could never obtain the Favour of his Company in a Morning before Breakfast which would have been the most convenient time to read over the Letters and papers, deliberate on their contents, and decide upon the Substance of the Answers. It was late when he breakfasted, and as soon as Breakfast

was over, a crowd of Carriages came to his Levee or if you like the term better to his Lodgings, with all sorts of People . . . but by far the greater part were Women and Children, come to have the honour to see the great Franklin. . . . I should have been happy to have done all the Business or rather all the Drudgery, if I could have been favoured with a few moments in a day to receive his Advice concerning the manner in which it ought to be done. But this condescension was not attainable.

Franklin's style of diplomacy, which looked to Adams like continual dissipation, had won 20 million livres in loans and gifts to the United States by 1782, equal to 10 million pounds, sustaining the country's credit while Congress refused to levy taxes. Franklin did it by following the rules that made him such good company. He knew that it could be in France's interest to help the United States, but doing so was by no means a necessary policy. In fact, the sums he obtained went far toward bankrupting the French monarchy, in a cause that was fundamentally antimonarchical and perhaps more against the French government's interests than either side recognized. In return the least that a representative of the United States could do was show gratitude.

John Adams believed that gratitude was a sign of weakness, beneath the dignity of a sovereign nation, a betrayal of national interests. In 1779 Franklin was relieved of his embarrassing assistance and made plenipotentiary, a mission of one since Lee too was out of the picture. Adams returned to the United States but was back the next year, now empowered to negotiate the peace treaty with Great Britain whenever the war should be over. Since the war was far from over and France had entered it, Adams took it upon himself to meddle in Franklin's conduct of relations with France. While Franklin had continually to solicit additional funds from France's foreign minister, the comte de Vergennes, Adams, fancying himself a military strategist, undertook to tell Vergennes in a series of letters just how France must deploy its forces in the field. Vergennes, furious, sent Adams's letters to Franklin and insisted that Franklin forward them to his superiors. In a letter to Samuel Huntington, the president of the Continental Congress, Franklin described his own mode of diplomacy and explained, as gently as possible, the friction that Adams was causing.

Comparison of Great Britain and America as to Credit, 1777

In the Affair of Borrowing Money, a Man's Credit depends on some or all of the following Particulars:

1. His known Conduct with regard to former Loans, in the Punctuality with which he discharg'd them.

2. His Industry in his Business.

3. His Frugality in his Expences.

4. The Solidity of his Funds, his Estate being good, and free of prior Debts, whence his undoubted Ability of Paying.

5. His well-founded Prospects of greater future Ability, by the Improvement of his Estate in Value, and by Aids from others.

6. His known Prudence in Managing his general Affairs, and the Advantage they will probably receive from the present Loan he desires.

7. His known Virtue, and honest Character manifested by his voluntary Discharge of Debts that he could not otherwise have been oblig'd to pay.

The same Circumstances that give a private Man Credit, ought to have and will have their Weight with Lenders of Money to publick Bodies or to Nations.

If then we consider and compare Britain and America in those several Lights, upon the Question to which it is safest to lend Money we shall find

1. *With Regard to former Loans;* that America which borrowed Ten Millions Sterling during the last War for the Maintenance of her Army of 25,000 Men and other Charges, had faithfully *discharg'd* and *paid* that Debt and all her other Debts, in 1772: whereas Britain during those ten years of Peace and profitable Commerce had made little or no Reduction of her Debt, but on the contrary from time to time diminish'd the Hopes of her Creditors by a wanton Diversion and Misapplication of the Sinking Fund which had been destin'd for the Discharge of it.

2. *With regard to Industry in Business.* Every Man in America is employ'd. The greatest Number in cultivating their own Lands; the rest in Handicrafts, Navigation and Commerce. An idle Man is a Rarity. Idleness and Inutility is a Character of Disgrace. In England the Quantity of that Character is immense. Fashion has spread it far and wide. Hence the Embarassment of private Fortunes and the daily Bankrupcies, arising from the universal

fondness for Appearance and expensive Pleasures. And hence in some degree the Mismanagement of their publick Business: For Habits of Business and Ability in it are acquired only by Practice; and where universal Dissipation and the perpetual Pursuit of Amusement are the Mode, the Youth who are educated in it, can rarely afterward acquire that patient Attention and close Application to Affairs, which are so necessary to a Statesman charg'd with the Care of National Welfare. Hence their frequent Errors in Policy. Hence the Weariness at Publick Councils and the Backwardness in going to them; the constant Unwillingness to engage in any Measure that requires Thought and Consideration; and the Readiness for postponing every new Proposition, which postponing is therefore the only Part of Business that they come to be expert in, an Expertness produc'd necessarily by so much daily Practice. Whereas in America, Men bred to close Employment, in their private Affairs, attend with habitual Ease to those of the Publick when engag'd in them, and nothing fails through Negligence.

3. *With regard to Frugality in Expences.* The Manner of Living in America, is in general more simple, and less Expensive than that in England. Plain Tables, plain Clothing, plain Furniture in Houses, few Carriages of Pleasure. In America an expensive Appearance hurts Credit, and is therefore avoided. In England it is often put on with a View of gaining Credit, and continued to Ruin. In publick Affairs the Difference is still greater. In England Salaries of Officers and Emoluments of Office are enormous. A King has a Millon Sterling per Annum, and yet cannot maintain his Family free of Debt, Secretaries of State, Lords of Treasury, Admiralty, &c. have vast Appointments, an Auditor of the Exchequer has, tis Said, 6 pence the Pound or a Fortieth Part of all publick Money expended by the Nation, so that when a War costs 40,000,000 there is a Million for him: an Inspector of the Mint in the last new Coinage received as his Fees £65,000 Sterling a Year, to which Rewards no Service these Gentlemen can render the Public is by any means equivalent. This is all paid by the People, who are oppress'd by the Taxes so occasion'd, and thereby render'd less able to contribute to the Payment of necessary national Debts. In America, Salaries where indispensible are extreamly low, but much of publick Business is done gratis. The Honour of serving the publick ably and faithfully is deemed sufficient. *Public Spirit* really exists there, and has great Effects. In

England it is universally deem'd a Non-Entity, and whoever pretends to it, is laugh'd at as a Fool, or suspected as a Knave. The Committees of Congress which form the Board of War, the Board of Treasury, the Naval Board, the Committee for Accounts, the Board of foreign Transactions for procuring Arms Ammunition, Clothing, &c. all attend the Business of their respective Functions without any Salary or Emolument whatever tho' they spend in it much more of their Time than any Lord of Treasury or Admiralty in England can afford from his Amusements. A late British Minister computed that the whole Expence of the Americans in their civil Government of 3,000,000 of People amounted to but £70,000 Sterling per Annum, and drew from thence a Conclusion that they ought to be taxed till their Expence equalled in proportion to what it cost Britain to govern Eight Millions: He had no Idea of a contrary Conclusion, that if 3,000,000 may be well governed for £70,000, Eight Millions may be as well governed for 3 times that Sum, and therefore the Expence of his own Government should be diminished. In that corrupted Nation, no Man is ashamed of being concern'd in lucrative Government Jobbs, in which the public Money is egregiously misapplied, and squandered; the Treasury pillaged; and more numerous and heavier Taxes are called for to the great Oppression of the People; while the Prospect of a greater Number of these Jobbs to be occasion'd by a War is an Inducement with many to cry out for War on all Occasions, and to oppose every Proposition of Peace. Hence the constant Increase of the National Debt, and the absolute Improbability of its ever being discharged.

4. *With Regard to the Solidity of Funds.* The whole 13 States of America are engag'd for the Payment of every Debt contracted by the Congress, and The Debt to be contracted by the present War is the only Debt they will have to pay, all or nearly all the former Debts of particular Colonies being already discharged. Whereas England will have to pay not only the enormous Debt this War must occasion, but all their vast preceding Debt on the Interest of it; and while America is enriching itself by Prizes made upon the British Commerce, more than it ever did by any Commerce of its own, under the Restraints of a British Monopoly, Britain is growing poorer by the Loss of that Monopoly, the Diminution of its Revenues, and of course less able to discharge the present indiscreet Encrease of its Expences.

5. *With Regard to Prospects of greater future Ability.* Britain has none such. Her islands are circumscrib'd by the Ocean. Excepting a few Parks or Forests she has no new Land to cultivate, and cannot therefore extend her Improvements. Her Numbers of People too, instead of Increasing from increas'd Subsistence, are continually diminishing from growing Luxury and the greater Difficulty of maintaining Families, which of course discourages early Marriage. Thus she will have fewer People to assist in paying her Debt, and that diminish'd Number will be poorer. America, on the contrary has besides her Lands already improved, a vast Territory yet to improve: The Lands cultivated continually increase in Value with the Encrease of People, and the People who double themselves by natural Propagation in 25 Years, will double yet faster by the Accession of Strangers as long as Lands are to be had for new Families; so that every 20 years there will be a double Number of Inhabitants oblig'd to discharge publick Debts, and those Inhabitants being more opulent may pay their Share with greater Ease.

6. *With Regard to Prudence in general Affairs and the Advantages they expect from the Loan desired.* The Americans are Cultivators of Land, those engag'd in Fishery and Commerce are a small Number compar'd with the Body of the People. They have ever conducted their several Governments with Wisdom, avoiding Wars and vain expensive Projects, delighting only in their peaceable Occupations, which must considering the Extent of their yet uncultivated Territory, find them Employment still for Ages: Whereas England ever unquiet, ambitious, avaritious, imprudent, and quarrelsome, is half her time engag'd in some War or other, always at an Expence infinitely greater than the Advantage proposed if it could be obtained. Thus she made a War against Spain in 1739 for a Claim of Debt of about £95,000 (scarce a Groat a Head for the Nation) spent £40,000,000 Sterling in the War, and 50,000 Men, and made Peace without obtaining the Satisfaction demanded. Indeed there is scarce a Nation in Europe against which she has not made War on some frivolous Pretext or other, and by this means has imprudently accumulated a Debt that has brought her on the Verge of Bankrupcy. But the most indiscrete of all her Wars is the present against America, with which she might for Ages have preserv'd her profitable Connection by only a just and equitable Conduct. She is now acting like a

mad Shopkeeper who should attempt by beating those that pass his Door to make them come in and be his Customers. America cannot submit to such Treatment without being first ruined, and being ruined her Custom will be worth nothing. And England to bring this to pass is adding to her Debt, and ruining herself effectually. America on the other Hand aims only at establishing her Liberty, and that Freedom of Commerce, which will be advantageous to all Europe, while the Abolishing of the Monopoly she has hitherto labour'd under will be an Advantage sufficiently ample to repay the Debt she may contract to accomplish it.

7. *With regard to Character in the honest Payment of Debts.* The Punctuality of America in Discharge of *Public Debts* is shown under the first head; the general Character of the People in that respect appears from their faithful Payment of *private Debts* to England since the Commencement of the War. There were not indeed wanting some half Politicians who propos'd stopping that Payment till Peace should be restor'd alledging that in the usual Course of Commerce and of the Credit given there was always a Debt existing equal to the Trade of 18 Months. That the Trade being for 5 Millions Sterling per Annum, the Debt must be Seven Million and an half. That this Sum paid to the British Merchants would operate to prevent the Distress intended to be brought on Britain by our Stoppage of Commerce with her: For the Merchants receiving this Money and no Orders with it for farther Supplies would either lay it out in the Funds, or in employing Manufacturers to accumulate Goods for a future hungry Market in America, upon an expected Accommodation, by which Means the Funds would be kept up and the Manufacturers prevented from Murmuring. But in Answer it was alledged that Injuries from Ministers should not be reveng'd on Merchants who were our Friends; that the Credit was in consequence of private Contracts made in Confidence of good Faith; that these ought to be held sacred and faithfully comply'd with; for that whatever publick Utility might be suppos'd to arise from a Breach of private Faith, it was unjust, and would in the End be found unwise, *Honesty* being in truth *the best Policy.* On this Principle the Proposition was universally rejected: And tho' the English prosecuted the War against us with unexampled Barbarity, burning our defenceless Towns in the midst of Winter and arming Savages against us, the Debt was punctually paid; and the Merchants of London have

testify'd to the Parliament and will testify to all the World that from their Experience in dealing with us they had before the War no Apprehensions of our Unfairness, and that since the War they have been convinc'd that their good Opinion of us was wellfounded. England on the Contrary, an old, corrupt, extravagant and profligate Nation, sees herself deep in Debt which she is in no Condition to pay, and yet is madly and dishonestly running deeper; despairing ever to satisfy her Creditors; and having no Prospect of discharging her Debts but by a Publick Bankrupcy.

On the whole it appears, that from the general Industry, Frugality, Ability, Prudence and Virtue of America, she is a much safer Debtor than Britain. To say nothing of the Satisfaction generous Minds must have in reflecting, that by Loans to America they are opposing Tyranny and aiding the Cause of Liberty which is the Cause of all Mankind.

Rough Draft of Affair of borrowing Money

John Adams's Diplomatic Blunders, 1780

Mr Adams has given Offence to the Court here by some Sentiments and Expressions contained in several of his Letters written to the Count de Vergennes. I mention this with Reluctance, tho' perhaps it would have been my Duty to acquaint you with such a Circumstance, even were it not required of me by the Minister himself. He has sent me Copies of the Correspondence, desiring I would communicate them to Congress; and I send them herewith. Mr Adams did not shew me his Letters before he sent them. I have in a former Letter to Mr [James] Lovell [Massachusetts delegate to the Continental Congress], mentioned some of the Inconveniencies that attend the having more than one Minister at the same Court; one of which Inconveniencies is, that they do not always hold the same Language, and that the Impressions made by one and intended for the Service of his Constituents, may be effaced by the Discourse of the other. It is true that Mr Adams's proper Business is elsewhere, but the Time not being come for that Business, and having nothing else here wherewith to employ himself, he seems to have endeavour'd supplying what he may suppose my Negociations defective in. He thinks as he tells me himself, that America has been too free in Expressions of Gratitude to France; for that she is more obliged to us than we to her; and that we should shew Spirit in our Applications. I apprehend that he mistakes his Ground, and that this Court is to be treated with Decency & Delicacy. The King, a young and virtuous Prince, has, I am persuaded, a Pleasure in reflecting on the generous Benevolence of the Action, in assisting an oppress'd People, and proposes it as a Part of the Glory of his Reign: I think it right to encrease this Pleasure by our thankful Acknowledgements; and that such an Expression of Gratitude is not only our Duty but our Interest. A different Conduct seems to me what is not only improper and unbecoming, but what may be hurtful to us. Mr Adams, on the other Hand, who at the same time means our Welfare and Interest as much as I, or any Man can do, seems to think a little apparent Stoutness and greater Air of Independence & Boldness in our Demands, will procure us more ample Assistance. It is for the Congress to judge and regulate their Affairs accordingly. M. De Vergennes, who appears much offended, told me yesterday, that he would enter into no further Discussions with Mr Adams, nor answer any more of his Letters. He [Adams] is gone to Holland to try, as he told me, whether something might not be done to render us a little less dependent on France. He says the Ideas of this Court & those of the People in America are so totally different, as that it is impossible for any Minister to please both. He ought to know America better than I do, having been there lately; and he may chuse to do what he thinks will best please the People of America: But when I consider the Expressions of Congress in many of their Publick Acts, and particularly in their Letter to the Chevr de la Luzerne [French minister to the United States] of the 24th of May last [specifically expressing "the grateful Sense Congress entertain" of the king's assistance], I cannot but imagine that he mistakes the Sentiments of a few for a general Opinion. It is my Intention while I stay here, to procure what Advantages I can for our Country, by endeavouring to please this Court; and I wish I could prevent anything being said by any of our Countrymen here that may have a contrary Effect, and increase an Opinion lately showing itself in Paris that we seek a Difference, and with a View of reconciling ourselves to England: Some of them have of late been very indiscreet in their Conversations.

17 A huckstered peace.

Franklin had thought from the beginning that the war was needless; he blamed it entirely on the British and could have forgiven them for it only if they had demonstrated repentance by offering reparations of a kind they were never likely to make. He was not empowered by Congress to engage in peace negotiations until 1781, but he was so fully identified with the American cause that would-be peacemakers in England began approaching him almost as soon as he arrived in France. One was James Hutton, a friend from his London days, who happened to be the leader of the pacifist Moravian Church. Hutton wanted to know what it would take to bring about a reconciliation between the two countries. Shortly before signing the treaties with France, Franklin gave his answer, laying out the continental view of the United States that he would later bring to the actual peace negotiations.

Although the task of negotiating peace with England had originally been entrusted to John Adams, on June 14, 1781, Congress transferred the task to a commission consisting of Adams, Franklin, John Jay of New York, Henry Laurens of South Carolina, and Thomas Jefferson. Although the fighting was effectively over with the surrender of Lord Cornwallis at Yorktown on October 19, 1781, the British did not send out feelers until March 1782, when the earl of Shelburne, an old friend of Franklin's, became secretary of state. In April, Shelburne sent Richard Oswald, a wealthy London merchant, to meet with Franklin, who was the only peace commissioner available and remained so for the next three months: Jefferson refused the commission, Laurens was captured at sea, Adams was still in the Netherlands seeking a loan, Jay stayed in Spain until June and then was incapacitated with influenza. Sometime early in April, unhampered by huckstering colleagues, as a basis for discussion Franklin had drafted some preliminary proposals for peace with reconciliation that were not much different from his unofficial proposals to Hutton four years before, probably without much hope that either the British or his American colleagues would agree to his proposals. He presented them to Oswald.

During the war Franklin had been pondering the needless suffering and destruction it imposed on noncombatants, and he hoped that the treaty could do something to alleviate their sufferings in future wars. Before Jay arrived, Franklin wrote out some proposals for "diminishing the Occasions & Mischiefs of War" in a letter to his friend and publisher Benjamin Vaughan, then expanded them in two essays, on privateering and the sugar islands. By the time Jay had recovered from his illness it was becoming clear that the actual peace treaty would be, as Franklin had predicted to Hutton, a product of huckstering, most of which he left to Jay and Adams. But the negotiations with Oswald, who was obliged continually to refer back to Shelburne in England, reached an impasse in November over reciprocal reparations for British destruction of American property and American confiscation of loyalist property. Franklin helped solve the problem by wording the provisions as recommendations rather than requirements. At the same time he proposed a clause in which both sides would forgo privateering in future wars.

Neither side really expected the recommendation of reparations to be followed, nor could Franklin have expected adoption, in the treaty, of his accompanying proposal to prohibit plunder and privateering. He nevertheless continued to press for the prohibition until the treaty was signed. He wanted it not as a concession from Britain but rather as a restraint on his own countrymen, who would be making the greater sacrifice in giving up privateering. Americans, he believed, because of geography could probably gain more from preying on "the rich commerce of Europe with the West Indies" than any other country could expect from seizing American merchant ships. But as he told David Hartley in May 1783, when the huckstering was in its final stages, "I do not wish to see our long extended Coast occupied by Piratical States." He still had his eye on an American political structure that would conform to his vision of greatness in more than size.

With the war ended and the peace negotiations completed, Franklin was obliged to stay on in France as official beggar for the United States. The Continental Congress that employed him had never exercised the power to tax, relying on the separate states to repay in the future the debts that Franklin had assumed in their name. But after a revolution that had begun as a protest against unjust taxes, the new state governments were slow to levy anything like the amounts needed, which would have been much larger than those Parliament had attempted to raise from the colonists. As a result the solvency of the United States rested on Franklin's continued borrowing, an increasingly precarious foundation for a new nation. As he complained to Adams, who was meeting rebuffs in his attempts to raise a loan in Holland, "When the States have not Faith enough in a Congress of their own chusing, to trust it with Money for the payment of their common Debt, how can they expect that Congress should meet with Credit when it wants to borrow more Money for their Use from Strangers?"

Ultimately it took a new Constitution and Alexander Hamilton to give the United States the credit that only Franklin's diplomacy had sustained during the war. He was not relieved of his mission until May 1785. While he remained in Paris, longing for home but enjoying the warmth of French hospitality, he renewed his ties with friends across the Channel, like George Whately, as we saw in chapter 1, and William Strahan, his oldest British friend, with whom he opened a familiar correspondence with an "I told you so" and a jocular comparison of republican and monarchical printing (with puns in printer's language that I leave to the reader to decipher). This letter concluded with a spoof about how Britain could recover America. After returning to Philadelphia, Franklin gave his final verdict on the costs of war in a letter to his sister Jane Mecom.

To James Hutton, 1778

My dear old Friend,   Passy Feb. 1. 1778

You desired that if I had no Propositions to make, I would at least give my Advice.

I think it is *Ariosto* who says, that all Things lost on Earth are to be found in the Moon; On which somebody remark'd that there must then be a great deal of Good Advice in the Moon. If so, there is among it a good deal of mine formerly given and lost in this Business. I will, however, at your Request give a little more; but without the least expectation that it will be followed; for none but God can at the same time give good Counsel and Wisdom to make Use of it.

You have lost by this mad War, and the Barbarity with which it has been carried on, not only the Government and Commerce of America, and the publick Revenues and private Wealth arising from that Commerce; but what is more, you have lost the Esteem, Respect, Friendship and Affection of all that great and growing People, who consider you at present, and whose Posterity will consider you as the worst and wickedest Nation upon Earth.

A Peace you may undoubtedly obtain, by dropping all your Pretensions to govern us. And by your superior Skill in huckstering Negotiation, you may possibly make such an apparently advantageous Treaty as shall be applauded in your Parliament. But if you do not with the Peace recover the Affections of that People, it will not be a lasting or a profitable one; nor will it afford you any Part of that Strength which you once had by your Union with them, and might (if you had been wise enough to take Advice) have still retained.

To recover their Respect and Affection, you must tread back the Steps you have taken.

Instead of honouring and rewarding the American Advisers and Promoters of this War, you should disgrace them with all those who have inflam'd the Nation against America by their malicious Writings; and all the Ministers and Generals who have prosecuted the war with such Inhumanity. This would show a national Change of Disposition, and a Disapprobation of what had passed.

In proposing Terms you should not only grant such as the Necessity of your Affairs may evidently oblige you to grant, but such additional Ones as may show your Generosity, and thereby demonstrate your Goodwill. For instance, perhaps you might by your Treaty retain all Canada, Nova Scotia, and the Floridas. But if you would have a real Friendly as well as able Ally in America, and avoid Occasions of future Discord, (which will otherwise be continually arising on your American Frontiers) you should throw in those Countries; and you may call it, if you please, an Indemnification for the needless and cruel Burning of their Towns; which Indemnification will otherwise be some time or other demanded.

I know your People cannot see the Utility of such Measures, and will never follow them. They will even call it Insolence and Impudence in me to mention them. I have however comply'd with your Desire, and am, as ever, Your affectionate Friend   B Franklin

Notes for a Conversation with Richard Oswald, 1782

Notes of Conversation.

To make a Peace durable what may give Occasion for future Wars, should, if practicable, be removed.

The Territory of the United States, and that of Canada, by long extended Frontiers touch each other.

The Settlers on the Frontiers of the American Provinces are generally the most disorderly of the People, who being far removed from the Eye & Controll of their respective Governments, are more bold in committing Offences against Neighbours, and are forever occasioning Complaints and furnishing Matter for fresh Differences between their States.

By the late Debates in Parliament, & publick Writings, it appears that Britain desires a *Reconciliation* with the Americans. It is a sweet Word. It means much more than a mere Peace, & what is heartily to be wish'd for. Nations may make a Peace whenever they are both weary of making War. But if one of them has made War upon the other unjustly, and has wantonly and unnecessarily done it great Injuries, and refuses Reparation; tho' there may for the present be Peace, the Resentment of those Injuries will remain, and will break out again in Vengeance, when Occasions offer. These Occasions will be watch'd for by one side, fear'd by the other; and the Peace will never be secure; nor can any Cordiality subsist between them.

Many Houses & Villages have been burnt in America by the English and their Allies the Indians. I do not know that the Americans will insist on Reparation. Perhaps they may. But would it not be better for England to offer it? Nothing could have a greater Tendenccy to conciliate? And much of the future Commerce & returning Intercourse between the two Countries may depend on the Reconciliation. Would not the Advantage of Reconciliation by such means be greater than the Expence?

If then a Way can be proposed which may tend to efface the Memory of Injuries, at the same time that it takes away the Occasions of fresh Quarrel & Mischief, will it not be worth considering, especially if it can be done not only without Expence but be a means of saving?

Britain possesses Canada. Her chief Advantage from that Possession consists in the Trade for Peltry. Her Expences in Governing and Defending that Settlement must be considerable. It might be humiliating to her to give it up on the Demand of America. Perhaps America will not demand it: Some of her politic Rulers may consider the fear of Such a Neighbour as a Means of keeping the 13 States more united among themselves, and more attentive to Military Discipline. But on the Minds of the People in general, would it not have an excellent Effect, if Britain Should voluntarily offer to give up this Province; tho' on these Conditions, that she shall in all times coming have & enjoy the Right of Free Trade thither, unincumbred with any Duties whatsoever; and that so much of the vacant Lands there shall be sold, as will raise a Sum sufficient to pay for the Houses burnt by the British Troops and their Indians; and also to indemnify the Royalists for the Confiscation of their Estates.

This is mere Conversation-matter between Mr. O & Mr. F. as the former is not impower'd to make Propositions, and the latter cannot make any without the Concurrence of his Colleagues. ——

Proposals for Diminishing the Occasions and Mischiefs of War, 1782

By the Original Law of Nations, War & Extirpation was the Punishment of Injury. Humanizing by degrees, it admitted Slavery instead of Death. A farther Step was, the Exchange of Prisoners instead of Slavery. Another, to respect more the property of private Persons under Conquest, & to be content with acquir'd Dominion. Why should not this Law of Nations go on improving? Ages have interven'd between its several Steps; but as Knowledge of late encreases rapidly, why should not those Steps be quicken'd? Why should it not be agreed to as the future Law of Nations that in any War hereafter the following Descriptions of Men should be undisturbed, have the Protection of both sides, & be permitted to follow their employments in Surety, viz

1. Cultivators of the Earth, because they labor for the Subsistance of Mankind.

2. Fishermen, for the same Reason.

3. Merchants & Traders, in unarm'd Ships; who accommodate different Nations by communicating & exchanging the Necessaries and Conveniencies of Life.

4. Artists & Mechanics, inhabiting & working in open Towns. It is hardly necessary to add that the Hospitals of Enemies should be unmolested; they ought to be assisted.

In short, I would have nobody fought with but those who are paid for Fighting. If obliged to take Corn from the Farmer, Friend or Enemy, I would pay him for it; the same for the Fish or Goods of the others.

This once established, that Encouragement to war which arises from Spirit of Rapine would be taken away, and Peace therefore more likely to continue & be lasting.

Thoughts on Privateering, 1782

It is for the Interest of Humanity in general, that the Occasions of War, and the Inducements to it, should be diminished.

If Rapine is abolished, one of the Encouragements to War is taken away, and Peace therefore more likely to continue and be lasting.

The Practice of Robbing Merchants on the high Seas, a Remnant of the Ancient Piracy, tho' it may be accidentally beneficial to particular Persons, is far from being profitable to all engaged in it, or to the Nation that authorizes it. In the Beginning of a War some rich Ships, not upon their Guard, are surprized and taken. This encourages the first Adventurers to fit out more arm'd Vessels, and many others to do the same. But the Enemy, at the same time, become more careful, arm their Merchant Ships better, and render them not so easy to be taken; they go also more under the Protection of Convoys, thus while the Privateers to take them are multiplied, the

Vessels subject to be taken, and the Chances of Profit are diminished; so that many Cruises are made wherein the Expences overgo the Gains; and as is the Case in other Lotteries, tho' particulars have got Prizes, the mass of Adventurers are Losers, the whole Expence of fitting out all the Privateers during a War, being much greater than the whole Amount of Goods taken. Then there is the National Loss of all the Labour of so many Men during the time they have been employed in Robbing; who, besides, spend what they get in Riot, Drunkenness and Debauchery, lose their Habits of Industry, are rarely fit for any Sober Business after a Peace, and serve only to encrease the Number of Highwaymen & House Breakers. Even the Undertakers, who have been fortunate, are, by sudden Wealth, led into expensive living, the Habit of which continues when the means of supporting it cease, and finally ruins them. A Just Punishment of their having wantonly & unfeelingly ruined many honest innocent Traders and their Families, whose Substance was employed in serving the common Interest of Mankind.

Thoughts Concerning the Sugar Colonies, 1782

Should it be agreed, & become a Part of the Law of Nations, that the Cultivators of the Earth are not to be molested or interrupted in their Peaceable and useful Employment, the Inhabitants of the Sugar Islands would perhaps come under the Protection of such a Regulation, which would be a great Advantage to the Nations who at present hold those Islands, since the Cost of Sugar to the Consumer in those Nations, consists not only in the Price he pays for it by the Pound, but in the accumulated Charge of all the Taxes he pays in every War to fit out Fleets and maintain Troops for the Defence of the Islands that raise the Sugar and the Ships that bring it home. But the Expence of Treasure is not all. A celebrated Philosophical Writer remarks, that when he consider'd the Wars made in Africa for Prisoners to raise Sugar in America, the Numbers slain in those Wars, the Number that being crowded in Ships perish in the Transportation, & the Numbers that die under the Severities of Slavery, he could scarce look on a Morsel of Sugar without conceiving it spotted with Human Blood. If he had consider'd also the Blood of one another which the white Nations shed in fighting for those Islands, he would have imagined his Sugar not as spotted only, but as thoroughly died red.—On these Accounts I am persuaded that the Subjects of the Emperor of Germany and the Empress of Russia, who have no Sugar Islands, consume Sugar cheaper at Vienna and Moscow, with all the Charge of transporting it after its Arrival in Europe, than the Citizens of London or of Paris. And I sincerely believe that if France & England were to decide by throwing Dice which should have the whole of their Sugar Islands, the Loser in the Throw would be the Gainer. The future Expence of defending them would be saved; the Sugars would be bought cheaper by all Europe if the Inhabitants might make it without Interruption, and whoever imported the Sugar, the same Revenue might be raised by Duties at the Custom Houses of the Nation that consumed it. And on the whole I conceive it would be better for the Nations now possessing Sugar Colonies to give up their Claim to them, let them govern themselves, and put them under the Protection of all the Powers of Europe as neutral Countries open to the Commerce of all, the Profits of the present Monopoly's being by no means equivalent to the Expence of maintaining them.

To William Strahan, 1784

. . .

You "fairly acknowledge that the late War terminated quite contrary to your Expectation." Your expectation was ill founded; for you would not believe your old Friend, who told you repeatedly that by those Measures England would lose Her Colonies, as Epictetus warn'd in vain his Master that he would break his Leg. You believ'd rather the Tales you heard of our Poltronery & Impotence of Body & Mind. Do you not remember the Story you told me of the Scotch Serjeant, who met with a Party of Forty American Soldiers, and tho' alone disarm'd them all and brought them in Prisoners: A Story almost as Improbable as that of the Irishman, who pretended to have alone taken and brought in Five of the Enemy, by *surrounding* them. And yet, my Friend, sensible and Judicious as you are, but partaking of the general Infatuation, you seemed to believe it.—The Word general puts me in mind of a General, your General [Sir Alured] Clarke, who had the Folly to say in my hearing at Sir John Pringle's, that with a Thousand British Grenadiers he would undertake to go from one end of America to the other and geld all the

Males partly by force and partly by a little Coaxing. It is plain he took us for a Species of Animals very little superior to Brutes. The Parliament too believ'd the Stories of another foolish General, I forget his Name, that the Yankies never *felt bold*. Yankey was understood to be a sort of Yahoo, and the Parliament did not think the Petitions of such Creatures were fit to be recieved and read in so wise an Assembly. What was the consequence of this monstrous Pride and Insolence? You first send small Armies to Subdue us, believing them more than sufficient, but soon found yourselves obliged to send greater; these whenever they ventured to penetrate our Country beyond the Protection of their Ships, were either repulsed and obliged to scamper out, or were surrounded, beaten, and taken Prisoners. An American Planter who had never seen Europe, was chosen by us to Command our Troops and continu'd during the whole War. This Man sent home to you, one after another, five of your best Generals, baffled, their Heads bare of Laurels, disgraced even in the Opinion of their Employers. Your Contempt of our Understandings in Comparison with your own appeared to be not much better founded than that of our Courage, if we may judge by this Circumstance, that in whatever Court of Europe a Yankey Negociator appeared, the wise British Minister was routed put in a passion, pick'd a quarrel with your Friends, and was sent home with a Flea in his Ear. But after all my dear Friend, do not imagine that I am vain enough to ascribe our Success to any superiority in any of those Points. I am too well acquainted with all the Springs and Levers of our Machine, not to see that our human means were unequal to our undertaking, and that if it had not been for the Justice of our Cause, and the consequent Interposition of Providence in which we had Faith we must have been ruined. If I had ever before been an Atheist I should now have been convinced of the Being and Government of a Deity. It is he who abases the Proud & favors the Humble! May we never forget his Goodness to us, and may our future Conduct manifest our Gratitude. —

But let us leave these serious Reflections and converse with our usual Pleasantry. I remember your observing once to me, as we sat together in the House of Commons, that no two Journeymen Printers within your Knowledge had met with such Success in the World as our selves. You were then at the head of your Profession, and soon afterward became a Member of that Parliament. I was an Agent for a few Provinces and now act for them all. But we have risen by different Modes. I as a Republican Printer, always lik'd a Form well *plaind down;* being averse to those *overbearing* Letters that hold their Heads so *high* as to hinder their Neighbours from *appearing.* You as a Monarchist chose to work upon *Crown* Paper, and found it profitable; while I work'd upon *Pro-patria* (often indeed call'd *Fools-Cap*) with no less advantage. Both our *Heaps hold out* very well, and we seem likely to make a pretty good days Work of it. With regard to Public Affairs, (to continue in the same stile) it seems to me that the Compositors in your Chapel do not *cast off their Copy* well, nor perfectly understand *Imposing.* Their *Forms* too are continually pester'd by the *Outs,* and *Doubles,* that are not easy to be corrected. And I think they were wrong in laying aside some *Faces,* and particularly certain *Head-pieces,* that would have been both useful and ornamental. But, Courage! The Business may still flourish with good Management; & the Master become as rich as any of the Company—

By the way, the rapid Growth and extension of the English language in America, must become greatly Advantageous to the Booksellers, & holders of Copy Rights in England. A vast audience is assembling there for English Authors, ancient, present and future, our People doubling every twenty Years; and this will demand large, and of course profitable, Impressions of your most valuable Books. I would therefore If I possessed such rights, entail them, if such a thing be practicable, upon my Posterity; for their Worth will be continually Augmenting. This may look a little like Advice, and yet I have drank no Madeira these Ten Months. The Subject however leads me to another thought, which is, that you do wrong to discourage the Emigration of Englishmen to America. In my piece on Population, I have proved, I think, that Emigration does not diminish but multiplies a Nation. You will not have fewer at home for those that go Abroad. And as every Man who comes among us, and takes up a piece of Land, becomes a Citizen, and by our Constitution has a Voice in Elections and a share in the Government of the Country, why should you be against acquiring by this fair Means a Repossession of it, and leave it to be taken by Foreigners of all Nations and Languages who by their Numbers may drown and stifle the English, which otherwise would probably become in the course of two Centuries the most extensive Language in the World, the Spanish only excepted. It is a fact that the Irish Emigrants and their Children are now in Possession of the Government of Pensilvania, by their Majority in the Assembly, as well as of a great part of the Territory; and I remember well the first Ship that brought any of them over. I am ever, my dear Friend, Yours most Affectionately   B Franklin

The Costs of War, 1787

I agree with you [his sister Jane Mecom] perfectly in your Disapprobation of War. Abstracted from the Inhumanity of it, I think it wrong in Point of Human Providence, for whatever Advantages one Nation would obtain from another, whether it be Part of their Territory, the Liberty of Commerce with them, free Passage on their Rivers, &c. &c. it would be much cheaper to purchase such Advantages with ready Money than to pay the Expense of acquiring it by War. An Army is a devouring Monster, and when you have rais'd it, you have, in order to subsist it, not only the fair Charges of Pay, Clothing, Provision, Arms & Ammunition, with numberless other contingent & just Charges to answer and satisfy, but you have all the additional Knavish Charges of the numerous Tribe of Contractors, to defray, with those of every other Dealer who furnishes the Articles wanted for your Army, and takes advantage of that want to demand exhorbitant Prices. It seems to me, that if Statesmen had a little more Arithmetick, or were more accustomed to Calculation, Wars would be much less frequent. I am confident that Canada might have been purchas'd from France for a tenth Part of the Money England spent in the Conquest of it. And if instead of fighting with us for the Power of Taxing us, she had kept us in a good Humour, by allowing us to dispose of our own Money, and now and then giving us a little of hers, by way of Donation to Colleges, or Hospitals, or for cutting Canals, or fortifying Posts, she might easily have drawn from us much more by our occasional voluntary Grants & Contributions, than ever she could by Taxes. Sensible People will give a Bucket or two of Water to a dry Pump, that they may afterwards get from it all they have occasion for. Her Ministry were deficient in that little Point of Common Sense;—And so they spent 100 Millions of her Money, and after all lost what they contended for.

18 The pretensions of wealth.

We have been following Franklin in his pursuit of the vision he first articulated in 1751. For thirty-odd years after that he had engaged himself in removing obstacles to what he saw as America's destiny, obstacles placed there first by British political folly and then by British military might. With the obstacles overcome, he had to think more directly about what, besides strength in numbers and resources, would make America great.

It went without saying that the existing dispersion of power among the several states had to give way to a more effective central government. He had first witnessed the evils of dispersion in the refusal of the colonies to join for their own protection against the French and against hostile Indians. But he had also witnessed the evils of an uninformed and irresponsible central control in the hands of the British ministry and Parliament. The independent states had created a more responsible central government in the Continental Congress, but they had limited its authority so narrowly in the Articles of Confederation of 1781 that it could never be the means for bringing America's potential to fruition.

In France his personal prestige had helped overcome the weakness of the Congress that appointed him, even as the feckless, unrestrained activities of the separate sovereign states continually hampered his mission. While he struggled to win funds for the United States, states like Virginia and South Carolina sent their own agents to borrow for themselves, leaving the French to wonder just how united the United States was. The states had similarly obstructed Washington's efforts to sustain the war by offering higher enlistment bounties in state militias than their delegates in Congress would allow the Continental Army to offer recruits. Thanks in no small measure to Washington and Franklin, the Revolution had nevertheless succeeded as a continental enterprise.

Both men rejoiced in its success, their success. But both knew that what they had done as Americans was threatened by the diffusion of power among the several states. Both waited for their countrymen to see what they saw, and both were present at the convention that corrected the situation. Washington's prestige and political judgment guaranteed that the national government would not become prey to the contentions and rivalries of the states. Franklin, however, too old now for public office, could contribute to the new union only by accepting much less than he thought best for America. At the convention he was one of the authors of the so-called Great Compromise, by which the states gained equal representation in the Senate, regardless of size, and a weight in proportion to their populations only in the House of Representatives. It was not truly a compromise but a concession by the large states. Franklin proposed it and agreed to it, though his own preference would have been a single legislative body based solely on population. Because he declined to press his own views on this and other public issues when it became clear that he could not prevail, his hopes for America seldom figure in the public record of the founding.

Franklin never drafted a plan of the government he wanted, but one thing he did not want is clear: he did not want the accumulation of wealth to result in the accumulation of power. It is ironic that Franklin should be remembered today for those aphorisms of Poor Richard that extolled the way industry and thrift could generate and multiply wealth. Published in a pamphlet under the title (not his choice) *The Way to Wealth* in 1758, they have probably had a wider circulation ever since than anything else he wrote or said. Unfortunately the pamphlet omitted Poor Richard's frequent warnings against making a fetish of wealth.

Content and Riches seldom meet together.

He does not possess wealth, it possesses him.

He that is of Opinion Money will do every Thing, may well be suspected of doing every Thing for Money.

If your Riches are yours, why don't you take them with you to the t'other World?

During his years in England, Franklin had found himself contending with the inordinate power that wealth gave its possessors in every aspect of government and politics. The members of the House of Lords enjoyed their seats because of the excessive wealth of their ancestors, and the House of Commons was filled with men rich enough to buy their way into it. What Franklin wanted for America can be read in his strictures on the government of Britain. William Pitt, Lord Chatham, who had played a leading role in winning Canada for Britain, was one of the few men of influence who would listen to Franklin's warnings against Britain's imminent loss of the colonies. In January 1775, after conferring with Franklin, he made a last-minute effort to reverse British policy in a resolution he presented to the House of Lords. Franklin was in the gallery as Chatham's guest and recorded the Lords' contemptuous rejection of the resolution and his own contempt for the role of heredity in Britain's government.

As he indicates, Franklin had no better opinion of the Commons than he did of the Lords. In his view, a principal source of corruption was the sinecures, salaries, and perquisites of office that enabled the king's ministry to buy or bribe a majority in the House of Commons. At the Constitutional Convention he made a strong plea against paying the executive, whether a council or a single president, any "salary, stipend, Fee, or reward whatsoever for their services," lest they follow the British example. He seems not to have recognized that his proposal would have limited the executive office to persons of private means. His suggestion, as James Madison recorded, "was treated with great respect, but rather for the author of it, than from any apparent conviction of its expediency or practicability."

But if the perquisites of the ministry corrupted British government, the root of the trouble lay in the elevation of property rights over human rights, expressed in the savage punishments authorized by English law for crimes against property, punishments out of all proportion to the offenses. When his London friend Benjamin Vaughan sent Franklin a pamphlet

(Martin Madan's *Thoughts on Executive Justice*) defending this disparity, he answered in a letter deriding the practice and outlining a view of property and its relation to government that distinguished him from most of his contemporaries, whether in England or the United States. Franklin had already expressed this view with regard to taxes and public property more succinctly in a letter to Robert Morris, superintendent of finance in the Continental Congress.

Franklin believed literally that people came before property. And the appropriate political expression of that priority was a government in which a single, popularly elected legislative assembly exercised supreme power. Most of the independent states, drafting their constitutions during the Revolution, had followed the advice of John Adams's *Thoughts on Government* (1776) and made their legislatures bicameral. The "upper" house was designed for persons of distinction, which usually translated to persons with considerable property. It was sometimes even said that the upper house represented property. The superior wisdom that was held to accompany a superiority of property would act as a brake on hasty measures that might appeal to the general public, especially measures (like paper-money bills) that threatened the sanctity of property.

In 1776 Franklin had presided over the convention that drafted the Pennsylvania state constitution. Almost alone among the new constitutions, it placed virtually all power in the hands of a popularly elected unicameral legislature. No records of the convention debates have survived, but a partial first draft of the Pennsylvania constitution does. It contains a clause, omitted from the final document, that conforms to Franklin's view of the hazards of great wealth: "that an enormous Proportion of Property vested in a few Individuals is dangerous to the Rights, and destructive of the Common Happiness of Mankind; and therefore every free State hath a Right by its Laws to discourage the Possession of such property." Whether this was Franklin's contribution to the debate is not clear, but its final omission was probably not to Franklin's liking. What is abundantly clear is that he approved of the Pennsylvania constitution of 1776 with its allocation of power to a single assembly and its denial of special favors to men of property. It is equally clear that men of property did not subscribe to his philosophy.

When he arrived home from France, Franklin found the state divided into Constitutionalists, who were satisfied with the state constitution, and Anti-Constitutionalists, who were not. In the vain hope that he could reconcile the two factions, he was immediately elected president of Pennsylvania, an honorary title for the presiding officer of an executive council that itself had little power. The constitution seemed to be working as expected, but by 1789 the Anti-Constitutionalists had prevailed in calling for a convention to meet in 1790 to draft a new constitution that would presumably (as it, in fact, did) give the Pennsylvania legislature an upper house and a stronger executive. A writer in the *Federal Gazette* offered "Hints for the Members of Convention," hints that included property qualifications for voting, a single executive, a bicameral legislature, and long terms of office. Franklin wrote an answer that gives, with some passion, his views on property and its place, or lack of it, in government. The convention did not establish property qualifications for voting in Pennsylvania, but in other respects it gave men of property what they wanted.

The life history of many individuals reads, like the caption in group pictures, from left to right. It would be too much to say that Benjamin Franklin's life reads from right to left, but the things that came from his pen in his last years sound more like "away with wealth" than a way to it. Among the things he put his name to, besides his denunciation of the proposals for the new Pennsylvania constitution, were a petition to the U.S. Congress to abolish slavery and the essay satirizing the congressional rejection of this petition, which appears in chapter 11.

Whatever discouragement with the American world these pieces may show, it would not be fair to leave them as his view of America. In the last chapter Franklin will voice once again his confidence in the country and the people he had served so long and so well.

Thoughts on the House of Lords, 1775

To hear so many of these *Hereditary* Legislators declaiming so vehemently against, not the Adopting merely, but even the *Consideration* of a

Proposal [for granting American rights] so important in its Nature, offered by a Person of so weighty a Character [William Pitt], one of the first Statesman of the Age, who had taken up this Country when in the lowest Despondency, and conducted it to Victory and Glory thro' a War with two of the mightiest Kingdoms in Europe; to hear them censuring his Plan not only for their own Misunderstandings of what was in it, but for their Imaginations of what was not in it, which they would not give themselves an Opportunity of rectifying by a second Reading; to perceive the total Ignorance of the Subject in some, the Prejudice and Passion of others, and the wilful Perversion of Plain Truth in several of the Ministers; and upon the whole to see it so ignominiously rejected by so great a Majority, and so hastily too, in Breach of all Decency and prudent Regard to the Character and Dignity of their Body as a third Part of the National Legislature, gave me an exceeding mean Opinion of their Abilities, and made their Claim of Sovereignty over three Millions of virtuous sensible People in America, seem the greatest of Absurdities, since they appear'd to have scarce Discretion enough to govern a Herd of Swine. Hereditary Legislators! thought I. There would be more Propriety, because less Hazard of Mischief, in having (as in some University of Germany,) Hereditary Professors of Mathematicks! But this was a hasty Reflection: For the *elected* House of Commons is no better, nor ever will be while the Electors receive Money for their Votes, and pay Money where with Ministers may bribe their Representatives when chosen.

Convention Speech on Salaries, 1787

June 2, 1787

Sir,

It is with Reluctance that I rise to express a Disapprobation of any one Article of the Plan for which we are so much obliged to the honourable Gentleman who laid it before us. From its first Reading I have borne a good Will to it, and in general wish'd it Success. In this Particular of Salaries to the Executive Branch, I happen to differ; and as my Opinion may appear new and chimerical, it is only from a Persuasion that it is right, and from a

Sense of Duty that I hazard it. The Committee will judge of my Reasons when they have heard them, and their Judgment may possibly change mine.—I think I see Inconveniencies in the Appointment of Salaries, I see none in refusing them, but on the contrary great Advantages.

Sir, There are two Passions which have a powerful Influence in the Affairs of Men. These are *Ambition* and *Avarice;* the Love of Power, and the Love of Money. Separately each of these has great Force in prompting Men to Action; but when united in View of the same Object, they have in many Minds the most violent Effects. Place before the Eyes of such Men, a Post of *Honour* that shall at the same time be a Place of *Profit,* and they will move Heaven and Earth to obtain it. The vast Number of such Places it is that renders the British Government so tempestuous. The Struggles for them are the true Source of all those Factions which are perpetually dividing the Nation, distracting its Councils, hurrying it sometimes into fruitless, & mischievous Wars, and often compelling a Submission to dishonourable Terms of Peace.

And of what kind are the Men that will strive for this profitable Pre-eminence, thro' all the Bustle of Cabal, the Heat of Contention, the infinite mutual Abuse of Parties, tearing to Pieces the best of Characters? It will not be the wise and moderate, the Lovers of Peace and good Order, the Men fittest for the Trust. It will be the Bold and the Violent, the Men of strong Passions and in indefatigable Activity in their selfish Pursuits. These will thrust themselves to your Government and be your Rulers. And these too will be mistaken in the expected Happiness of their Situation: For their vanquish'd Competitors of the same Spirit and from the same Motives will perpetually be endeavouring to distress their Administration, thwart their Measures, and render them odious to the People.

Besides these Evils, Sir, tho' we may set out in the Beginning with moderate Salaries, we shall find that such will not be of long Continuance. Reasons will never be wanting for propos'd Augmentations. And there will always be a Party for giving more to the Rulers, that the Rulers may be able in Return to give more to them. Hence as all History informs us, there has been in every State & Kingdom a constant kind of Warfare between the Governing & the Governed: the one striving to obtain more for its Support, and the other to pay less. And this has alone occasion'd great Convulsions, actual civil Wars, ending either in dethroning of the Princes or enslaving of the People. Generally indeed the Ruling Power carries its Point, and we see the Revenues of Princes constantly increasing, and we see that they are never satisfied, but always in want of more. The more the People are discontented with the Oppression of Taxes; the greater Need the Prince has of Money to distribute among his Partisans & pay the Troops that are to suppress all Resistance, and enable him to plunder at Pleasure. There is scarce a King in a hundred who would not, if he could, follow the Example of Pharoah, get first all the Peoples Money, then all their Lands, and then make them & their Children Servants forever. It will be said, that we don't propose to establish Kings. —I know it. —But there is a natural Inclination in Mankind to Kingly Government. It sometimes relieves them from Aristocratic Domination. They had rather have one Tyrant than 500. It gives more of the Appearance of Equality among Citizens; and that they like. I am apprehensive, therefore, perhaps too apprehensive, that the Government of these States, may in future times end in a Monarchy. But this Catastrophe I think may be long delay'd, if in our propos'd System we do not sow the Seeds of Contention, Faction & Tumult by making our Posts of Honour Places of Profit. If we do, I fear that tho' we employ at first a Number and not a single Person, the Number will in time be set aside, it will only nourish the Fœtus of a King, (as the honourable Gentleman from Virg[ini]a [Edmund Randolph] very aptly express'd it) and a King will the sooner be set over us.

It may be imagined by some that this is an Utopian Idea, and that we can never find Men to serve us in the Executive Department, without paying them well for their Services. I conceive this to be a Mistake. Some existing Facts present themselves to me, which incline me to a contrary Opinion. The High Sheriff of a County in England is an honourable Office, but it is not a profitable one. It is rather expensive, and therefore not sought for. But yet it is executed, & well executed, and usually by some of the principal Gentlemen of the County. In France, the Office of Counsellor or Member of their judiciary Parliaments, is more honourable. It is therefore purchas'd at a high Price: There are indeed Fees on the Law Proceedings, which are divided among them, but these Fees do not amount to more than three per Ct on the Sum paid for the Place. Therefore as legal Interest is there at five per Cent they in fact pay two per Ct. for being allow'd to do the Judiciary Business of the Nation, which is at the same time entirely exempt from the Burthen of Paying them any Salaries for their Services. I do not however mean to recommend this as an eligible Mode for our judiciary Department. I only bring the Instance to shew that the Pleasure of doing Good & Serving their Country, and the Respect such Conduct entitles them to, are sufficient Motives with some Minds to give up a great Portion of their Time to the Public, without the mean Inducement of pecuniary Satisfaction.

Another Instance is that of a respectable Society, who have made the Experiment, and practis'd it with Success now more than a hundred Years.—I mean the Quakers. It is an establish'd Rule with them that they are not to go to Law, but in their Controversies they must apply to their Monthly, Quarterly & Yearly Meetings. Committees of these sit with Patience to hear the Parties, and spend much Time in composing their Differences. In doing this, they are supported by a Sense of Duty; & the Respect paid to Usefulness. It is honourable to be so employ'd, but it was never made profitable by Salaries, Fees, or Perquisites. And indeed in all Cases of public Service, the less the Profit the greater the Honour.

To bring the Matter nearer home, have we not seen the great and most important of our Offices, that of General of our Armies, executed for Eight Years together, without the smallest Salary, by a Patriot whom I will not now offend by any other Praise; and this thro' Fatigues & Distresses in common with the other brave Men his Military Friends & Companions, and the constant Anxieties peculiar to his Station? and shall we doubt finding three or four Men in all the United States, with public Spirit enough to bear Sitting in peaceful Council, for perhaps an equal Term, merely to preside over our civil Concerns, & see that our Laws are duly executed. Sir, I have a better Opinion of our Country. I think we shall never be without a sufficient Number of wise and good Men to undertake and execute well & faithfully the Office in question.

Sir, The Saving of the Salaries, that may at first be propos'd, is not an Object with me. The subsequent Mischiefs of proposing them are what I apprehend. And therefore it is that I move the Amendment. If it is not seconded or accepted, I must be contented with the Satisfaction of having deliver'd my Opinion frankly, and done my Duty.

Property Rights and Human Rights, 1785

Superfluous Property is the Creature of Society. Simple and mild Laws were sufficient to guard the Property that was merely necessary. The Savage's Bow, his Hatchet, & his Coat of Skins, were sufficiently secured without Law by the Fear of personal Resentment & Retaliation. When by virtue of the first Laws Part of the Society accumulated Wealth & grew Powerful, they enacted others more severe, and would protect their Property at the Expence of Humanity. This was abusing their Power, and commencing a Tyranny. If a Savage before he enter'd into Society had been told, Your Neighbour by this Means may become Owner of 100 Deer, but if your Brother, or your Son, or yourself, having no Deer of your own, and being hungry should kill one of them, an infamous Death must be the Consequence; he would probably have preferr'd his Liberty, & his common Right of killing any Deer, to all the Advantages of Society that might be propos'd to him.

That it is better 100 guilty Persons should escape, than that one innocent Person should suffer, is a Maxim that has been long & generally approv'd, never that I know of controverted. Even the sanguinary Author [Martin Madan] of the *Thoughts* [*on Executive Justice* (1785)] agrees to it page 163, adding well, that "the very Thought of *injured* Innocence, and much more that of *suffering* Innocence, must awaken all our tenderest and most compassionate Feelings, and at the same time raise our highest Indignation against the Instruments of it. — But, he adds, there is no Danger of *either* from a strict Adherence to the Laws." — Really? — Is it then impossible to make an unjust Law? — And if the Law it self be unjust, may it not be the very "Instrument" which ought to "raise the Author's, & every body's, highest Indignation." I read in the last Newspaper from London, that a Woman is capitally convicted at the Old Bailey for privately stealing out of a Shop some Gause value 14 Shillings and threepence. Is there any Proportion between the Injury done by a Theft value 14/3, and the Punishment of a human Creature by Death on a Gibbet? Might not that Woman by her

Labour have made the Reparation ordain'd by God, in paying four-fold? Is not all Punishment inflicted beyond the Merit of the Offence, so much Punishment of Innocence? In this light, how vast is the annual Quantity of not only *injured* but *suffering* Innocence, in almost all the civilized States of Europe!

But it seems to have been thought that this kind of Innocence may be punish'd by way of *preventing* Crimes. I have read indeed of a cruel Turk in Barbary, who whenever he bought a new Christian Slave, ordered him immediately to be hung up by the Legs & to receive an 100 Blows of a Cudgel on the Soles of his Feet, that the severe Sense of the Punishment, and Fear of incurring it thereafter, might prevent the Faults that should merit it. — Our Author himself would hardly approve entirely of this Turk's Conduct in the Government of Slaves, and yet he appears to recommend something like it for the government of English Subjects, when he applauds, Page 105, the Reply of Judge [Sir Thomas] Burnet to the convict Horsestealer, who being ask'd what he had to say why Judgment of Death should not pass against him, & answering that it was hard to hang a Man for *only* stealing a Horse, was told by the Judge, "Man thou art not to be hang'd *only* for stealing a Horse, but that Horses may not be stolen." The Man's Answer, if candidly examin'd, will I imagine, appear reasonable, as being founded on the Eternal Principle of Justice & Equity, that Punishments should be proportion'd to Offences: and the Judge's Reply brutal and unreasonable; tho' the Writer "wishes all Judges to carry it with them whenever they go the Circuit, and to bear it in their Minds, as containing a wise Reason for all the *penal Statutes* which they are called upon to put in Execution: — it at once illustrates, says he, the true Grounds and Reasons of ALL CAPITAL PUNISHMENT's whatsoever, namely, that every man's Property *as well as his Life* may be held sacred and inviolate." Is there then no difference in Value between Property and Life? If I think it right that the Crime of Murder should be punished with Death, not only as an equal Punishment of the Crime, but to prevent other Murders, does it follow that I must approve of inflicting the same Punishment for a little Invasion of my *Property* by Theft? If I am not myself so barbarous, so bloody-minded and revengeful, as to kill a Fellow Creature for stealing from me 14/3, how can I approve of a Law that does it?

The Moral Obligation of Taxes, 1783

The Remissness of our People in Paying Taxes is highly blameable, the Unwillingness to pay them is still more so. I see in some Resolutions of Town-Meetings, a Remonstrance against giving Congress a Power to take as they call it, *the People's Money* out of their Pockets tho' only to pay the Interest and Principal of Debts duly contracted. They seem to mistake the Point. Money justly due from the People is their Creditors' Money, and no longer the Money of the People, who, if they withold it, should be compell'd to pay by some Law. All Property indeed, except the Savage's temporary Cabin, his Bow, his Matchcoat, and other little Acquisitions absolutely necessary for his Subsistence, seems to me to be the Creature of public Convention. Hence the Public has the Right of Regulating Descents & all other Conveyances of Property, and even of limiting the Quantity & the Uses of it. All the Property that is necessary to a Man for the Conservation of the Individual & the Propagation of the Species, is his natural Right which none can justly deprive him of: But all Property superfluous to such purposes is the Property of the Publick, who by their Laws have created it, and who may therefore by other Laws dispose of it, whenever the Welfare of the Publick shall demand such Disposition. He that does not like civil Society on these Terms, let him retire & live among Savages.— He can have no right to the Benefits of Society who will not pay his Club towards the Support of it.

Queries and Remarks on "Hints for the Members of the Pennsylvania Convention," 1789

Queries & Remarks on a Paper entitled "Hints for the Members of Convention No II" in the Federal Gazette of Tuesday Nov 3d 1789.

Hint 1. Of the Executive Branch.
"Your Executive should consist of a single Person."
On this I would ask, Is he to have no Council? How is he to be informed of the State and Circumstances of the different Counties, their Wants, their Abilities, their Dispositions, and the Characters of the principal People, respecting their Integrity, Capacities and Qualifications for Offices? Does

not the present Construction of our Executive provide well for these Particulars? And during the Number of Years it has existed, has its Errors or Failures in answering the End of its Appointment been more or greater than might have been expected from a single Person?

"But an Individual is more easily watched and controuled than any greater Number."

On this I would ask, Who is to watch & controul him? And by what Means is he to be controuled? Will not those Means, whatever they are, and in whatever Body vested, be subject to the same Inconveniences of Expence, Delay, Obstruction of good Intentions &c. which are objected to the present Executive?

2. The Duration of the Appointment.

"This should be governed by the following Principles—the Independency of the Magistrate and the Stability of his Administration; neither of which can be secured but by putting both beyond the Reach of every annual Gust of Folly and of Faction."

On this it may be asked, Ought it not also to be put beyond the Reach of every *triennial, quinquennial* or *septennial* Gust of Folly and of Faction; and in short beyond the Reach of Folly and of Faction at any Period whatever? Does not this Reasoning aim at establishing a Monarchy at least for Life, like that of Poland? Or, to prevent the Inconveniences, such as that Kingdom is subject to in a new Election on every Decease, does it not point to an hereditary Succession? Are the Freemen of Pennsylvania convinced, from a View of the History of such Governments, that it will be for their Advantage to submit themselves to a Government of such Construction?

"On the Legislative Branch."

"A plural Legislature is as necessary to good Government, as a single Executive. It is not enough that your Legislature should be numerous, it should also be divided. Numbers alone are not a sufficient Barrier against the Impulses of Passion, the Combinations of Interest, the Intrigues of Faction, the Haste of Folly, or the Spirit of Encroachment. One Division should watch over and controul the other; supply its Wants, correct its Blunders and cross its Designs, should they be criminal or erroneous. Wisdom is the specific Quality of the

Legislature, grows out of the Number of the Body, and is made up of the Portions of Sense and Knowledge which each Member brings to it."

On this it may be asked, May not the Wisdom brought to the Legislature by each Member be as effectual a Barrier against the Impulses of Passion, &c. when the Members are united in one Body as when they are divided? If one Part of the Legislature may controul the Operations of the other, may not the Impulses of Passion, the Combinations of Interest, the Intrigues of Faction, the Haste of Folly, or the Spirit of Encroachment in the one of those Bodies obstruct the Good proposed by the other and frustrate its Advantages to the Public? Have we not experienced in this Colony, when a Province under the Government of the Proprietors [the Penn family, descendants of William Penn, who had originally owned all the land in the colony], the Mischiefs of a second Branch existing in the Proprietary-Family, countenanced and aided by an Aristocratic Counsel? How many Delays & what great Expences were occasioned in carrying on the public Business; and what a Train of Mischiefs, even to the preventing of the Defence of the Province during several Years, when distressed by an Indian War, by the iniquitous Demand, that the Proprietary Property should be exempt from Taxation? The Wisdom of a few Members in one single Legislative Body may it not frequently stifle bad Motions in their Infancy, and so prevent their being adopted; whereas if those wise Men, in Case of a double Legislature, should happen to be in that Branch wherein the Motion did not arise, may it not, after being adopted by the other occasion lengthy Disputes and Contentions between the two Bodies, expensive to the Public, obstructing the public Business and promoting Factions among the People, many Tempers naturally adhering obstinately to Measures they have once publicly adopted? Have we not seen in one of our neighbouring States a bad Measure adopted by one Branch of the Legislature for Want of the Assistance of some more intelligent Members, who had been packed into the other, occasion many Debates, conducted with much Asperity, which could not be settled but by an expensive, general Appeal to the People? [a dispute in Maryland over a bill for paper money passed by the House of Delegates but rejected by the Senate]. And have we not seen, in another neighbouring State [New York] a similar Difference between the two

Branches, occasioning long Debates and Contentions, whereby the State was prevented, for many Months, enjoying the Advantage of having Senators in the Congress of the United States? And has our present Legislative in one Assembly committed any Errors of Importance, which they have not remedied, or may not easily remedy; more easily probably than if divided into two Branches? And if the Wisdom brought by the Members to the Assembly is divided into two Branches may it not be too weak in each to support a good Measure, or obstruct a bad one? The Division of the Legislature into two or three Branches in England, was it the Product of Wisdom or the Effect of Necessity, arising from the preexisting Prevalence of an odious Feudal System? which Government notwithstanding this Division is now become in Fact an absolute Monarchy, since the King, by bribing the Representatives with the People's Money, carries, by his Ministers, all the Measures that please him, which is equivalent to governing without a Parliament, and renders the Machine of Government much more complex and expensive, and from its being more complex, more easily put out of Order? Has not the famous political Fable of the Snake with two Heads and one Body some useful Instruction contained in it? She was going to a Brook to drink, and in her Way was to pass thro' a Hedge, a Twig of which opposed her direct Course; one Head chose to go on the right Side of the Twig, the other on the left; so that Time was spent in the Contest, and before the Decision was completed, the poor Snake died with Thurst.

"*Hence it is that the two Branches should be elected by Persons differently qualified; and in short, that, as far as possible, they should be made to represent different Interests.*

"*Under this Reasoning I would establish a Legislature of two Houses. The Upper should represent the Property; the lower the Population of the State. The upper should be chosen by Freemen possessing in Lands & Houses one thousand Pounds, the lower by all such as had resided four Years in the Country and paid Taxes. The first should be chosen for four, the last for two Years; They should in Authority be coequal.*"

Several Questions may arise upon this Proposition. 1st. What is the Proportion of Freemen possessing Lands & Houses of one thousand Pounds Value compared to that of Freemen whose Possessions are inferior? Are they as one to ten? Are they even as one to twenty? I should doubt whether [that is, "fear that"] they are as one to fifty. If this Minority is to chuse a Body expresly to controul that which is to be chosen by the great Majority of the Freemen, what have this great Majority done to forfeit so great a Portion of their Right in Elections? Why is this Power of Controul, contrary to the Spirit of all Democracies, to be vested in a Minority, instead of a Majority? Then is it intended or is it not that the Rich should have a Vote in the Choice of Members for the lower House, while those of inferior Property are deprived of the Right of voting for Members of the upper House? And why should the upper House, chosen by a Minority have equal Power with the lower, chosen by a Majority? Is it supposed that Wisdom is the necessary Concomitant of Riches, and that one Man worth a thousand Pound must have as much Wisdom as twenty, who have each only 999? And why is Property to be represented at all? —Suppose one of our Indian Nations should now agree to form a civil Society, each Individual would bring into the Stock of the Society little more Property than his Gun & his Blanket; for at present he has no other; we know that when one of them has attempted to keep a few Swine, he has not been able to maintain a Property in them, his Neighbours thinking they have a Right to kill and eat them whenever they want Provision; it being one of their Maxims, that Hunting is free for all: the Accumulation therefore of Property in such a Society, and its Security to Individuals in every Society must be an Effect of the Protection afforded to it by the joint Strength of the Society, in the Execution of its Laws; private Property therefore is a Creature of Society & is subject to the Calls of that Society whenever its Necessities shall require it, even to its last Farthing; its Contributions therefore to the public Exigencies are not to be considered as conferring a Benefit on the Public, entitling the Contributors to the Distinctions of Honour and Power; but as the Return of an Obligation previously received or the Payment of a just Debt. The Combinations of Civil Society are not like those of a Set of Merchants who club their Property in different Proportions for Building & Freighting a Ship, and may therefore have some Right to vote in the Disposition of the Voyage in a greater or less Degree according to their respective Contributions; but the important Ends of Civil Society are the personal Securities of Life and Liberty; these remain the same in every Member of the Society, and the poorest continues to have an equal Claim to them with the most opulent, whatever Difference Time, Chance or Industry may occasion in their Circumstances.—On these Considerations I am sorry to see the Signs this Paper I have been considering affords of a Disposition among some of our People to commence an Aristocracy, by giving the Rich a Predominancy in Government, a Choice peculiar to themselves in one half the Legislature, to be proudly called the UPPER House, and the other Branch chosen by the Majority of the People degraded by the Denomination of the LOWER, and giving to this *upper House* a Permanency of four Years, & but two to the *lower.* I hope therefore that our Representatives in the Convention will not hastily go into these Innovations, but take the Advice of the Prophet, "*Stand in the old Ways, view the ancient Paths, consider them well, and be not among those that are given to Change.*"

19 America.

We noticed earlier that Franklin wanted America to go it alone in its bid for independence, without soliciting help from abroad. His confidence in the country's growth and strength persuaded him that there was no way the Revolution could fail. But even he was surprised by how quickly it showed its strength, as he noted in a conversation with his fellow commissioner to France, Arthur Lee.

After the war, when the officers of the Continental Army formed a society, designed to be hereditary, he mocked them for indulging in this European style of perpetuating empty titles. The Society of the Cincinnati quickly abandoned its hereditary qualification, but not before Franklin had time to make fun of it in a letter to his daughter, Sarah Bache.

Franklin wrote the letter while still in France, and there he was continually solicited by people who wished to honor America with their presence: craftsmen willing to set up shop there in return for a monopoly on, say, glassmaking, landowners who would accept a few hundred rich acres, politicians who could show Americans how to build a perfect government if given a suitable sum for their expertise. Franklin, they all believed, could surely get these things for them: he was America's potentate in France, with the plenary powers potentates always had. In 1784, tired of explaining to these importunate supplicants that America was not like that, he printed a little pamphlet, *Information to Those Who Would Remove to America.* In its celebration of a "happy mediocrity," it describes an America Franklin had not seen for some years. Is it also his wishful prescription for an ideal America? He gave another prescription, and a prediction, for his

America in the speech that closed the Constitutional Convention of 1787, which states in a few words the beliefs that infuse so many of the preceding pages.

After Franklin had made his appeal to the convention and emerged from Independence Hall, according to the recollection of another delegate, a woman approached him and asked, "Well, Doctor, what have we got, a republic or a monarchy?' "A republic," he answered, "if you can keep it." Although it was not quite the republic he wanted, it was a republic worth keeping. Most of us believe we have kept it, however precariously. It has survived the corrosion of excessive wealth. It harbors pockets of poverty equal to those that shocked Franklin in Ireland and Scotland. But it survived the Civil War and abolished the slavery that he only belatedly learned to abhor. It survives. And unless we have indeed become so corrupted as to welcome despotism, it may yet free itself from the evils that Franklin feared and we continue to face.

Arthur Lee's Conversation with Franklin About the Miracle of the Revolution, 1777

Having some conversation with Dr. F. upon the present state of things, he seemed to agree with me in thinking that France and Spain mistook their interest and opportunity in not making an alliance with us now, when they might have better terms than they could expect hereafter. That it was well for us they left us to work out our own salvation; which the efforts we had hitherto made, and the resources we had opened, gave us the fairest reason to hope we should be able to do. He told me the manner in which the whole of this business had been conducted, was such a miracle in human affairs, that if he had not been in the midst of it, and seen all the movements, he could not have comprehended how it was effected. To comprehend it we must view a whole people for some months without any laws or government at all. In this state their civil governments were to be formed, an army and navy were to be provided by those who had neither a ship of war, a company of soldiers, nor magazines, arms, artillery or ammunition. Alliance were to be formed, for they had none. All this was to be done, not at leisure nor in a time of tranquillity and communication with other nations, but in the face of a most formidable invasion, by the most powerful nation, fully provided with armies, fleets, and all the instruments of destruction, powerfully allied and aided, the commerce with other nations in a great measure stopped up, and every power from whom they could expect to procure arms, artillery, and ammunition, having by the influence of their enemies forbade their subjects to supply them on any pretence whatever. Nor was this all; they had internal opposition to encounter, which alone would seem sufficient to have frustrated all their efforts. The Scotch, who in many places were numerous, were secret or open foes as opportunity offered. The Quakers, a powerful body in Pennsylvania, gave every opposition their art, abilities and influence could suggest. To these were added all those whom contrariety of opinion, tory principles, personal animosities, fear of so dreadful and dubious an undertaking, joined with the artful promises and threats of the enemy rendered open or concealed opposers, or timid neutrals, or lukewarm friends to the proposed revolution. It was, however, formed and established in despite of all these obstacles, with an expedition, energy, wisdom, and success of which most certainly the whole history of human affairs has not, hitherto, given an example. To account for it we must remember that the revolution was not directed by the leaders of faction, but by the opinion and voice of the majority of the people; that the grounds and principles upon which it was formed were known, weighed and approved by every individual of that majority. It was not a tumultuous revolution, but a deliberate system. Consequently, the feebleness, irresolution, and inaction which generally, nay, almost invariably attends and frustrates hasty popular proceedings, did not influence this. On the contrary, every man gave his assistance to execute what he had soberly determined, and the sense of the magnitude and danger of the undertaking served only to quicken their activity, rouse their resources, and animate their exertions. Those who acted in council bestowed their whole thoughts upon the public; those who took the field did [so], with what weapons, ammunition and accomodation they could procure. In commerce, such profits were offered as tempted the individuals of almost all nations, to break through the prohibition of their governments, and furnish arms and ammunition, for which they received from a people ready to sacrifice every thing to the common cause, a thousand fold.

The effects of anarchy were prevented by the influence of public shame, pursuing the man who offered to take a dishonest advantage of the want of law. So little was the effects of this situation felt, that a gentleman, who thought their deliberations on the establishment of a form of government too slow, gave it as his opinion that the people were likely to find out that laws were not necessary, and might therefore be disposed to reject what they proposed, if it were delayed. Dr. Franklin assured me that upon an average he gave twelve hours in the twenty-four to public business. One may conceive what progress must be made from such exertions of such an understanding, aided by the co-operation of a multitude of others upon such business, not of inferior abilities. The consequence was, that in a few months, the governments were established; codes of law were formed, which, for wisdom and justice, are the admiration of all the wise and thinking men in Europe. Ships of war were built, a multitude of cruisers were fitted out, which have done more injury to the British commerce than it ever suffered before. Armies of offence and defence were formed, and kept the field, through all the rigours of winter, in the most rigorous climate. Repeated losses, inevitable in a defensive war, as it soon became, served only to renew exertions that quickly repaired them. The enemy was every where resisted, repulsed, or beseiged. On the ocean, in the channel, in their very ports, their ships were taken, and their commerce obstructed. The greatest revolution the world ever saw, is likely to be effected in a few years; and the power that has for centuries made all Europe tremble, assisted by 20,000 German mercenaries, and favoured by the universal concurrence of Europe to prohibit the sale of warlike stores, the sale of prizes, or the admission of the armed vessels of America, will be effectually humbled by those whom she insulted and injured, because she conceived they had neither spirit nor power to resist or revenge it.

To Sarah Bache, 1784

My dear Child   Passy, Jany. 26th. 1784

Your Care in sending me the Newspapers is very agreable to me. I receiv'd by Capt. Barney those relating to the Cincinnati. My Opinion of the Institution cannot be of much Importance. I only wonder that when the united Wisdom of our Nation had, in the Articles of Confederation, manifested their Dislike of establishing Ranks of Nobility, by Authority either of the Congress or of any particular State, a Number of private Persons should think proper to distinguish themselves and their Posterity from their Fellow Citizens, and form an Order of hereditary Knights, in direct Opposition to the solemnly declared Sense of their Country. I imagine it must be likewise contrary to the Good Sense of most of those drawn into it, by the Persuasion of its Projectors, who have been too much struck with the Ribbands & Crosses they have seen among them, hanging to the Button-holes of Foreign Officers. And I suppose those who disapprove of it have not hitherto given it much Opposition, from a Principle a little like that of your Mother, relating to punctilious Persons, who are always exacting little Observances of Respect, that *if People can be pleased with small Matters, it is pity but they should have them.* In this View, perhaps I should not myself, if my Advice had been asked, have objected to their Wearing their Ribband and Badge according to their Fancy, tho' I certainly should to the entailing it as an Honour on their Posterity. For Honour worthily obtain'd, as that for Example of our Officers, is in its Nature a personal Thing, and incommunicable to any but those who had some Share in obtaining it. Thus among the Chinese, the most antient, and, from long Experience, the wisest of Nations, Honour does not *descend* but *ascends*. If a Man from his Learning, his Wisdom or his Valour, is promoted by the Emperor to the Rank of Mandarin, his Parents are immediately intitled to all the same Ceremonies of Respect from the People, that are establish'd as due to the Mandarin himself; on this Supposition, that it must have been owing to the Education, Instruction, and good Example afforded him by his Parents that he was rendered capable of Serving the Publick. This *ascending Honour* is therefore useful to the State as it encourages Parents to give their Children a good and virtuous Education. But the *descending Honour,* to Posterity who could have had no Share in obtaining it, is not only groundless & absurd, but often hurtful to Posterity, since it is apt to make them proud, disdaining to be employed in useful Arts, & thence falling into Poverty and all the Meannesses, Servility and Wretchedness attending it; which is the present case with much of what is called the *Noblesse* in Europe. Or if, to keep up the Dignity of the Family, Estates are entailed entire on the Eldest Male Heir, another Pest to Industry and Improvement of the Country is introduced, which will be follow'd by all the odious Mixture of Pride & Beggary, & Idleness that have half depopulated Spain, occasioning continual Extinction of Families by the Discouragements of Marriage and improvement of Estates. I wish therefore that the Cincinnati, if they must go on with their Project, would direct the Badges of their Order to be worn by their Parents instead of handing them down to their Children. It would be a good Precedent, & might have good Effects. It would also be a kind of Obedience to the fourth Commandment, in which God enjoins us to *honour* our Father & Mother, but has no where directed us to *honour* our Children. And certainly no Mode of honouring those immediate Authors of our Being can be more effectual, than that of doing praiseworthy Actions, which reflect honour on those who gave us our Education, or more becoming than that of manifesting by some public Expression or Token that it is to their Instruction & Example we ascribe the Merit of those Actions.

. . .

The Gentleman who made the Voyage to France to provide the Rib-bands & Medals has executed his Commission. To me they seem tolerably done, but all such Things are criticised. Some find fault with the Latin, as wanting classic Elegance & Correctness; and since our Nine Universities were not able to furnish better Latin, it was Pity, they say, that the Mottos had not been in English. Others object to the Title, as not properly assumable by any but Gen. Washington, who serv'd without Pay. Others object to the Bald Eagle, as looking too much like a *Dindon*, or Turkey. For my own part I wish the Bald Eagle had not been chosen as the Representative of our Country. He is a Bird of bad moral Character. He does not get his Living honestly. You may have seen him perch'd on some dead Tree near the River, where, too lazy to fish for himself, he watches the Labour of the Fishing Hawk [osprey]; and when that diligent Bird has at length taken a Fish, and is bearing it to his Nest for the Support of his Mate and young Ones, the Bald Eagle pursues him & takes it from him. With all this Injustice, he is never in good Case but like those among Men who live by Sharping & Robbing he is generally poor and often very lousy. Besides he is a rank Coward: The little *King Bird* not bigger than a Sparrow attacks him boldly & drives him out of the District. He is therefore by no means a proper Emblem for the brave and honest Cincinnati of America who have driven all the *King birds* from our Country, tho' exactly fit for that Order of Knights which the French call *Chevaliers de l'Industrie.* I am on this account not displeas'd that the Figure is not known as a Bald Eagle, but looks more like a Turky. For in Truth the Turky is in Comparison a much more respectable Bird, and withal a true original Native of America. Eagles have been found in all Countries, but the Turky was peculiar to ours, the first of the Species seen in Europe being brought to France by the Jesuits from Canada, and serv'd up at the Wedding Table of Charles the ninth. He is besides, tho' a little vain and silly, a Bird of Courage, and would not hesitate to attack a Grenadier of the British Guards who should presume to invade his Farm Yard with a red Coat on.

I shall not enter into the Criticisms made upon their Latin. The gallant Officers of America may not have the Merit of being great Scholars, but they undoubtedly merit much as brave Soldiers from their Country, which should therefore not leave them merely to *Fame* for their *Virtutis Premium* [reward of virtue], which is one of their Latin Mottos. Their *Esto perpetua* [Let it be perpetual] another is an excellent Wish, if they mean it for their Country, bad, if intended for their Order. The States should not only restore to them the *Omnia* of their first Motto *Omnia reliquit servare Rempublicam* [He gave up everything to serve the republic], which many of them have left and lost, but pay them justly, & reward them generously. They should not be suffered to remain with their new-created Chivalry *entirely* in the Situation of the Gentleman in the Story, which their *Omnia reliquit* reminds me of. You know every thing makes me recollect some Story. He had built a very fine House, & thereby much impair'd his Fortune. He had a Pride however in showing it to his Acquaintance. One of them after viewing it all, remark'd a Motto over the Door, O̅IA VANITAS. What, says he, is the Meaning of this OIA? 'tis a Word I don't understand. I will tell you says the Gentleman, I had a mind to have the Motto cut on a Piece of smooth Marble, but there was not room for it between the Ornaments to be put in Characters large enough to be read. I therefore made use of a Contraction antiently very common in Latin Manuscripts, by which the m's & n's in Words are omitted, and the Omission noted by a little Dash above, which you may see there, so that the

Word is *Omnia, Omnia Vanitas* [All is vanity]. O, says his Friend, I now comprehend the Meaning of your Motto, it relates to your Edifice; and signifies, that if you have abridged your *Omnia,* you have nevertheless left your V A N I T A S legible at full length.

I am ever, Your Affectionate Father
B Franklin

Information to Those Who Would Remove to America, 1784

MANY Persons in Europe having directly or by Letters, express'd to the Writer of this, who is well acquainted with North-America, their Desire of transporting and establishing themselves in that Country; but who appear to him to have formed thro' Ignorance, mistaken Ideas & Expectations of what is to be obtained there; he thinks it may be useful, and prevent inconvenient, expensive & fruitless Removals and Voyages of improper Persons, if he gives some clearer & truer Notions of that Part of the World than appear to have hitherto prevailed.

He finds it is imagined by Numbers that the Inhabitants of North-America are rich, capable of rewarding, and dispos'd to reward all sorts of Ingenuity; that they are at the same time ignorant of all the Sciences; & consequently that strangers possessing Talents in the Belles-Letters, fine Arts, &c. must be highly esteemed, and so well paid as to become easily rich themselves; that there are also abundance of profitable Offices to be disposed of, which the natives are not qualified to fill; and that having few Persons of Family among them, Strangers of Birth must be greatly respected, and of course easily obtain the best of those Offices, which will make all their Fortunes; that the Governments too, to encourage Emigrations from Europe, not only pay the expence of personal Transportation, but give Lands gratis to Strangers, with Negroes to work for them, Utensils of Husbandry, & Stocks of Cattle. These are all wild Imaginations; and those who go to America with Expectations founded upon them, will surely find themselves disappointed.

The Truth is, that tho' there are in that Country few People so miserable as the Poor of Europe, there are also very few that in Europe would be called rich: it is rather a general happy Mediocrity that prevails. There are few great Proprietors of the Soil, and few Tenants; most People cultivate their own Lands, or follow some Handicraft or Merchandise; very few rich enough to live idly upon their Rents or Incomes; or to pay the high Prices given in Europe, for Paintings, Statues, Architecture and the other Works of Art that are more curious than useful. Hence the natural Geniuses that have arisen in America, with such Talents, have uniformly quitted that Country for Europe, where they can be more suitably rewarded. It is true that Letters and mathematical Knowledge are in Esteem there, but they are at the same time more common than is apprehended; there being already existing nine Colleges or Universities, viz. four in New-England, and one in each of the Provinces of New-York, New-Jersey, Pensilvania, Maryland and Virginia, all furnish'd with learned Professors; besides a number of smaller Academies: These educate many of their Youth in the Languages and those Sciences that qualify Men for the Professions of Divinity, Law or Physick [Medicine]. Strangers indeed are by no means excluded from exercising those Professions, and the quick Increase of Inhabitants every where gives them a Chance of Employ, which they have in common with the Natives. Of civil Offices or Employments there are few; no superfluous Ones as in Europe; and it is a Rule establish'd in some of the States, that no Office should be so profitable as to make it desirable. The 36 Article of the Constitution of Pensilvania, runs expresly in these Words: *As every Freeman, to preserve his Independance, (if he has not a sufficient Estate) ought to have some Profession, Calling, Trade or Farm, whereby he may honestly subsist, there can be no Necessity for, nor Use in, establishing Offices of Profit; the usual Effects of which are Dependance and Servility, unbecoming Freemen, in the Possessors and Expectants; Faction, Contention, Corruption, and Disorder among the People. Wherefore whenever an Office, thro' Increase of Fees otherwise, becomes so profitable as to occasion many to apply for it, the Profits ought to be lessened by the Legislature.*

These Ideas prevailing more or less in all the United States, it cannot be worth any man's while, who has a means of Living at home, to expatriate himself in hopes of obtaining a profitable civil Office in America; and as to military Offices, they are at an End with the War; the Armies being disbanded. Much less is it adviseable for a Person to go thither who has no other Quality to recommend him but his Birth. In Europe it has indeed its

Value, but it is a Commodity that cannot be carried to a worse Market than to that of America, where People do not enquire concerning a Stranger, *What IS he?* but *What can he DO?* If he has any useful Art, he is welcome; and if he exercises it and behaves well, he will be respected by all that know him; but a mere Man of Quality, who on that Account wants to live upon the Public, by some Office or Salary, will be despis'd and disregarded. The Husbandman is in honor there, & even the Mechanic, because their Employments are useful. The people have a Saying, that God Almighty is himself a Mechanic, the greatest in the Universe; and he is respected and admired more for the Variety, Ingenuity and Utility of his Handiworks, than for the Antiquity of his Family. They are pleas'd with the Observation of a Negro, and frequently mention it, that *Boccarorra* (meaning the White-man) make de Blackman workee, make de Horse workee, make de Ox workee, make ebery ting workee; only de Hog. He de Hog, no workee; he eat, he drink, he walk about, he go to sleep when he please, *he libb like a Gentleman.* According to these Opinions of the Americans, one of them would think himself more oblig'd to a Genealogist, who could prove for him that his Ancestors & Relations for ten Generations had been Plough-men, Smiths, Carpenters, Turners, Weavers, Tanners, or even Shoemakers, & consequently that they were useful Members of Society; than if he could only prove that they were Gentlemen, doing nothing of Value, but living idly on the Labour of others, mere *fruges consumere nati,** and otherwise *good* for *nothing,* till by their Death, their Estates like the Carcase of the Negro's Gentleman-Hog, come to be *cut up.*

With Regard to Encouragements for Strangers from Government, they are really only what are derived from good Laws & Liberty. Strangers are welcome because there is room enough for them all, and therefore the old Inhabitants are not jealous of them; the Laws protect them sufficiently, so that they have no need of the Patronage of great Men; and every one will enjoy securely the Profits of his Industry. But if he does not bring a Fortune with him, he must work and be industrious to live. One or two Years Residence give him all the Rights of a Citizen; but the Government does

*There are a Number of us born
 Merely to eat up the Corn. WATTS.

not at present, whatever it may have done in former times, hire People to become Settlers, by Paying their Passages, giving Land, Negroes, Utensils, Stock, or any other kind of Emolument whatsoever. In short America is the Land of Labour, and by no means what the English call *Lubberland*, and the French *Pays de Cocagne* [land of plenty], where the Streets are said to be pav'd with half-peck Loaves, the Houses til'd with Pancakes, and where the Fowls fly about ready roasted, crying, *Come eat me!*

Who then are the kind of Persons to whom an Emigration to America may be advantageous? and what are the Advantages they may reasonably expect?

Land being cheap in that Country, from the vast Forests still void of Inhabitants, and not likely to be occupied in an Age to come, insomuch that the Propriety of an hundred Acres of fertile Soil full of Wood may be obtained near the Frontiers in many Places for eight or ten Guineas, hearty young Labouring Men, who understand the Husbandry of Corn and Cattle, which is nearly the same in that Country as in Europe, may easily establish themselves there. A little Money sav'd of the good Wages they receive there while they work for others, enables them to buy the Land and begin their Plantation, in which they are assisted by the Good Will of their Neighbours and some Credit. Multitudes of poor People from England, Ireland, Scotland and Germany, have by this means in a few Years become wealthy Farmers, who in their own Countries, where all the Lands are fully occupied, and the Wages of Labour low, could never have emerged from the mean Condition wherein they were born.

From the Salubrity of the Air, the Healthiness of the Climate, the Plenty of good Provisions, and the Encouragement to early Marriages, by the certainty of Subsistance in cultivating the Earth, the Increase of Inhabitants by natural Generation is very rapid in America, and becomes still more so by the Accession of Strangers; hence there is a continual Demand for more Artisans of all the necessary and useful kinds, to supply those Cultivators of the Earth with Houses, and with Furniture & Utensils of the grosser Sorts which cannot so well be brought from Europe. Tolerably good Workmen in any of those mechanic Arts, are sure to find Employ, and to be well paid for their Work, there being no Restraints preventing Strangers from exercising any Art they understand, nor any Permission necessary. If they are poor, they begin first as Servants or Journeymen; and if they are sober, industrious & frugal, they soon become Masters, establish themselves in Business, marry, raise Families, and become respectable Citizens.

Also, Persons of moderate Fortunes and Capitals, who having a Number of Children to provide for, are desirous of bringing them up to Industry, and to secure Estates for their Posterity, have Opportunities of doing it in America, which Europe does not afford. There they may be taught & practice profitable mechanic Arts, without incurring Disgrace on that Account; but on the contrary acquiring Respect by such Abilities. There small Capitals laid out in Lands, which daily become more valuable by the Increase of People, afford a solid Prospect of ample Fortunes thereafter for those Children. The Writer of this has known several Instances of large Tracts of Land, bought on what was then the Frontier of Pensilvania, for ten Pounds per hundred Acres, which, after twenty Years, when the Settlements had been extended far beyond them, sold readily, without any Improvement made upon them, for three Pounds per Acre. The Acre in America is the same with the English Acre or the Acre of Normandy.

Those who desire to understand the State of Government in America, would do well to read the Constitutions of the several States, and the Articles of Confederation that bind the whole together for general Purposes under the Direction of one Assembly called the Congress. These Constitutions have been printed by order of Congress in America; two Editions of them have also been printed in London, and a good Translation of them into French has lately been published at Paris.

Several of the Princes of Europe having of late Years, from an Opinion of Advantage to arise by producing all Commodities & Manufactures within their own Dominions, so as to diminish or render useless their Importations, have endeavoured to entice Workmen from other Countries, by high Salaries, Privileges, &c. Many Persons pretending to be skilled in various great Manufactures, imagining that America must be in Want of them, and that the Congress would probably be dispos'd to imitate the Princes above mentioned, have proposed to go over, on Condition of having their Passages paid, Lands given, Salaries appointed, exclusive Privileges for Terms of Years, &c. Such persons on reading the Articles of Confederation will find that the Congress have no Power committed to them, or Money put into their Hands, for such purposes; and that if any such Encouragement is given, it must be by the Government of some separate State. This however has rarely been done in America; and when it has been done it has rarely succeeded, so as to establish a Manufacture which the Country was not yet so ripe for as to encourage private Persons to set it up; Labour being generally too dear there, & Hands difficult to be kept together, every one desiring to be a Master, and the Cheapness of Land enclining many to leave Trades for Agriculture. Some indeed have met with Success, and are carried on to Advantage; but they are generally such as require only a few Hands, or wherein great Part of the Work is perform'd by Machines. Goods that are bulky, & of so small Value as not well to bear the Expence of Freight, may often be made cheaper in the Country than they can be imported; and the Manufacture of such Goods will be profitable wherever there is a sufficient Demand. The Farmers in America produce indeed a good deal of Wool & Flax; and none is exported, it is all work'd up; but it is in the Way of Domestic Manufacture for the Use of the Family. The buying up Quantities of Wool & Flax with the Design to employ Spinners, Weavers, &c. and form great Establishments, producing Quantities of Linen and Woollen Goods for Sale, has been several times attempted in different Provinces; but those Projects have generally failed, Goods of equal Value being imported cheaper. And when the Governments have been solicited to support such Schemes or Encouragements, in Money, or by imposing Duties on Importation of such Goods, it has been generally refused, on this Principle, that if the Country is ripe for the Manufacture, it may be carried on by private Persons to Advantage; and if not, it is a Folly to think of forceing Nature. Great Establishments of Manufacture, require great Numbers of Poor to do the Work for small Wages; these Poor are to be found in Europe, but will not be found in America, till the Lands are all taken up and cultivated, and the excess of People who cannot get Land, want Employment. The Manufacture of Silk, they say, is natural in France, as that of Cloth in England, because each Country produces in Plenty the first Material: But if England will have a Manufacture of Silk as well as that of Cloth, and France one of Cloth as well as that of Silk, these unnatural Operations must be supported by mutual Prohibitions or high Duties on the Importation of each others Goods, by which means the Workmen are enabled to tax the home-Consumer by greater Prices, while the higher Wages they receive makes them neither happier nor richer, since they only drink more and work less. Therefore Governments in America do nothing to encourage such Projects. The People by this Means are not impos'd on, either by the Merchant or Mechanic; if the Merchant demands too much Profit on imported Shoes, they buy of the Shoemaker: and if he asks too high a Price, they take them of the Merchant: thus the two Professions are Checks on each other. The Shoemaker however has on the whole a considerable Profit upon his Labour in America, beyond what he had in Europe, as he can add to his Price a Sum nearly equal to all the Expences of Freight & Commission, Risque or Insurance, &c. necessarily charged by the Merchant. And the Case is the same with the Workmen in every other Mechanic Art. Hence it is that Artisans generally live better and more easily in America than in Europe, and such as are good Œconomists make a comfortable Provision for Age, & for their Children. Such may therefore remove with Advantage to America.

In the old longsettled Countries of Europe, all Arts, Trades, Professions, Farms, &c. are so full that it is difficult for a poor Man who has Children, to place them where they may gain, or learn to gain a decent Livelihood. The Artisans, who fear creating future Rivals in Business, refuse to take Apprentices, but upon Conditions of Money, Maintenance or the like, which the Parents are unable to comply with. Hence the Youth are dragg'd up in Ignorance of every gainful Art, and oblig'd to become Soldiers or Servants or Thieves, for a Subsistance. In America the rapid Increase of Inhabitants takes away that Fear of Rivalship, & Artisans willingly receive Apprentices from the hope of Profit by their Labour during the Remainder of the Time stipulated after they shall be instructed. Hence it is easy for poor Families to get their Children instructed; for the Artisans are so desirous of Apprentices, that many of them will even give Money to the Parents to have Boys from ten to fifteen Years of Age bound Apprentices to them till the Age of twenty one; and many poor Parents have by that means, on their Arrival in the Country, raised Money enough to buy Land sufficient to establish themselves, and to subsist the rest of their Family by Agriculture. The

Contracts for Apprentices are made before a Magistrate, who regulates the Agreement according to Reason and Justice; and having in view the Formation of a future useful Citizen, obliges the Master to engage by a written Indenture, not only that during the time of Service stipulated, the Apprentice shall be duly provided with Meat, Drink, Apparel, washing & Lodging, and at its Expiration with a compleat new suit of Clothes, but also that he shall be taught to read, write & cast Accompts, & that he shall be well instructed in the Art or Profession of his Master, or some other, by which he may afterwards gain a Livelihood, and be able in his turn to raise a Family. A Copy of this Indenture is given to the Apprentice or his Friends, & the Magistrate keeps a Record of it, to which Recourse may be had, in case of Failure by the Master in any Point of Performance. This Desire among the Masters to have more Hands employ'd in working for them, induces them to pay the Passages of young Persons, of both Sexes, who on their Arrival agree to serve them one, two, three or four Years; those who have already learnt a Trade agreeing for a shorter Term in Proportion to their Skill and the consequent immediate Value of their Service; and those who have none, agreeing for a longer Term, in Consideration of being taught an Art their Poverty would not permit them to acquire in their own Country.

The almost general Mediocrity of Fortune that prevails in America, obliging its People to follow some Business for Subsistance, those Vices that arise usually from Idleness are in a great Measure prevented. Industry and constant Employment are great Preservatives of the Morals and Virtue of a Nation. Hence bad Examples to Youth are more rare in America, which must be a comfortable Consideration to Parents. To this may be truly added, that serious Religion under its various Denominations, is not only tolerated but respected and practised. Atheism is unknown there, Infidelity rare & secret, so that Persons may live to a great Age in that Country without having their Piety shock'd by meeting with either an Atheist or an Infidel. And the Divine Being seems to have manifested his Approbation of the mutual Forbearance and Kindness with which the different Sects treat each other, by the remarkable Prosperity with which he has been pleased to favour the whole Country.

Speech in the Convention on the Constitution, 1787

Mr President

I confess that I do not entirely approve this Constitution at present, but Sir, I am not sure I shall never approve it: For having lived long, I have experienced many Instances of being oblig'd, by better Information or fuller Consideration, to change Opinions even on importnt Subjects, which I once thought right, but found to be otherwise. It is therefore that the older I grow the more apt I am to doubt my own Judgment, and to pay more Respect to the Judgment of others. Most Men indeed as well as most Sects in Religion, think themselves in Possession of all Truth, and that wherever others differ from them it is so far Error. [Sir Richard] Steele, a Protestant, in a Dedication tells the Pope, that the only Difference between our two Churches in their Opinions of the Certainty of their Doctrine, is, the Romish Church is infallible, and the Church of England is never in the Wrong. But tho' many private Persons think almost as highly of their own Infallibility, as of that of their Sect, few express it so naturally as a certain French Lady, who in a little Dispute with her Sister, said, I don't know how it happens, Sister, but I meet with no body but myself that's *always* in the right. *Il n'y a que moi qui a toujours raison.*

In these Sentiments, Sir, I agree to this Constitution, with all its Faults, if they are such; because I think a General Government necessary for us, and there is no *Form* of Government but what may be a Blessing to the People if well administred; and I believe farther that this is likely to be well administred for a Course of Years, and can only end in Despotism as other Forms have done before it, when the People shall become so corrupted as to need Despotic Government, being incapable of any other. I doubt too whether any other Convention we can obtain, may be able to make a better Constitution: For when you assemble a Number of Men to have the Advantage of their joint Wisdom, you inevitably assemble with those Men all their Prejudices, their Passions, their Errors of Opinion, their local Interests, and their selfish Views. From such an Assembly can a perfect Production be expected? It therefore astonishes me, Sir, to find this System approaching so near to Perfection as it does; and I think it will astonish our Enemies, who are waiting with Confidence to hear that our Councils are confounded, like those of the Builders of Babel, and that our States are on the Point of Separation, only to meet hereafter for the Purpose of cutting one anothers Throats. Thus I consent, Sir, to this Constitution because I expect no better, and because I am not sure that it is not the best. The Opinions I have had of its Errors, I sacrifice to the Public Good. I have never whisper'd a Syllable of them abroad. Within these Walls they were born, and here they shall die. If every one of us in returning to our Constituents were to report the Objections he has had to it, and endeavour to gain Partizans in support of them, we might prevent its being generally received, and thereby lose all the salutary Effects & great Advantages resulting naturally in our favour among foreign Nations, as well as among ourselves, from our real or apparent Unanimity. Much of the Strength and Efficiency of any Government in procuring & securing Happiness to the People depends on Opinion, on the general Opinion of the Goodness of that Government as well as of the Wisdom & Integrity of its Governors. I hope therefore that for our own Sakes, as a Part of the People, and for the Sake of our Posterity we shall act heartily & unanimously in recommending this Constitution, wherever our Influence may extend, and turn our future Thoughts and Endeavours to the Means of having it well administred.

On the whole, Sir, I cannot help expressing a Wish, that every Member of the Convention, who may still have Objections to it, would with me on this Occasion doubt a little of his own Infallibility, and to make *manifest* our *Unanimity,* put his Name to this Instrument.

Chronology.

1706   born January 17
1718   apprenticed to brother James, printer
1723   goes to Philadelphia
1724   sails to London, November 5
1726   sails for home, July 21
1727   forms Junto
1729   acquires *Pennsylvania Gazette;* son William born, mother unknown
1730   enters into common-law marriage with Deborah Read
1732   publishes first *Poor Richard's Almanack*
1736   appointed clerk of Pennsylvania Assembly
1737   appointed postmaster of Philadelphia
1745   begins electrical experiments
1747   organizes Pennsylvania militia
1748   forms printing partnership with David Hall and retires from business
1748–50   experiments with lightning
1751   elected to Pennsylvania Assembly
1753   appointed joint deputy postmaster general of North America
1754   attends Albany Congress
1757   sails to London as agent of Pennsylvania Assembly
1762   returns to Philadelphia
1764   sails to London with petition for royal government
1765   opposes Stamp Act

1766   supports repeal of Stamp Act in examination by the British
        House of Commons
1772   sends Hutchinson-Oliver letters to Massachusetts
1774   denounced by Alexander Wedderburn and dismissed from
        Post Office, January 31; negotiates with Lord Howe against
        Parliamentary measures; Deborah Franklin dies in
        Philadelphia, December 19
1775   returns to Philadelphia; elected to Second Continental
        Congress
1776   goes to Canada and returns; helps write Declaration of
        Independence; sails to France, October 27, arrives December 3
1778   signs treaties with France, February 6
1782   helps negotiate peace with England
1785   returns to Philadelphia
1787   attends Constitutional Convention
1790   petitions against slavery; dies April 17

Credits.

Page 92: Ascension of Montgolfier Balloon, September 19, 1783. Comte de la Vaulx, Paul Tissandier, and Charles Dollfus, *L'Aeronautiques: des origines à 1922* (Paris, Floury, 1922), ill. 6.

Pages 98–111: Benjamin Franklin, Sketches from a letter to Julien-David Le Roy, begun at Passy, February 1784, finished at sea, August 1785: fig. 11 (p. 98); fig. 12 (p. 99); fig. 13 (p. 100); fig. 14 (p. 101); fig. 26 (p. 110); fig. 27 (p. 110). Papers of Benjamin Franklin, Manuscript Division, Library of Congress, Washington, D.C.

Pages 104–5: James Poupard after George-Louis Le Rouge, *A Chart of the Gulf Stream,* 1786, in Benjamin Franklin, "Maritime Observations," *Transactions of the American Philosophical Society* 2 (1786). Courtesy Yale University Library.

Page 114: Lewis Evans, Illustration to Benjamin Franklin, "Opinions and Conjectures concerning the Properties and Effects of the Electrical Matter, arising from Experiments and Observations made in Philadelphia, 1749," sec. 21. Reproduced by permission of the American Academy of Arts and Sciences.

Page 172: Benjamin Franklin, "Join, or Die," *Pennsylvania Gazette,* May 9, 1754. Courtesy Yale University Library.

Texts

"Abigail Adams on Madame Helvétius," excerpted from "Abigail Adams to Lucy Cranch," September 5, 1784, *The Adams Papers: Adams Family Correspondence,* Vols. 5 & 6: *October 1782–December 1785,* ed. Richard Alan Ryerson, Joanna Revelas, Celeste Walker, Gregg L. Lint, and Humphrey Costello. Cambridge: The Belknap Press of Harvard University Press, Copyright © 1993 by the Massachusetts Historical Society. Reprinted by permission of the publisher.

"The Open Window: From the Autobiography of John Adams," 1776, excerpted from *The Adams Papers: Diary and Autobiography of John Adams,* Vol. 3: *Diary, 1782–1804, Autobiography to 1776,* ed. L. H. Butterfield. Cambridge: The Belknap Press of Harvard University Press, Copyright © 1961 by the Massachusetts Historical Society. Reprinted by permission of the publisher.

"On Transported Felons," from *The Pennsylvania Gazette,* April 11, 1751.

The following are from *The Papers of Benjamin Franklin*, ed. Leonard W. Labaree (vols. 1–14), William B. Willcox (vols. 15–26), Claude A. Lopez (vol. 27), Barbara B. Oberg (vols. 28–35), and Ellen R. Cohn (vols. 36–). New Haven: Yale University Press, 1959– . Copyright © by the American Philosophical Society Held at Philadelphia for Promoting Useful Knowledge and by Yale University. Reprinted by permission. Works from published volumes are cited by title, date, volume, and page numbers; works from forthcoming volumes are cited by title and date.

"Journal of a Voyage," 1726 (excerpt), vol. 1, pp. 72–99.

"To George Whatley [Whately]," May 23, 1785 (excerpt).

"Rules for Making Oneself a Disagreeable Companion," November 15, 1750, vol. 4, pp. 73–74.

"To Catharine Ray," September 11, 1755 (excerpt), vol. 6, pp. 182–86.

"To Mary Stevenson," September 14, 1767, vol. 14, pp. 250–55.

"To Anna Mordaunt Shipley," August 12 [*i.e.*, 13], 1771, vol. 18, pp. 199–202.

"To Madame Brillon," March 10, 1778, vol. 26, pp. 85–86.

"To Emma Thompson," February 8, 1777 (excerpt), vol. 23, pp. 296–99.

"The Speech of Miss Polly Baker," April 15, 1747, vol. 3, pp. 120–25.

"Leaping Whales," from " 'A Traveller': News-Writers' Nonsense," [May 20, 1765], vol. 12, pp. 132–35.

"Remarks Concerning the Savages of North-America," [before January 7, 1784].

"To Josiah and Abiah Franklin," April 13, 1738 (excerpt), vol. 2, pp. 202–4.

"To Joseph Huey," June 6, 1753, vol. 4, pp. 503–6.

"To Jane Mecom," September 16, 1758 (excerpt), vol. 8, pp. 152–55.

"On the Benefits of Moist Fresh Air," excerpted from "To Thomas Percival," [October 15, 1773], vol. 20, pp. 442–45.

"On Fresh Air," excerpted from "To Jan Ingenhousz," August 28, 1785.

"To Benjamin Vaughan," July 31, 1786.

"Mesmerism," excerpted from "To La Sablière de la Condamine," March 19, 1784.

"To Jared Eliot," February 13, 1749 / 50 (excerpt), vol. 3, pp. 463–66.

"To Peter Collinson," August 25, 1755, vol. 6, pp. 167–68.

"To Edward Nairne," November 13, 1780[–October 18, 1783] (excerpt), vol. 33, pp. 518–23.

"To James Bowdoin," December 2, 1758, vol. 8, pp. 194–98.

"To Sir Joseph Banks," August 30, 1783 (excerpt).

"On the Motion of Vessels," "The Gulf Stream," and "Advice for Travelers," excerpted from "To Julien-David Le Roy," [February 1784–August 1785].

"Note on the Similarities Between Electricity and Lightning" (1749), excerpted from "To John Lining," March 18, 1755, vol. 5, pp. 521–27.

"Experiment to Determine Whether the Clouds That Contain Lightning Are Electrified," excerpted from "Opinions and Conjectures," [July 29, 1750], vol. 4, pp. 9–34.

"Joseph Priestley's Account of Franklin's Kite Experiment," excerpted from "The Kite Experiment," October 19, 1752, vol. 4, pp. 360–69.

"How to Secure Houses, &c. from Lightning," excerpted from "Poor Richard Improved," 1753, vol. 4, pp. 403–9.

"Of Lightning, and the Method (Now Used in America) of Securing Buildings and Persons from Its Mischievous Effects," September 1767, vol. 14, pp. 260–64.

"To Peter Collinson," September 1753, vol. 5, pp. 68–79.

"To the Abbé Soulavie," from "To Jean-Louis Giraud Soulavie," September 22, 1782, vol. 38, pp. 123–27.

"Loose Thoughts on a Universal Fluid, &c.," excerpted from "To David Rittenhouse," June 25, 1784[–June 20, 1788].

"Felons and Rattlesnakes," May 9, 1751, vol. 4, pp. 130–33.

"Thoughts on Immigrants," excerpted from "To James Parker," March 20, 1750/1, vol. 4, pp. 117–22.

"Observations Concerning the Increase of Mankind," 1751, vol. 4, pp. 225–34.

"Indians and Germans," excerpted from "To Peter Collinson," May 9, 1753, vol. 4, pp. 477–86.

"To Joshua Babcock," January 13, 1772, vol. 19, pp. 6–7.

"To John Waring," December 17, 1763 (excerpt), vol. 10, pp. 395–96.

"The Speech of Sidi Mehemet Ibrahim," from "Benjamin Franklin to the Federal Gazette," March 23, 1790.

"To James Parker," March 20, 1750/1 (excerpt), vol. 4, pp. 117–22.

"The Albany Plan of Union," [July 10, 1754], vol. 5, pp. 374–92.

"The Interest of Great Britain Considered," 1760 (excerpt), vol. 9, pp. 47–100.

"To Peter Collinson," April 30, 1764 (excerpt), vol. 11, pp. 180–84.

"To William Franklin," November 9, 1765 (excerpt), vol. 12, pp. 361–65.

"Peace Is Sought by War," from " 'Pacificus': Pax Quaeritur Bello," January 23, 1766, vol. 13, pp. 54–58.

"Franklin's Examination Before the Committee of the House of Commons," excerpted from "Examination Before the Committee of the Whole of the House of Commons," [February 13, 1766], vol. 13, pp. 124–62.

"To David Hall," February 24, 1766 (excerpt), vol. 13, pp. 169–70.

"To William Shirley," December 22, 1754, vol. 5, pp. 449–51.

"On the Disputes with America," excerpted from "To Lord Kames," February 25, 1767, vol. 14, pp. 62–71.

"New Fables," January 2, 1770, vol. 17, pp. 3–4.

"To Samuel Cooper," June 8, 1770 (excerpt), vol. 17, pp. 160–65.

"An Edict by the King of Prussia," September 22, 1773, vol. 20, pp. 413–18.

"To Joseph Galloway," February 25, 1775 (excerpt), vol. 21, pp. 508–10.

"To David Hartley," October 3, 1775 (excerpt), vol. 22, pp. 216–17.

"To Jonathan Shipley," July 7, 1775 (excerpt), vol. 22, pp. 93–98.

"To Joseph Priestley," October 3, 1775, vol. 22, pp. 217–18.

"To Admiral Lord Howe," from "To Lord Howe," July 20, 1776, vol. 22, pp. 518–21.

"Sketch of Propositions for a Peace," [after September 26 and before October 25, 1776], vol. 22, pp. 630–33.

"Comparison of Great Britain and America as to Credit, in 1777," [before September 8, 1777], vol. 24, pp. 508–14.

"John Adams's Diplomatic Blunders," excerpted from "To Samuel Huntington," August 9, 1780, vol. 33, pp. 160–66.

"To James Hutton," February 1, 1778, vol. 25, pp. 562–63.

"Notes for a Conversation with Richard Oswald," from "Franklin: Notes for a Conversation with Oswald," [on or before April 19, 1782], vol. 37, pp. 169–72.

"Proposals for Diminishing the Occasions and Mischiefs of War," excerpted from "To Benjamin Vaughan," July 10, 1782, vol. 37, pp. 608–11.

"Thoughts on Privateering" and "Thoughts Concerning the Sugar Colonies," from "Franklin's Thoughts on Privateering and the Sugar Islands: Two Essays," [after July 10, 1782], vol. 37, pp. 617–20.

"To William Strahan," August 19, 1784 (excerpt).

"The Costs of War," excerpted from "To Jane Mecom," September 20, 1787.

"Thoughts on the House of Lords," excerpted from "To William Franklin: Journal of Negotiations in London," March 22, 1775, vol. 21, pp. 540–99.

"Convention Speech on Salaries," from "Benjamin Franklin: Convention Speech on Salaries," June 2, 1787.

"Property Rights and Human Rights," excerpted from "To Benjamin Vaughan," March 1, 1785.

"The Moral Obligation of Taxes," excerpted from "To Robert Morris," December 25, 1783.

"Queries and Remarks on 'Hints for the Members of the Pennsylvania Convention,'" from "Benjamin Franklin: Queries and Remarks on 'Hints for the Members of Pennsylvania Convention,'" [after November 3, 1789].

"Arthur Lee's Conversation with Franklin About the Miracle of the Revolution," from "Franklin on the Miracle of the Revolution," [October 25, 1777], vol. 25, pp. 100–102.

"To Sarah Bache," January 26, 1784 (excerpt).

"Information to Those Who Would Remove to America," [before March 9, 1784].

"Speech in the Convention on the Constitution," excerpted from "From Benjamin Franklin: Speech in the Convention on the Constitution," [September 17, 1787].

Index